T0361277

ROUTLEDGE LIBRARY EDITIONS:
INTERNATIONAL TRADE POLICY

Volume 18

A NATIONAL POLICY FOR ORGANIZED FREE TRADE

A NATIONAL POLICY FOR ORGANIZED FREE TRADE

The Case of U. S. Foreign Trade Policy for Steel, 1976–1978

MICHAEL W. HODIN

LONDON AND NEW YORK

First published in 1987 by Garland Publishing, Inc.

This edition first published in 2018
by Routledge
2 Park Square, Milton Park, Abingdon, Oxon OX14 4RN

and by Routledge
711 Third Avenue, New York, NY 10017

Routledge is an imprint of the Taylor & Francis Group, an informa business

British Library Cataloguing in Publication Data
A catalogue record for this book is available from the British Library

ISBN: 978-1-138-06323-5 (Set)
ISBN: 978-1-315-14339-2 (Set) (ebk)
ISBN: 978-1-138-29770-8 (Volume 18) (hbk)
ISBN: 978-0-203-73140-6 (Volume 18) (ebk)

Publisher's Note
The publisher has gone to great lengths to ensure the quality of this reprint but points out that some imperfections in the original copies may be apparent.

Disclaimer
The publisher has made every effort to trace copyright holders and would welcome correspondence from those they have been unable to trace.

FOREIGN ECONOMIC POLICY OF THE UNITED STATES

A National Policy for Organized Free Trade:

The Case of U. S. Foreign Trade Policy for Steel

1976–1978

MICHAEL W. HODIN

GARLAND PUBLISHING, INC.
NEW YORK & LONDON • 1987

For a complete list of the titles in this series, see the final pages of this volume.

Library of Congress Cataloging-in-Publication Data

Hodin, Michael W.
A national policy for organized free trade.

(Foreign economic policy of the United States)
Originally presented as the author's thesis (Ph. D.)--Columbia, 1979.
Bibliography: p.
1. Steel industry and trade--United States. 2. Steel industry and trade. 3. United States--Commercial policy. 4. Free trade and protection--Protection. I. Title. II. Series.
HD9515.H59 1987 382'.45669142'0973 87-23719
ISBN 0-8240-8085-8

All volumes in this series are printed on acid-free, 250-year-life paper.

Printed in the United States of America

PREFACE TO GARLAND EDITION

Since completion of the original writing in mid 1978, several important events have come to pass, which have served to underscore the importance and relevance of the study of the U.S. foreign trade policy toward steel in the late seventies. First, by year-end 1979, the Tokyo Round of Trade Negotiations were complete; accompanying amendments to U.S. Trade Law were also adopted, thus ensuring conformity between the two. Ironically, while both events were heralded as monuments to liberal trade, there was a good deal in both which made it easier, and more "GATT" legal to impose restrictions on trade. But the U.S. was not alone as the Europeans, for example, continued their subsidy regimes for agricultural, steel and other products; and, the Japanese their panoply of non-tariff barriers maintaining its byzantine complex into which foreign goods and services still could not easily be marketed. U.S. policy reaction, as in steel, would be applied to sector after sector since 1978.

Secondly, the trend of continued deterioration of the U.S. trade position persisted. Moreover, any debate over what the real meaning of the trade deficit should be -- does it simply mean, as the Wall Street Journal articulately argued, that the deficit is really a symbol of the strength, durability and predictability of the U.S. market to attract imports and that a trade deficit therefore really is a healthy sign? -- evaporated by 1985, when it became all too clear that the current accounts (including capital and direct investment flows) had come into deficit as well. Therefore, to the degree that the deficits fed what was already a growing protectionist trend among the developed countries, the recognition of the deficit in the U.S. current account merely gave greater and more urgent support for such tendencies here.

By early 1986, no fewer than 300 pieces of legislation in the U.S. Congress dealt with trade issues, and most were clearly protectionist in one way or another. Moreover, the years since 1978, experienced a growing list of "affected sectors" for which protectionism was meant as a solution: to textiles, steel and autos, was added consumer electronics, microchips, and even the symbolic, if not actual cutting edge of American technological capability, computers.

A third important trend which came to characterize U.S. Trade policy in the period since original writing in 1978, has became a keystone of President Reagan's trade policy: that the answer to increased competition to American Industry in the U.S. lay not in protecting ourselves at the border through tariffs, voluntary restraint agreements or other forms of quantitative restrictions, but by encouraging the opening of others' markets. This policy approach began to take shape in President Reagan's first term, and addressed investment as well as trade, both in the goods and service sectors. This was articulated in the Presidential Statement on International Investment which reversed the policy of President Carter whose Administration insisted on a policy of "neutrality" toward American business overseas. President Reagan, on the other hand went forthrightly in support of active advocacy of American business interests overseas: "...The United States will pursue an active policy aimed at reducing foreign government actions that impede or distort investment flows, and at developing an international system based on national treatment and most favored nation principles that permits investment flows to respond more freely to market forces. The United States will work to protect U.S. investment abroad from treatment which is discriminatory or otherwise inconsistent with international law standards..."

But the approach to encourage others to open their markets took even more penetrating forms. These came in the Trade and Tariff Act of 1984 which included basic changes to the character of U.S. Trade Laws, primarily reflected in its efforts to address investment issues through action toward other countries' market conditions. Section 303 required the USTR office to make an annual report to Congress, in which it would identify barriers to U.S. exports of goods, services and overseas direct investments.

Still another provision of the 1984 Act is that newly industrializing countries receiving preferential treatment (GSP) for its exports to the U.S., (including increasing amounts of steel) must in return ensure its intellectual property right laws respect the fruits of U.S. research and technology sold in their country. Perhaps even more fundamental, the 1984 Amendments redefined Section 301, so that it would become an effective cutting edge of U.S. efforts to open others' markets. Critically, the redefined Section 301 also provided self-initiation by the President, to be implemented by his Special Trade Negotiator.

By early 1985, the USTR office served notice to the Mexicans that their GSP had been put in jeopardy as a result of protectionist market policies. By late 1985, President Reagan began using Section 301 with respect to the Koreans lack of intellectual property protection of U.S. goods and their restriction on U.S. services such as insurance seeking to do business in Korea; the Japanese burdensome requirements on U.S. tobacco to be sold there; and the Brazilians with respect to their elaborate controls on the ability of U.S. (or non-Brazilian) computers to be sold there.

The mood which came to prevail, and as of Summer 1986 began to produce results, was accurately summed up in a November 17 Fortune Magazine interview, "The Korean case was really a watershed, says a Washington trade consultant. We've finally turned around and said, 'Look Korea, if you don't stop, we're going to close our market to you.'" As of this writing, the Koreans have agreed to change their intellectual property laws to assure patent and trademark protection to U.S. goods; the Japanese appear to be opening their market to more U.S. tobacco; and the Brazilians, while not yet motivated on the computer issue, have gotten the message.

Consistent with the 1984 Amendments to U.S. Trade Law, was the increasing focus on trade related problems associated with intellectual property protection, also as a means of rendering others' markets more hospitable to U.S. goods and services. On April 7, 1986, President Reagan's Property Rights Policy Statement was issued in support of the Administration sponsored "Intellectual Property Rights Improvement Act of 1986." The first underlying premise of this statement was that all countries' economic growth and international competitiveness can be enhanced by strong domestic intellectual property protection. The second was that if countries do not provide strong protection of intellectual property rights, and an effective system of international enforcement does not exist, then substantial distortions in international trade will result.

The final significant event which the reader should have as background brings us full circle to the 1976-78 period, namely, the Agreement at Punta del Este, Uruguay in September 1986 by the 92 members of the GATT to begin the 8th Round of Trade Talks. A number of the issues to be addressed in the 8th Round are the ones that have plagued U.S. trade policy in the years since 1979. Moreover, U.S. objectives for the new Round of GATT Talks will be to continue to get others to open their markets as an additional way to manage the otherwise unrelenting tendencies toward protectionism.

In this context, one can read the story of U.S. trade policy toward steel, 1977-79, as a critical step in the path which has been moving the U.S. from a policy of organized free trade to one where increasing scope is allowed to market forces. Coping with the protectionist impulse will surely always be with us, as it has since the beginning of the Mercantile Period in the Fifteenth Century. However, the case of steel in the late seventies underscored that the great strides toward freer and more open market trade policies that were made immediately following World War II were largely a function of American management of the international economic system and its concomitant ability to absorb many of the protectionist impulses. As American management broke down it became more and more difficult to resist the protectionist impulse since there was no one to absorb it, and the Case of Steel, 1976-78 illuminates the breadth and scope of the issues. Thus, the U.S. Government's efforts in the current period to encourage others to absorb elements of these protectionist impulses represent a new hope for the strengthening of the structure known as liberal trade.

New York City
November 11, 1986

TABLE OF CONTENTS

Page

LIST OF CHARTS

CHAPTER 1

U.S. FOREIGN TRADE DECISIONMAKING FOR INDUSTRIAL SECTORS

I. Introduction

In 1971, for the first time since the creation of the Bretton Woods System, the United States experienced a balance of trade deficit; in 1973 and 1975, it reported small surpluses, and it has reverted to ever-increasing deficits since.[1] While it is of course true that oil comprises a substantial percentage of imports into the United States,[2] and that this basic commodity figures as a central factor in the global political economy, the explanation for what has become an annual and increasing United States trade deficit is more complicated. In the "non-petroleum merchandise trade," for example, the amount of imports increased from $71 billion in 1975, to roughly $128 billion in 1978, or an increase of slightly over

---

[1]United States Department of Commerce, Bureau of Economic Analysis, Balance of Payments Division (November 28, 1978.)

[2]Petroleum imports, according to the Department of Commerce' were $27 billion in 1975, $34.6 million in 1976, $45 billion in 1977, and $43.2 billion in 1978 (where 1978 figure is annualized based on first and second quarter data available), November 28, 1978.

eighty percent. By contrast, the petroleum imports during the same period increased by fifty-nine percent.[1] Thus, the United States trade balance, which went from a surplus of slightly more than $9 billion in 1975, to a deficit of almost $45 billion in 1978,[2] must be explained by more than the oil import factor.

There is also more to the United States balance of trade deficit than a matter of recessionary cycles.[3] What at first appeared almost exclusively as a cyclical downturn of the industrial economies in 1974-75, is now pointed to as part of a larger and more serious structural dilemma -- the problems associated with changes in the

---

[1]United States Department of Commerce, Bureau of Economic Analysis, Balance of Payments Division (November 28, 1978).

[2]Ibid.; also see, "Machinery, Manufactured Goods Replace Oil As Top U.S. Import," New York Times (July 5, 1978), p. 1. Also note that the steel balance of trade deficit in 1978 was approximately $6 billion, or 13.3 percent of the total United States Balance of Trade Deficit.

[3]Good discussions on the cyclical and structural problems in the industrial economies of Europe, the United States, and Japan, are found in: William Diebold, Jr., "Adapting Economies to Structural Change: The International Aspect," International Affairs (Fall 1978); Susan Strange, "The Management of Surplus Capacity; Or, How Does Theory Stand Up to Protectionism 1970s Style?" (xerox: Fall 1978); and Richard Blackhurst, Nicolas Marian, and Jan Tumlir, "Trade Liberalization, Protectionism, and Interdependence," No. 5 (Geneva, November 1977); Joan Spero, The Politics of International Economic Relations (New York: St. Martin's Press 1977), especially pp. 72-75.

global pattern of production and competition. As distinguished from passing recessionary phases, a structural change involves lasting shifts in the way resources are used.[1] These shifts may be the result of changes in technology, patterns of production, consumption, demand/supply ratios, and trade, as well as government responses to one or all of them. Understandably, some parts of the manufacturing sector experience different degrees of structural change at different points in time than others. Such changes lead to the threat, or actual displacement of workers and is accompanied by various degrees of instability in domestic society. Predictably, there is a politicization of issues for the industries and in those parts of society most affected.

Steel is representative of those industries experiencing a worldwide structural crisis. And so, it is also a sector where governments are responding to the pressures from their domestic constituencies for protection from the adverse dislocative impact of industrial development. In some cases these pressures come from the difficulties societies have in adjusting to the results of a natural decline in the rate of growth of

---

[1]For an excellent discussion of "structural change" see, William Diebold, Jr., International Affairs, "Adapting Economies to Structural Change: The International Aspect," pp. 563-588.

of consumption experienced by advanced industrial economies. But quite often these pressures are more the results of other governments' economic strategies and foreign economic policies which tend to push their own economic adjustment problem onto others. In effect the first set of circumstances is exacerbated by the second; the result is an intricate web of economic conditions and government policies which produce overcapacity and oversupply in international industries.

Steel is such an industry plagued by a condition of global overcapacity and oversupply, which itself is but a symptom of the structural crisis. It is primarily this condition which has led the governments of Europe, Japan and the United States to alter their domestic and foreign policies for steel. In the United States, where the steel industry has been a net importer since 1960, the emphasis for policy development has been in the area of foreign trade policy, and the major change has come in 1976-78.

The study of the making of United States foreign trade policy for steel, 1976-78, therefore, provides a way of examining the United States response to two related problems of international trade: 1) the structural changes in the global economy; and 2) the resultant trend toward protection among the industrial nations. Both lead to the politicization of industrial sector issues in the domestic and international arenas.

While the development of U.S. foreign trade policy for steel, 1976-78, is studied as a representative case of how the U.S. conducts its foreign trade policy for industrial sector cases, it should be recognized that there are special characteristics of steel which distinguish it from the others of its kind. We shall argue, however, that these special characteristics add strength to the argument that the steel case, in and of itself, is an important and worthwhile study, even as these characteristics are understood as limitations on the degree to which this particular study may be applicable to other sectors. The characteristics of steel which distinguish it from other industrial sectors are:

First, in the developed as well as the developing worlds, governments have taken a unique interest in promoting and maintaining their steel industries. This special interest in steel is due to the perception that steel is necessary for industrial development, economic health, and to ensure a secure and adequate national defense. The result has been a unique participation by governments around the world in the steel industries.

A second characteristic of the steel industry which distinguishes it from other industrial sectors is the pattern of geographical concentration. In the United

State the steel industry is concentrated in the older industrial regions of the Northeast and Midwest which tend to suffer more severely from the burdens of an aging economy. Because the steel industry is located in the older, relatively economically depressed regions of the country, it is more difficult to adjust the labor force from one sector to another, than it would be for a sector located in more vibrant growth regions like the Southwestern part of the country. Hence, the "locational factor" leads to rather effective concentrated clusters of political pressures on government, which are not easily alleviated by economic adjustment.

A final characteristic which sets the steel industry apart from other industrial sectors in the United States is its investment practices and attendant political interests. The steel industry in the United States has not engaged in investment in foreign markets. It will be conspicuous throughout this study that the steel industry's interests in the United States lie almost entirely in production for the home market; there has been negligible investment by U.S. steel firms outside the United States, and there is therefore little concern of any significant political consequence in foreign markets or imports into the U.S. market from foreign subsidiaries of U.S. firms. Consider for example, an article written for the Oxford Economic Papers by G.K. Helleiner, in which he expressed the view that the balance in U.S. trade policy is largely determined by the interests of the industries involved. "Where U.S. firms are not internationally oriented," he wrote in 1977, "they are likely to ally with labor and to achieve some success in generating protection from competitive imports."[1] The steel industry in the United States has not become transnational, nor internationally oriented, and it is therefore solely interested in protecting its own position in the home -- i.e., United States -- market.

Thus, all three factors -- pervasive government involvement around the world, its geographical concentration which leads to higher degrees of politicization in regions unable to adjust to poor economic conditions, and little foreign investment of any political significance -- distinguish the steel case from other cases on U.S. foreign trade policy for industrial sectors. The case is not a perfect representative, but that is

---

[1]G.K. Helleiner, "Transnational Enterprises and the New Political Economy of U.S. Trade Policy," Oxford Economic Papers, volume 29, number 1, March 1977, pp. 115-16. For a discussion of Transnational Enterprises and their effects on U.S. foreign trade policy, also see, Robert Gilpin, "The Politics of Transnational Economic Relations," in Transnational Relations and World Politics, ed. by Robert O. Keohane and Joseph S. Nye, Sr. (Cambridge: Harvard University Press, 1973); Joseph S. Nye, Sr., and Robert O. Keohane, their introduction and conclusion in the book they edited on Transnational Relations and World Politics.

probably true of most, if not all, case studies; imperfect application of specific cases to the general categories should be expected. Nevertheless, there is enough about the steel case which makes it both an important study about a very specific element in U.S. foreign trade policy, and one from which we can learn about how the United States is likely to develop policy for other industrial sector cases.

For steel, as with a number of other sectors receiving various forms of government assistance through the use of foreign trade policy tools, the largest proportion of domestic interests lie in controlling imports into the domestic marketplace.

As the steel issue became politicized in the United States, policymakers found that traditional liberal trade policy responses were no longer adequate. There has developed a willingness within the chambers of American government trade policymaking circles to talk of the global trading order in terms of organizing markets, monitoring production levels, limiting imports, and setting price guidelines. All of these point to an orientation different from the liberal ideas advocated by Cordell Hull, and codified in the General Agreement on Trade and Tariffs (GATT). Hence, the United States, in some respects as a reaction to the policies of its major trading partners, seems to be concluding that the system of (classical) free trade[1] is no longer applicable. But the neoprotectionist policies of the thirties,[2] and against which the post-war liberal trading order was created, are not looked upon as acceptable either.

So, U.S. policymakers found that domestic pressures forced them to consider policies of intervention in the steel trade to protect affected constituencies from the adjustment costs largely created by the international political economy of steel. The willingness, indeed the political necessity, to develop strategies for intervening in international trade represents a change in how U.S. policymakers view the policy options available to them -- i.e., the kinds of operating procedures they

---

[1]For a good, clear description of classical free trade, see Stephen Krasner, "State Power and the Structure of International Trade," World Politics (April 1976). As Krasner explains, the concept of classical free trade is best illustrated by the period beginning in about 1860, when Britain and France signed the Cobden-Chevalier Treaty. The Cobden-Chevalier Treaty virtually eliminated trade barriers between the countries involved, and lasted for some twenty years; and Richard N. Gardner, Sterling Dollar Diplomacy: The Origins and Prospects of Our International Economic Order (New York: McGraw Hill, new expanded version, 1969). For an excellent discussion of the development of the ideas of "free trade" and "protectionism," see, Edward L. Morse, Modernization and the Transformation of International Relations (London: The Free Press, 1976). Morse also examines the relationship between classic forms of protectionism and free trade, and their contemporary counterparts.

[2]See, for example, Charles P. Kindelberger, The World in Depression (Berkeley: The University of California Press, 1973); and Clair Wilcox, A Charter for World Trade (New York: MacMillan, 1949).

will apply to the complex questions of international trade in industrial sectors. This change marks a departure from liberal trade policies where there is minimal government policy of involvement in international trade, to an interventionist trade policy where government assumes an active role in assisting its domestic constituencies to cope with the dislocative effects of the international trading order.

The basic proposition of this study, therefore, is that the operating procedures of the United States foreign trade policy are changing, and that the change represents a successful effort to move from liberal policies toward a new principle of the international trading order -- intervention. The central question, then, is how and why the United States is developing the capabilities to do this.

Implicit in the central question is that systemic shifts have occurred, and that the United States is shaping its policy to adapt to the changed conditions. But as the United States tries to adapt and we ask how and the degree to which its operating procedures change, we must also ask about the policymaking process itself. Thus, an important effect of this kind of policy development is that it questions the appropriateness of classic decisionmaking approaches.

As U.S. policy assumes the responsibility of

assisting domestic constituencies -- by intervening in international trade -- there is an associated shift in the focus of the policymaking process istself, from one on legislation to one on administrative and adjudicatory functions of the Executive. Part of the reason for this is the integration of international negotiations by sectors into the policymaking process at the national level. The policymaking process, in other words, must account both for international negotiations by sectors as well as the more traditional domestic pressures; at the same time the researcher must develop new approaches in which to study the decisionmaking process. The central theoretical question of this study, therefore, is how and why the study of the making of U.S. foreign trade policy for industrial sectors like steel require new approaches for analysis of the decisionmaking process? And, as a related question, who are the major participants in the process, and what are their roles?

To answer these questions we shall examine the national decisionmaking level of analysis in a way that may take account of both the international and domestic pressures on U.S. policymakers. Thus in trying to balance these two pressures -- domestic constituencies from "below," and its trading partners from "above" -- the United States foreign trade policymakers developed two policies for steel during the period under study: the Trigger Price

Mechanism (TPM), and the International Steel Committee (ISC).[1]

In both cases we shall see that there are central elements which support the general hypothesis that U.S. trade policy is adapting to the protectionist strategies of its trading partners by also intervening in international trade. As we have indicated above, however, there is a marked unwillingness on the part of U.S. decisionmakers simply to abandon the principles and operating procedures associated with the liberal trading order. Accordingly, they adopt a set of goals and objectives which effectively straddle the two positions.

These goals and objectives make up what will be referred to in this study as an "Administration policy." Analytically, therefore, the decisionmaking process is separated into two stages: first, the development of the Administration's goals and objectives, conditioned by large and comprehensive policy concerns such as the commitment to trade liberalization, and by overall global political-economic factors such as the effects of other governments' economic strategies and foreign economic policies. Second is the development of specific policies for steel. Since the U.S. policymakers seek to manage the effects of the non-tariff barriers on the domestic

---

[1]We shall examine both programs in Chapters 5 and 6.

political economy, they must integrate into the policy-making process the pressures from its trading partners which are responsible for non-tariff barrier effects, as well as the pressures from its domestic constituencies.

In summary, the researcher is faced with the case of steel in foreign trade decisionmaking, which appears not to fit into classic decisionmaking theory. In this first chapter, therefore, we will set forth a framework for analysis to focus attention on those areas which distinguish industrial sector trade policy cases from the more traditional study of foreign trade issues. Having developed the framework for analysis it will then be possible in Chapters 2 and 3 to examine the pressures on the Administration creating the terms in which a steel policy developed. In Chapter 4, we shall move to the actual political process from which the Administration's steel plan grew. Chapters 5 and 6 will offer a description and analysis of the U.S. steel policy, 1976-78. And, in the concluding chapter, we shall re-examine the central theoretical and analytical hypotheses in light of the evidence.

II. Foreign Trade Policy and the International Economic System: Independent Variables

This is a dissertation about United States foreign trade policy in the case of steel, and not about the international economic system, nor about the international steel trade per se.[1] The emphasis, therefore, is on decisionmaking in the United States. But, it is decisionmaking on an issue which is affected by conditions in the international system, as foreign trade policy is a process wherein policymakers seek to make domestic politics compatible with the international political economy.[2] These conditions of the international system will be viewed as the independent variables to which the U.S. foreign trade policy for steel responded. For it was in the context of this international system -- characterized, as it were, by a dwindling pie of benefits -- that the U.S. trade policy for steel, 1976-78, developed. And it was in the light of this

---

[1]Stephen Krasner makes this important distinction in his *Defending the National Interest: Raw Materials Investment and U.S. Foreign Policy* (Princeton: Princeton University Press, 1978).

[2]Peter J. Katzenstein, "Introduction: Domestic and International Forces and Strategies of Foreign Economic Policy," *International Organization* (Fall 1977) p. 588.

situation that policymakers were forced by the pressures from domestic constituencies to question the value of a strictly liberal -- i.e., non-interventionist -- trade policy. Let us examine, therefore, the nature and scope of the changes in the international trading order which promoted different kinds of relationships both at the national level -- between governments and their domestic constituencies, and at the international level -- between governments.

Those who write of the breakup of the international trading order write also of the loss of power of the United States. They argue that a dominant economic power is necessary to furnish the resources upon which the system of openness rests. As a leading proponent of this theory, Stephen Krasner has written:

> . . . openness is most likely to occur during periods when a hegemonic state is in its ascendancy. Such a state has the interests and the resources to create a structure characterized by lower tariffs, rising trade proportions, and less regionalism.[1]

Until recently, America's relationship to the international economic system fit this description.

Further elaborating Krasner's point, Charles Maier explains that American policy could no longer support the trading system in the way "everyone" had come to enjoy,

---

[1]Stephen Krasner, "State Power and the Structure of International Trade," p. 325.

and so the system began to weaken: "Hegemony remains successful only when it achieves advances for the whole international structure within which it is exercised . . . . Indeed, once the system ceased to pay off, it began to founder."[1]

The system, in a number of ways, has ceased to benefit other states.[2] Clearly, that has been the perception of governments in Europe, Japan and the United States. Problems in concluding the Tokyo Round of the MTN under the GATT are symptomatic of a basic mistrust of the benefits which can be gained from trade liberalization. As an illustration, consider the statement by Ambassador Alonzo McDonald, the U.S. Deputy Special Representative for Trade Negotiations and head of the United States Delegation to the Tokyo Round:

---

[1]Charles Maier, "The Politics of Productivity: Foundations of American International Economic Policy After World War II," International Organization (Autumn 1977). p. 631-632.

[2]Of course, not everyone holds the view put forth here. Among the most notable dissenters: David P. Calleo and Benjamin M. Rowland, America and the World Political Economy (Indiana University Press, 1973). Here they are critical of the American hegemonic role in the world political economy. Their view is stated straightforwardly in the first chapter when they write: ". . . given our post-war position of hegemony, and ideology stressing outward looking transatlantic interdependence and denigrating inward-looking nationalism is transparently convenient for imperialist purposes." p. 7; also, Joyce and Gabriel Kolko, The Limits of Power: The World and the United States Foreign Policy (New York: Harper and Row, 1972).

> In my view we should not anticipate another round of the MTN for a very long time, if ever. The Tokyo Round may well be the last comprehensive, long-range multilateral effort at trade liberalization. Its slow start reflects its complexity, its comprehensiveness, and constant stream of pitfalls inviting failure. The political difficulties we in the United States had in obtaining our mandate were formidable in 1974. They would be nearly insurmountable in our country today, and among our trading partners.

McDonald's pessimism was echoed even more recently by a British diplomat responsible for international trade issues. The diplomat said of the MTN:

> There are some [European governments] that are not now certain they want to go through with it [completion of the negotiations] . . . the political consequences [domestically] may be too great . . .[1]

Since there is no society which today is capable of absorbing the political and social costs associated with increasing levels of unemployment and inflation, governments are more apt to promote domestic economic strategies of intervention in their own markets that lead to foreign economic policies which export domestic adjustment costs onto others. This phenomenon of individual governmental strategies of protection prompted Harald Malmgram to write in 1970 of what he feared might

---

[1]Both statements were made during discussions with the author. Ambassador McDonald's comments were made in February 1978, and subsequently formalized in a speech delivered in Geneva. Comments by the British diplomat were made in November 1978.

be the emergence of powerful economic blocs ushering in a period of "neomercantalism." The threat of neo-mercantalism came, in his terms, as an

> . . . attempt to pass onto other countries some or all of the economic and social costs of domestic adjustment . . . . Neo-mercantalism sector by sector, whether aimed at industry relief or at rural poverty, must inevitably repress the interests of other countries in particular sectors, in particular regions.[1]

Writing eight years later, Susan Strange was unequivocal in how she assessed the condition of the international trading order:

> Whether we like it or not, the time has come to recognize the 1970s as a decade characterized by protectionism in trade policy. It has been a period of marked retrogression in trade liberal-ization in which states have put more and bigger obstacles in the way of foreign imports and greater restrictions on foreign enterprises.

Thus, confirming Malmgram's fears, she concluded, "The trend has been unmistakably away from free trade and toward protection of the national economic interests."[2]

A Change in Economic Power Relations

Industrial economies have experienced widespread demand for increased protection. One senses the breakup of structures and the inadequacy of traditional ideas in

---

[1]Harald Malmgram, "Coming Trade Wars," Foreign Policy (Winter 1970), p. 137.

[2]Susan Strange, "The Management of Surplus Capacity, Or How Does Theory Stand Up to Protectionism 1970s Style?" p. 1.

stages. By historical terms it has come of a sudden: one saw, for example, the 1971 devaluation of the dollar, OPEC's cartelization policy and subsequent control over world oil prices which threw all the industrial states in a tailspin, and the United States turnabout from world trade surplus to deficit accompanied by an astonishing rise in the power of the West German and Japanese exports.

The authors cited above have written of a system in which the United States was the dominant economic and political power, promoting the "politics of productivity";[1] a system intended to benefit the American producer while aiming for higher world levels of "exchange and welfare." Thus, many purport to explain what they regard as the impending collapse of the liberal trading order by the failure of American economic power to continue to provide the benefits which supported the system. Underlying this theme is the premise that other states increased their power at the same time the U.S. lost its power, and that the two phenomena perpetuated each other. In their study on Power and Interdependence,[2] for example, Robert Keohane and Joseph Nye write:

---

[1]Charles Maier, "The Politics of Productivity," International Organization (Fall 1977).

[2]Robert O. Keohane and Joseph Nye, Power and Interdependence: World Politics in Transition (Little Brown and Company 1977).

> Ironically, the benefits of the hegemônial system, and the extent to which they are shared, may bring about its collapse. As their economic power increases, secondary states change their assumptions . . . . Thus as the rulemaking and rule-enforcing powers of the hegemonial state begins to erode, the policies of the secondary states are likely to change. But so are the policies of the hegemonic state.[1]

They write of the erosion of the "international regime,"[2] to explain the changes in this international system -- the independent variables of this study. But they are quick to point out that the international systems model "does not . . . focus directly on national policy, but on the development and decline of international regimes." Therefore, they write, "Those who are trying to explain the policies of particular states will find these models too abstract. Our level of analysis is the world system, rather than national policy."[3]

So, the focus of this paper is not on the international system per se, but on how U.S. policy is responding to conditions in it. Keohane and Nye do suggest that U.S. policy is changing when they write that "the rulemaking and rule-enforcing" powers of the dominant state have begun to erode. But their purpose is to determine whether the

---

[1]Ibid., p. 45.

[2]Ibid., p. 223.

[3]Ibid., p. 223.

United States will continue to manage the international economic system, how this will affect the stability of the system, and how the system might change if the United States doesn't manage it, or manages it differently. For this paper, these are the independent variables which are accepted as external constraints on the U.S. policy-making process -- our central concern.

Indeed, it is the hypothesis of this paper that U.S. foreign trade policymakers are turning with greater frequency to the use of interventionist policies. A central assumption is that the United States is attempting to maintain control over the system, and that it seeks to develop a set of operating procedures which support the liberal trading order. In light of the structural changes in the international political economy this is a difficult task. Underscoring this dilemma, the Congressional Budget Office has argued in a recent study prepared as background for Congressional consideration of the MTN that the "most difficult questions facing U.S. makers of trade policy are how a liberal trading system can be made to work effectively and equitably despite a variety of influences with the potential to disrupt international trade patterns."[1]

---

[1]"U.S. Trade Policy and the Tokyo Round of the Multilateral Trade Negotiations," The Congressional Budget Office of the United States (xerox: March 1979), p. 35.

Faced with contradictory pressures from its domestic constituencies to intervene to equalize what are regarded as unfair advantages against them, and other impulses to pursue liberal trade policies, U.S. policymakers must balance the two. As we shall see in the next section, this situation has led also to a change in focus for U.S. policymakers: from the traditional emphasis on legislation and the lawmaking process, where a number of issues across a wide variety of sectors are bargained against one another,[1] to a complex bargaining process among governments focused on individual sectors.

---

[1]This point is elaborated in the next section. Also see my section on the Congress in Chapter 4, and my conclusions.

III. A Framework for Decisionmaking

Analysis

Steel policy has been debated much in the past two or three years, both at the international and domestic levels. For the United States it has been a part of the general policy debate in the Executive branch, and it has been the subject of hearings, markup sessions, legislation, and floor debate in the Congress.[1] Even at the community level, there has been political action. It is an issue area with which policymakers have had to reckon. Precisely because the policy debate over steel did not begin with the development of a major piece of trade legislation, and that it therefore will not end in a neatly packaged bill sent to the President's desk for signature, it is perhaps more representative of how the United States conducts foreign trade policy in the seventies and beyond. Certainly, it is representative of the increasing number of cases -- textiles, electronics, nuts and bolts, etc. -- which require individual and ongoing policy considerations.

---

[1]A distinction should be made between major trade bills which become acts of law, i.e., the Trade Expansion Act of 1962, or the Trade Reform Act of 1974, and the flurry of legislation introduced by Congressmen which may not even get hearings in committee.

But it is also this aspect which makes it more difficult to fit into the existing models.[1] Indeed, the two most notable -- E.E. Schattschneider's work on the Smoot-Hawley Tariff, and Bauer Pool and Dexter's work on the Reciprocal Trade Act of 1953 and the Trade Expansion Act of 1962 -- took as their starting and finishing points pieces of major legislation. It is not this author's intention to discount the importance of these studies, but only to establish the difference between the industrial sector cases for which policy is made, and major trade bills. Recognizing the distinction will allow appropriate use of former research tools, such that they do not confuse further an already confusing situation.

One common feature that these studies share is the absence of an analytic home in the policymaking process for foreign interests. As policymakers formulate policy for industrial sectors, they must engage in the

---

[1]See, for example, E.E. Schattschneider _Politics, Pressure, and the Tariff_ (Englewood Cliffs, N.J.: Prentice Hall 1935); and Raymond A. Bauer, Ithiel De Sola Pool, and Lewis Anthony Dexter _American Business and Public Policy_ (Chicago: Aldine 1972); Theodore Lowi, "American Business, Public Policy, Case Studies, and Political Theory," _World Politics_, p. 16, (1964) pp. 677-715; Robert A. Pastor, "Legislative-Executive Relations and U.S. Foreign Trade Policy: The Case of the Trade Act of 1974," prepared for delivery at the 1976 Annual Meeting of the American Political Science Association (Chicago, September 2-5, 1976).

diplomacy of international economics. Thus foreign trade policymakers develop relationships with government officials in other countries, and with institutions and processes outside the United States domestic political arena. In addition, they are imbued with a sense of "national purpose," which I.M. Destler describes as a kind of pluralism "applying not just to the range of specific interests outside the government that seek to influence policy, but to legitimate competing objectives which the government itself pursues and must pursue."[1] As policymaking in industrial sectors emphasizes the administrative or adjudicatory process in the Executive branch, policymakers tend to develop a set of goals and objectives quite apart from constituent pressures for specific policy. As we shall see below, this is due in some respects to the absence of the Congress as an equal partner in the decisionmaking process, but also to the Administration's perception that it is formulating the nation's foreign policy and must conduct itself accordingly -- i.e., to consider trade policy as a part of its foreign policy and not just responding to domestic pressures. Former researchers have not provided for this.

---

[1] I.M. Destler, "Protection for Congress: The Politics of Trade Policy." Paper was prepared as background for June 26, 1978 meeting of the Joint Discussion Group on Executive-Congressional Relations, Council on Foreign Relations and the Carnegie Endowment for International Peace.

In the Schattschneider approach, domestic interest groups were signalled as the single most important factor. Indeed, he concluded that interest groups largely wrote the Smoot-Hawley Tariff Act.[1] He left little room for consideration of what later researchers believed to be critical, if not determining factors -- the beliefs and attitudes of Congressmen separate from the sum of the pressure groups' lobbying effort; or as the bureaucratic-politics approach[2] of a later vintage argued, the inter-agency disputes in the Executive where each agency represents different interests and promotes them largely for bureaucratic rewards, i.e., bigger budgets, larger staffs, and more power. While the Bauer Pool and Dexter study refined the classic pressure group model, it offers little help analytically in dealing with foreign trade policy as a complex phenomenon which is characterized by the trading off of domestic and international political economic factors.

Messrs. Bauer, Pool and Dexter do conclude that legislators vote the way they do because of a "Congressional transformation process"; that the decisionmaker does make his own decisions but he is influenced, directly

---

[1]Schattschneider, Politics, Pressure and the Tariff.

[2]Graham Allison The Essence of Decision (Boston, Little Brown and Company, 1971); and Morton Halperin Bureaucratic Politics and Foreign Policy (Washington, D.C.: The Brookings Institution, 1974).

or indirectly, by pressure groups. They dispelled a good deal of the naivete about how trade law is made,[1] but didn't offer much in the way of how it is implemented or managed.

A newer version of how trade policy is made in the United States is offered by Robert Pastor.[2] In his study of the Trade Act of 1974, Pastor offers us what he calls the "Institutional-Bias Model." It explains foreign policy, and particularly foreign trade policy, as an interaction between two institutions -- the Executive and Legislative branches of government. In his words, "The model defines foreign policy as the resultant of sometimes subtle or tacit, sometimes forceful or conflictual, interactive process between two institutions, the Executive and Congress."[3] The model has a great deal of value,

---

[1]For example, Bauer, Pool and Dexter are clear on the point that Congress no longer plays a major role in the making of the country's trade policy. Indeed, it is underscored in the introduction to their volume that Congress has been "giving up" that role since the passage of the Smoot-Hawley Tariff. See, Bauer, Pool and Dexter, American Business and Public Policy, pp. 11-12, 1972 revised edition.

[2]Robert A. Pastor, "Legislative-Executive Relations and U.S. Foreign Trade Policy: The Case of the Trade Act of 1974"; prepared for delivery at the 1976 Annual Meeting of the American Political Science Association, Chicago, September 2-5, 1976 (hereafter cited Pastor, Legislative-Executive Relations).

[3]Ibid., p. 6.

and probably explains the relatively equal give-and-take between the Congress and the Executive better than previous theories were able to do. But in this model we still lose the ability to account for conditions that operate outside the lawmaking process per se. It does not adequately account for the role other governments play in how the United States conducts its foreign policy, nor for the broad conditions that affect trade policy -- either the broad economic conditions, or trade policy conditions themselves such as bargaining between and among trading partners. It does not allow us to discuss international relations within the context of the foreign trade policy-making process.

The difficulty with each of these approaches is their inability to account analytically for interests that do not fundamentally derive from domestic pressure groups. Pastor goes furthest in discounting the pressure group theory of old, but he also does not provide the conceptual framework in which we might understand the relationship between the United States and its major trading partners.

An additional problem is that steel, as with the cases of which it is representative, is kept from the Congress. So these theories are inadequate in still another way: in his skillful and perceptive presentation of the "institutional-biased" model -- an altogether appropriate model to explain the classic trade bill process -- Pastor leaves us with an inappropriate description of the Executive-Legislative relationship in the trade policy process for industrial sectors. Unlike their relationship in the lawmaking process, the Executive and the Congress are unequal in the policy process for cases like steel. Since the issues are ongoing, tend to be independent of one another, and are directly connected to the trade policies of other governments, it is understandable that the Executive plays a much larger role than the Congress. Partly of its own making, and partly due to the nature of these issues, Congress participates in the process largely as the most influential among equals lobbying the Executive.

If it is assumed that the Congress and the Executive participate in a relatively equal relationship, as suggested by plural theories of decisionmaking, one can be particularly confused by Congressional actions. If it is understood, on the other hand, that Congress is acting more as a pressure on the Executive than as an institutional equal to it, events may be more easily interpreted. Consider, for example, three sets of actions taken by the Congress at the end of its 95th Congress. Each one is a product of Congressional response to individual sectors, and intended only to signal precise messages to the Administration about how to conduct the

Nation's trade policy: first, the failure of the 95th Congress to grant the President an extension of the countervailing duty waiver -- a condition for negotiation of a subsidy code, which has been considered one of the more critical and most difficult to negotiate of the non-tariff barrier negotiations, in the GATT.[1] Second, the persistence, and qualified success, of the "textile" lobby, supported by other special interest groups, to prevail on the United States negotiating team in Geneva to withdraw U.S. textile tariff concessions from the trade talks.[2] Their objective has been to avoid further liberalization of United States policy with regard to the percentage of textile and apparel goods imported into the United States. The two measures -- nonaction in the case of the countervailing duty issue, and action in the case of textiles -- caused enough of a stire internationally for the Economist to comment:

---

[1]As of writing, both Houses of the 96th Congress have passed the Waiver Extension. Most of the groups opposing the extension of the waiver during the 95th Congress, notably the sugar and textile lobbies, have negotiated satisfactory arrangements with the Administration.

[2]Senator Hollings (D.-S.C.) led the textile fight in the Senate during the 95th Congress. The issue reached the floor of the United States Senate for the first time on September 29, 1978. For the debate see the Congressional Record, September 29, 1978, pp. 16634-S.16643.

> The two measures produced instant anger from the EEC Ministers meeting in Luxembourg . . . the two sides [the Europeans and the Americans] now have widely differing ideas about what should be done . . . the Europeans are adopting this overt bloody-mindedness [about the overall MTN package].[1]

The third development, also in the last frenetic days of the 95th Congress, was the passage of a bill tightening meat import quotas -- another concrete indication of the strength and willingness to take protective measures.

Indeed, each had a rather direct effect on slowing the progress of an already troubled MTN. And yet, there is still another, seemingly contradictory signal to be read from these actions: the textile proposal was dropped from a bill which would have been difficult for the President to veto, and instead attached to one that easily could be vetoed -- a Jesse Helms Carson City Silver Dollar Bill. Both the textile and meat import bills were vetoed by the President, but what's more important, is that they were vetoable.

The countervailing duty issue has proved more difficult. Still, the tenor of the negotiations between the U.S., and the European Community (which happens to be most affected by it) has been more one of accommodation and compromise than one of conflict. As one Senate staff aide put it:

---

[1]"Congress and the Trade Act," The Economist (October 21, 1978) pp. 109-10.

> No one is looking for a way to defeat the countervailing duty waiver . . . when the President sends a bill to the 96th Congress asking for an extension of the waiver . . . Senators will want to support it . . . it is not like the SALT Treaty were groups conspire to defeat it . . . they will want to do their duty and support free trade.[1]

In fact, when the President finally did send the bill to extend the waiver on countervailing duties to the 96th Congress, the Congress supported it. Congressmen were able to support the President because affected constituent interests had been helped in other areas of trade policy.

What we learn from all of this is that the Congress has learned, rather effectively, to play trade politics with the Executive without taking the ultimate responsibility for policy. By playing that role, the Congress can successfully keep issues separate -- Congressional caucuses push the Administration for an international steel agreement, better concessions for textiles at the MTN, and market sharing arrangements for colored televisions -- and avoid the unpleasant responsibility of trading off one issue for the other as so often happened in the classic trade bill debates.[2] Congress can give the impression that it will represent each industry equally, though the amount it can do for any one is limited.

---

[1]Interview, November 20, 1978.

[2]See Schattschneider, Politics, Pressure, and the Tariff; and Bauer, Pool, and Dexter, American Business and Public Policy.

As we shall see in the case of steel, Congress can pressure the Administration through a number of available tools -- letters to the President or his Special Trade Representative, introduction of legislation, speeches on the House or Senate floors, committee hearings -- but stops short of writing provisions into the law as in the case of a trade bill.

Probably the most dramatic example of the way Congress has learned to finesse its responsibilities in trade matters is reflected in its consideration of the Multilateral Trade Agreement. According to the Trade Act of 1974, the Congress can only vote the final Agreement "up or down"; the provisions in the Trade Act state quite explicitly that no amendments either in the committee or on the floor are allowed, that it be a privileged motion and cannot be recommitted to committee, and that the final vote must be taken after only twenty hours of debate.[1] In effect, the Congress tied its own hands, effectively fluffing off the responsibility of satisfying domestic constituencies to the Administration. This unique situation for consideration of the Multilateral Trade Agreement applies in a general way to other trade matters involving industrial sectors. Congress circumscribes its own power. Conversely, the Executive takes

---

[1]1974 Trade Act, P.L. 93-618.

on proportionately more power. The Executive therefore has the ability and the incentive to develop and promote a set of goals and objectives of its own.

Finally, existing theories do not help us interpret what happens after the legislation becomes law, a critical part of the trade policy process for industrial sectors. There is an ongoing process of trade policy where trade bills are no more than landmarks subject to interpretation through an administrative or adjudicatory process. More precisely, it is not clear from the log-rolling process through which trade bills become law, or from the final Act itself, how particular provisions of trade law will be implemented. The Trade Act of 1974, for example, is pointed to by some analysts as a "free trade bill." It does indeed contain a number of provisions which merit such an interpretation. For example, it delegated unprecedented powers to the President to negotiate another trade liberalization round under the GATT.[1] At the same time, however, it is equally arguable that the "escape clause" provisions were amended to afford interest groups easier access to protection from foreign competition.[2] Even the President's negotiating authority, in certain respects legislated to him so generously, is contingent on equally

---

[1]Ibid. This point is elaborated in Chapter 2.

[2]Ibid.

unprecedented consultative links with the Congress. One simply does not know from the language of the Trade Act, or even from the bargaining process between the Executive and the Legislature during the lawmaking process, the degree Congress may wish to use its "consultative rights," and even if it does to a large degree, whether that will push policy in the direction of freer trade or protection. Therefore, an analytic framework which purports to explain and describe the decisionmaking process should address questions regarding the implementation of laws as well.

IV. An Approach for U.S. Foreign Trade Policy Decisionmaking in Industrial Sectors

The attractiveness of the pressure group theory, as with the related bureaucratic-politics approach, for students of international relations, is that it broke down the "black box" or "billiard ball approach,"[1] in which the state was assumed to be a unified and rational actor. In the latter, two assumptions had to be made: first, that the state is stronger than the society -- i.e., the government, and not domestic constituencies, determined the tenor and direction of policy -- and second, that the state acts autonomously. Both assumptions were unacceptable to the liberal-pluralist theories.[2] Rather, policy was understood to be a function of which groups in society could most effectively apply pressure; the group, not the state, was considered dominant. Besides, empirical

---

[1]Arnold Wolfers describes the international system as a system in which states appeared as unified actors, and where action was viewed as a function of something called "national interest." (Taken from Robert W. Cox, class lecture notes, Columbia University, September 1974).

[2]Krasner, _Defending the National Interest_, especially where he explains that the pluralists agreed that the central feature of American politics was the fragmentation and dispersion of power. See p. 61.

evidence could prove that interest groups actually did play the determinant role in the policymaking process.[1]

Indeed, compared to other countries, the United States government is weak relative to its society -- certainly weaker than the authoritarian or totalitarian types, but also weaker than other democratic types which resolve more and more issues in the domain of public policy.[2] In some sense, then, it is accurate to characterize governmental policy in the United States as a reflection of whichever groups in society hold and use power. However, the concept of a public or national interest, or one of state objectives and goals, different from the vector summation of the interests of all groups in the society, had no real home in liberal-pluralist thinking. This was predictable since the liberal-pluralist thinkers sought to do exactly opposite from what was represented by the "national interest" concept.

---

[1]See, for example, Robert Dahl *Who Governs?* (New Haven: Yale University Press, 1961).

[2]For excellent studies on this point see Andrew Shonfield, *Modern Capitalism: The Changing Balance of Public and Private Power* (London, New York, Toronto: Oxford University Press, 1965); Peter J. Katzenstein, ed. *Between Power and Plenty: Foreign Economic Policies of Advanced Industrial States* (Madison, Wisconsin: University of Wisconsin Press 1978); John Zysman, *Political Strategies for Industrial Order: State, Market, and Industry in France* (Berkeley: University of California Press 1977); William Diebold, Jr., *The United States and the Industrial World: American Foreign Economic Policy in the 1970s* (New York: Praeger 1972); and *Joseph A. Schumpeter, Capitalism, Socialism, and Democracy* (New York: Harper and Brothers 1942).

But, in opening up the black box, an entirely necessary and good development in political science theory, all that accompanied it was discarded. It became heresy to suggest that there might be a set of state objectives different from those developed through the policymaking process, i.e., that an Administration could have a particular set of interests it pursues which are not entirely the product of the pressures from domestic constituencies. For one thing, the ideological overtones -- that the state is more powerful than the society -- were frightful. And it was entirely right to be fearful of such a development. For another, from where could one have presumed these objectives might have come anyway, if not from interest groups?

This study assumes that United States foreign trade policy develops from a process in which there are many competing interests, and where one of those interests is represented by an Administration policy -- a set of goals and objectives which form the foundation for a bargaining process out of which policy is derived. In formulating policy for industrial sectors like steel, policymakers in the Administration respond to pressures from non-domestic groups such as foreign governments and foreign private interests, in addition to domestic constituencies. This process has been institutionalized in the development of a clearly defined group of individuals throughout the federal bureaucracy who formulate industrial trade policy. Ironically, because of the apparently diffuse nature of trade policy -- virtually every agency in the federal bureaucracy has an office of trade policy which seeks to claim jurisdiction over some aspect -- the lead agencies[1] and representatives from the White House staff meet and develop positions, goals, and objectives on issues. Thus when one refers to the Administration, one is really talking about a three-tier committee structure which varies according to sector. For example, experts on steel from the Special Trade Representative's Office (STR) and the Departments of Treasury, State, Commerce, and Labor, consider issues and formulate policy.

The three-tier structure consists of 1) the Trade Policy Committee as the senior policymaking level comprised of the Secretaries from the lead agencies and chaired by the President's Special Trade Representative (STR) for Trade Negotiations; 2) the Trade Policy Review Group (TPRG), a second level, is comprised of the Assistant or Undersecretary representatives from the lead agencies, and chaired by the Assistant to the President's STR; 3) the Trade Policy Staff Committee level is comprised

---

[1]The "lead agencies" in U.S. Trade Policy are: the Special Trade Representative's office, Departments of State, Treasury, Commerce, and Labor.

of working staff representatives from the lead agencies and chaired by a senior civil servant from the STR's office, according to sector.[1] Predictably, most of the work is done by the Trade Policy Staff Committee, though decisions are typically made by the TPRG.

Thus there are individuals across the federal bureaucracy who develop an Administration position for individual sectors -- positions on steel, textiles, electronics, and shoes, for example. It is this position which represents the Administration's interest in the bargaining process among government, domestic constituencies, and foreign interests. So in this study, government will be understood to mean more than what Bentley suggested when he said: "The interest groups create the government and work through it . . ."[2] And, the process of government, too, will be understood

---

[1]Understandably, there is only one representative from an agency for the Trade Policy Committee since this group is comprised of the Secretaries of the Departments, and the Special Trade Representative. For the second tier -- the Trade Policy Review Group -- the representative is likely to change according to issues. For example, the textile and steel representative is likely to be a different individual. In the case of the third tier -- the Trade Policy Staff Committee -- it is virtually certain that different sets of individuals represent their departments depending upon the sector.

[2]Arthur F. Bentley, "The Process of Government," quoted in <u>Essays on the Scientific Study of Politics</u>, ed. Herbert J. Storing, article by Leo Weinstein "The Group Approach," (New York: Holt Reinhart and Winston, 1962) p. 270.

as something different from -- indeed more than -- interest group participation.

Hence, the concept of a "national interest," amended, does have a place in developing an analytic framework which purports to explain how the United States conducts its foreign trade policy for industrial sectors. Stephen Krasner has developed a carefully reasoned argument which concludes that there is a national interest separate from what evolves out of group pressure on government. There is a distinction, he writes, between the state and society in which the state may be viewed as an autonomous actor.[1] That is, the state -- effectively represented by one, two, or all three of the policy groups listed above -- creates a position for itself distinct from any one position offered by domestic or foreign interests, though trying to balance the two. According to Krasner, "A statist paradigm views the state as an autonomous actor. The objectives sought by the state cannot be reduced to some summation of private desires. These objectives can be called appropriately the national interest."[2]

While not adhering strictly to Krasner's statist paradigm, an analytic framework derived from that thought

---

[1]Stephen Krasner, Defending the National Interest.

[2]Ibid., p. 5.

should help the researcher avoid the pitfalls of both pluralist thinking and systems theory. In the first case one tends to overlook the participants external to the state, concentrating on groups and actions in the society and/or agencies in the Executive branch jockeying for power. In addition, one fails to account for a particularly strong Executive, not only as compared to groups in society, but also compared to the Legislature, i.e., it doesn't allow us to consider policy tools outside the legislative process.

In the second case, one loses sight of how active and dynamic the state, qua nation state, continues to be, but often assumes that the growth of transnational or supranational organizations have superseded it.[1]

None of these accurately depict the process involved in the burgeoning number of industrial sector cases which comprise an ever-growing part of the United States foreign trade policy process. The state appears to be growing stronger, while at the same time, interests outside the society affect policy.

It is not this author's intention to revert to a theory which suffered from serious misunderstandings

---

[1]Stephen Krasner, "State Power and Structure of International Trade," where he writes: "In recent years, students of international relations have multinationalized, bureaucratized, and transgovernmentalized the state until it has virtually ceased to exist as an analytic construct." p. 317.

about relations between state and society in liberal-democratic systems. But, the analytic dissolution of the state -- from the society "below," or from the international system "above" -- is not acceptable either.
In the case of steel -- 1976-78 -- there have been changes at the level of United States operating procedures which come about from the interaction of forces in the domestic society with those in the international system. The intervening force between these two levels is the U.S. government, represented in very large proportion by the Executive. The relationship among the three occurs through a bargaining process, which is characterized by a dynamic where the "Administration policy" is considered greater than a creation of the policymaking process as pluralist theory understands it, i.e., the Administration adopts certain goals and objectives of its own in order to accommodate both sets of pressures -- international and domestic. We shall approach our examination of the development of the U.S. foreign trade policy for steel in this framework.

INTRODUCTION TO PART I

The steel issue in the United States did not suddenly erupt as a foreign trade problem in the mid-seventies. It had been a persistent source of tension in U.S. trade policy since 1963, when Roger M. Blough, representing the steel industry, and David J. McDonald, president of the United Steelworkers of America together appealed to President Kennedy to "help block the dumping of foreign steel sold here at prices below those charged in the manufacturing country."[1]

Indeed, prior to that period, the USW and the industry were more accustomed to meeting each other as adversaries across the collective bargaining table; only three years earlier McDonald was still blaming the government's domestic policy, and implicating industry's internal decisions, for the depressed conditions in the steel sector: "The real trouble in steel is not the imports but the business conditions at home. If we were to take decisive measures to strengthen our economy and thereby expand job opportunities there would be no problem concerning imports."[2]

---

[1]"McDonald, Blough to See President Kennedy," Steel Labor, September 1963 (Indianapolis, Indiana, Sept. 1963).

[2]Ibid.

But, by 1963 the industry and the USW together filed a petition against dumping, and alleged:

> The dumping problem has assumed such proportions since 1959 that it threatens the most serious consequences for American Pipe Producers and his employers . . . [We] believe in free trade under fair conditions. We are certain that under such conditions our steel industry can compete effectively with foreign steel companies . . .[1]

Tensions continued to mount as import tonnage for the industry as a whole reached ten million net tons in 1965, accounting for over ten percent of apparent domestic consumption.[2] That was considerably higher, and resulted in a deeper trade deficit for steel than ever had been experienced in the country.[3] Imports continued to rise over the next three years, reaching 18 million tons or about 17 percent of apparent consumption by 1968. So, by 1968, the steel import situation had become a problem for steel industry and labor, and would become one for the government. For that level of import penetration, according to industry spokesmen, contributed significantly to maintaining reasonable profits needed to finance the modernization of facilities. And, in fair trade parlance, it was blamed on other countries' economic strategies.

---

[1]Ibid.

[2]William Hogan, <u>1970s: The Critical Years for Steel</u> (Lexington: Lexington Books 1972) Chapter 3.

[3]See N 1, "Introduction to the Political Economy of Steel."

"If foreign steel producing industries were run like prudent private enterprises in this country,"[1] the industry argued before the Finance Committee in 1968, "the problems of the U.S. steel industry would be less troublesome."

This period also marked a change in the nature of the relationship between government and industry. Until 1968, the government-industry relationship was characterized by what a Senate Finance Committee Report described as "friction arising over decisions by the steel industry."[2] Indeed, prior to this period it was quite noticeable that industry and government confronted each other in adversarial terms. Industry didn't have much need for government, and Washington didn't care much for what it believed was industry's interference in free market competition. From the turn of the century, U.S. Steel, and others, had been accused time and again of monopolistic, anticompetitive practices; in 1949 President Truman threatened to expand steelmaking capacity by seizing some of the country's major steel mills -- an event he claimed was in the national interest since the steel industry, it was felt, could not be relied upon to

---

[1]U.S. Congress, Senate Committee on Finance, Report on Steel Imports, 90th Congress, 2d Session (Washington, D.C.: Government Printing Office), December 19, 1967, p.xxi.

[2]Ibid.

produce quantities of steel necessary for the Korean war effort; in 1962 President Kennedy confronted the industry's decision to raise prices, and forced a rollback; and so forth.[1]

By the mid-sixties when the industry turned its attention to the effects that international trade were having on its competitive position, they found that a different kind of atmosphere between themselves and government was necessary. Since their competitive position -- "its ability to maintain reasonable profit levels and its need to finance the modernization of facilities"[2] -- was now related not only to an ability to raise prices and control domestic market forces, but also to competition from foreign producers, the industry (and labor) recognized that they would have to

---

[1]William T. Hogan, Economic History of the Iron and Steel Industry in the United States, 5 volumes. (See especially volumes 4 and 5, Part VI) (Lexington, Massachusetts: Lexington Books, 1971); Gertrude Schroder, The Growth of the Major Steel Companies, 1900-1950 (Baltimore: The Johns Hopkins Press, 1953); Maeva Marcus, Truman and the Steel Seizure Case: The Limits of Presidential Power (New York: Columbia University Press 1977); Steel Labor, "The Voice of United Steelworkers of America," 1943-1971 (Indianapolis, Indiana, published monthly); Walter Adams, "The Steel Industry," The Structure of American Industry; Walter Adams, ed. (New York: Macmillan, 1977); U.S. Tariff Commission, Report Series, No. 128, Iron and Steel (Washington, D.C.: Government Printing Office 1938).

[2]U.S. Senate Finance Committee Report on Steel Imports, December 1967, p. xxi.

go to Washington for programs to offset what they argued were it foreign competitors' unfair advantages. As a first step they enlisted the Congress. In its Report on "Steel Imports," the Senate Finance Committee was sympathetic:

> No private enterprise industry can, in the long run, survive in competition with foreign industries that have become "instruments of government," unless its own government lends assistance against subsidized imports. . ."[1]

Simply put, that is what happened in 1967: the steel lobby (industry, labor, aided by special pressures from sympathetic Congressmen) asked its government to lend assistance -- assistance for a condition which was described by the Senate Finance Committee:

> World overcapacity of steelmaking facilities [that] caused some foreign steel industries to unload their surplus production on the U.S. market at prices at or below cost. In some countries they have been abetted by governments through the remission of taxes and through subsidies.[2]

So, after some controversy the Johnson Administration in December 1969, entered into a Voluntary Restraint Agreement (VRA) for basic steel with Japan and the six members of the European Coal and Steel Community (ECSC): they agreed to limit total steel imports into the United State to fourteen million tons for 1969, divided 41

---

[1]Ibid., p. xxiii.

[2]Ibid., p. xxii.

percent for Japan and the ECSC, each, and 18 percent for the rest of the world.[1]

For 1969, imports were recorded at fourteen million tons; in 1970 they fell to 13.4 million.[2] But, in 1971 they rose again to an all-time high of 18.3 million tons.[3] Thus negotiations among the United States, Japan, and the ECSC, began again in mid-1971 to renew or extend the 1968 VRA.[4] Agreement was finally reached and signed in May 1972.[5]

But the steel issue wouldn't go away. In 1973, the industrial countries experienced what is now nostalgically referred to as a "boom year," and international economic problems among them seemed to fade. Like a sore pimple -- in the immediate sense a derivative of the unhealthy European conditions, but from the long term perspective, a result of the effects the precipitous Japanese growth had on international trade -- the problem returned again in 1975, but U.S. policymakers were hopeful that "it could be kept on the back burner."[6] It couldn't.

---

[1]William Hogan, 1970s: The Critical Years for Steel, p. 52.

[2]Ibid., pp. 52-53.

[3]Ibid.

[4]Ibid., p. 55.

[5]Ibid., p. 70.

[6]Interview, November 2, 1978.

And so, industry and labor again went to Washington for assistance. But by 1977, the idea that the U.S. government could actively intervene in the international trade of industrial products had been well established. For steel it was about ten years old, for textiles even older, and other sectors were quickly catching on. Still, the programs developed for steel in 1976-78, carved out new conceptual ground for U.S. industrial trade policy in its domestic and international aspects. In part this was because of the recognition that the issue was not only persistent, but getting worse. This was also because of the peculiar circumstances of the period -- the structural crisis was exacerbated by imposing recessionary conditions. What had been evolving since the mid-sixties reached a critical stage in terms of policy development by 1976. However, the structural changes which characterize the world steel industry in the 1970s raised even more serious questions about the economic viability and political advisability of a foreign trade policy for the United States based on, and wedded in, principles of liberalism. United States policymakers found that the squeeze between an economic liberalism and political internationalism on the one hand, and an economic nationalism on the other, got more difficult to balance. Of course, there is the view stated by Susan Strange that we need not choose between the two propositions. Ms. Strange argues, "If both tendencies are ever-present in the international political economy, both doctrines may be valid. National interest may require both trade liberalization and trade protection."[1]

The dilemma posed by the two policy extremes -- trade liberalism and trade protection -- have led U.S. policymakers to a compromised "interventionism" in the market through strategies of "market-sharing diplomacy" and other forms of collective protection. Specific details and arrangements obtain in each individual case involving industrial sectors. For steel -- as with other international products like textiles, electronics, or shoes -- U.S. policymakers operate from a set of goals and objectives derived in part from general level policy concerns, and in part from the specifics of each case. The prescriptions for the margins of policy -- those points beyond which policymakers perceived they could not tread, and around which the specific details for policy evolved -- comprise the qualities which shall be referred to in this paper as "national policy," i.e., the Administration's goals and objectives. These are the parameters which define

---

[1]Susan Strange, "The Management of Surplus Capacity: Or, How Does Theory Stand Up to Protectionism 1970s Style?" (London, 1978, xeroxed), p. 1.

the Administration's, i.e., the Executive branch, foreign trade policy.

In Part I we shall discuss the conditions in which the United States policy for steel, 1976-78, evolved. Chapter 2 of this section will focus on the general U.S. context -- i.e., the political climate largely shaped by the terms of the Multilateral Trade Negotiations, the debate over U.S. trade law, and the ideological changes in how U.S. policymakers have come to view the relationship between politics and the market. In Chapter 3 we shall turn our attention to the global context from which U.S. trade policy for steel developed. There we shall address specifically the political economic conditions of steel outside the United States insofar as these conditions affected the U.S. policy itself. Together, Chapter 2 -- the U.S. policy context -- and Chapter 3 -- the global political-economic context -- will be viewed as constraints on U.S. policymakers as they developed a foreign trade policy for steel.

CHAPTER 2

PARAMETERS FOR AN ADMINISTRATION POSITION

I. Introduction

The United States foreign trade policy for steel was shaped against a background of three conditions in U.S. politics: the Multilateral Trade Negotiations (MTN) in Geneva which formed the overall political climate effectively absorbing the steel issue; an ongoing debate over how to interpret the import relief provisions of domestic trade law, a process that largely determined the legal and administrative bounds in which the steel issue was set; and, the increased use of market-sharing arrangements by U.S. policymakers in other industrial sectors, an indicator of important changes in the ideological background of what was acceptable to do in industrial trade policy. Each of these conditions were hopelessly intertwined, though for analytic purposes will be treated separately in this chapter.

In their own ways they set the parameters outside of which the steel policy could not have developed. Whether it was the political climate, the legal claims, or the ideological background, each acted as pressures on those who participated in the development of a foreign trade policy for steel.

Interestingly, the one constant drawing together each of these three elements was the Trade Act of 1974 -- an ambiguous document which reflected the reality of interlocking, and sometimes conflicting, views among the Administration, the Congress, and domestic interests. The steel issue was not itself contained by the Trade Act, but the pressures which did shape it were themselves dependent on the Act. After all, the Trade Act is the formal foundation for U.S. trade policy. And yet, it offers little help in understanding the development of the steel policy, apart from its relationship as part of the dynamic which made up each separate condition. Therefore, let us turn first to a discussion of the Trade Act as it affected the political climate. We shall then begin to examine how all three broad pressures formed the background against which the foreign trade policy for steel developed.

II. Commitment to the MTN -- The Political Climate

The commitment to, and completion of, a successful Multilateral Trade Agreement has loomed in the background of virtually all trade matters involving the U.S. with Japan and Western Europe since 1973. According to one Senate staffer: "For a few years now, it has been the biggest game in town."[1] Indeed, some policy officials explicitly based their support of, and interest in, the Trade Act of 1974 on the grounds that it was a necessary condition for negotiating trade liberalization in the GATT. Henry Kissinger, clearly the leading foreign policy official of the Ford Administration, confirmed this when he said that the trade bill was necessary,

> [for] the trade negotiations to be conducted seriously . . . on the substantive issues . . . (the actual and potential trade disturbances of the energy situation are

---

[1]Interview, November 16, 1978.

urgent), and the authority contained in the trade bill is needed.[1]

President Ford, in his annual report to the Congress on "The Trade Agreements Program" stated that the launching of the seventh round of the multilateral trade negotiations is "the most important event in the international trade field . . . .[2]

Still more recently, when discussing the steel issue, an official at the State Department bluntly characterized the MTN as "the key to the last four years . . . [the goal elsewhere] has been to not upset the applecart in Geneva."[3] But, during the course of these negotiations, the debate in the United States has in many ways paralleled the debate over the interpretation of the Trade Act of 1974. Therefore, let us look at the terms of that debate.

The Trade Act, the MTN, and the U.S. Commitment to Liberalization

The Trade Act of 1974 authorizes the Executive

---

[1]U.S. Congress, Senate Committee on Finance, The Trade Reform Act of 1973, "Digest of Testimony Received on H.R. 10710," 93rd Congress, 2d Session (Washington, D.C.: Government Printing Office, October 1974). p. 1.

[2]The Eighteenth Annual Report on the Trade Agreements Program: Message from the President of the United States, August 8, 1974. (Washington, D.C.: Government Printing Office 1974). p. 13.

[3]Interview, November 2, 1978.

to enter into trade agreements -- an implicit condition for trade liberalization. According to the "Summary of Provisions," a document used far more than the Public Law itself by staff and Congressmen alike when dealing with matters of international trade:

> The Act gives strong emphasis to the need for establishing fair and equitable conditions of trade, including reform of the General Agreement on Trade and Tariffs . . . for the purpose of harmonizing, reducing, or eliminating tariff and non-tariff barriers to, and other distortions of, international trade . . . .[1]

But not everyone agreed on what "fair and equitable conditions of trade" meant -- a phrase which effectively sums up the whole of the trade policy debate in the United States and among its major trading partners, since roughly 1965.[2] It is worth going into some detail here since the MTN -- as the condition creating the political climate into which the steel issue was absorbed -- was itself shaped in U.S. trade policy by the character of this debate.

---

[1]U.S. Congress, Senate and House Committees on Finance and Ways and Means, Trade Act of 1974, "Summary of Provisions of H.R. 10710," 93rd Congress, 2d Session (Washington, D.C.: December 30, 1974). p. 1.

[2]The term "fair trade" will be used throughout this paper. It is a phrase which was first used by industry and labor groups who believed they were unfairly discriminated against in international trade as a result of other governments' interference in the "free trade system." "Fair trade" has been regularly used since about the mid-sixties, when industrial sector constituencies in the United States -- steel, textiles, etc. -- began to ask Washington for assistance in international trade issues. It is typically used in a context preceded by, "I'm a free trader,

For some, "fair and equitable conditions of trade" did refer to the mandate needed to negotiate further liberalization of international trade in the GATT. Alan Wolff, now second in command for U.S. trade negotiations under Ambassador Strauss, took this view when he wrote:

> The Trade Act of 1974 was the most carefully studied enactment of trade legislation in the history of the United States. The result was a precisely drawn mandate which allows the Executive to enter into negotiations.[1]

And complete them, it might be added. A number of high level policy officials in Treasury also took this position -- Assistant Secretary C. Fred Bergsten, Under Secretary Anthony Solomon, and General Counsel Robert Mundheim, have all expressed this view at one

---

but . . . ," implicitly admitting that it is still not acceptable in U.S. trade politics to "be a protectionist." Indeed, many foreign trade policy officials in government have begun to use the term as well. In many ways, the term has begun to lose value since it is invoked so often. To be fair, however, there is still a distinction between terms of "fair trade," "free trade," and "protection"; in the United States pressures for "fair trade" are increasingly answered by various forms of market-sharing arrangements, i.e., "organized free trade." (We shall develop the concept of "organized free trade" throughout this paper.) For an interesting discussion of the "Free Trade"-"Fair Trade" debate see the Economist, "Free Trade to Fair Trade," 2/10/79, pp. 87, 88.

[1]Alan Wolff, "The U.S. Mandate for Trade Negotiations," Virginia Journal of International Law, volume 16, number 3 (Spring 1976)

time or another.[1] Bergsten, for example, commented at a Labor Department Conference on Unemployment that "The United States need not join the protectionist policies of its trading partners," and went on to say that the U.S. commitment to the MTN is grounded in the belief that "We ought to fight their [protectionist] policies [by being free traders]."[2] The position is also promoted regularly by those at State. As one business leader involved in the MTN commented, "You can count on State to support almost any position which

---

[1]Officials in Treasury -- notably Assistant Secretary C. Fred Bergsten, Under Secretary Anthony Solomon, General Counsel Robert Mundheim, and Assistant Secretary for Tariff Affairs, Peter Erenhaft -- have tended to continue to support a liberal trading order not substantially different from what we have been used to since 1945. In part this can be explained by Treasury's institutional relationship to corporate finance and multinationals which maintain an obvious stake in the liberal trading order (almost) regardless of how it may adversely affect domestic industries like steel, textiles, or shoes. Treasury's position in these matters is manifested in its enforcement, or lack thereof, of the anti-dumping and countervailing duty laws over which it has jurisdiction. Treasury has clearly favored a very liberal interpretation and enforcement of these laws, a position it has maintained over the decades, transcending Administrations. Predictably, this position tends to perpetuate itself in the type of high level policy official appointed to Treasury. As an example, see C. Fred Bergsten ed. The Future of the International Economic Order: An Agenda for Research (Washington, D.C.: The Brookings Institution 1974).

[2]Quoting C. Fred Bergsten at a U.S. Labor Department Conference on International Trade and Its Effects on Unemployment, 11/15/78, in personal files of author. Bergsten made his remarks in the context of a debate with former Secretary of Labor Dunlop. Dunlop was proposing that the United States should admit how its trading partners are acting -- policies of intervention in the

will lead to the conclusion of an Agreement."[1] While those in the Special Trade Representative's office generally didn't hold a free trade position on ideological grounds, as Bergsten at Treasury or Secretary Cooper at State,[2] it was the key agency negotiating the MTN and so went after an Agreement for the sake of an Agreement. In private sessions with the Finance Committee, top officials in the STR's office have revealed their desire ". . . to finish this unthankful job . . . spread the pain as evenly as possible by nicking instead of goring most interests' oxes."[3] Such was one man's implicit definition of "fair and equitable."

To others, however, "fair and equitable conditions" meant the need to redress the unfair trading

---

market -- and join in with those kinds of policies so as to give U.S. domestic producers a "fair chance." In response, Bergsten argued that the United States should fight those policies with fervent and diligent free trade policies. For an elaboration, see my conclusion, pp.

[1]Interview, December 17, 1978.

[2]See, for example, Richard N. Cooper, <u>The Economics of Interdependence: Economic Policy in the Atlantic Community</u> (New York: McGraw Hill, 1968); especially note Parts I and II; see also Bergsten, <u>The Future of the International Economic Order</u>.

[3]Quoted from Finance Committee closed session with the Special Trade Representative's office. On file in personal notes of author.

practices of their trading partners. Proponents of this view would promote what is now popularly called "fair trade."

Consider, for example, a statement by Russell Long, the powerful chairman of the Senate Finance Committee, where he indicated the hard line interpretation some would assign to the 1974 Trade Act. In March 1974, on the first day of a long series of hearings before the Senate Finance Committee, he included in his opening remarks a cautious prognosis about the U.S. role in world economic affairs. He said:

> I recognize that the United States must play a major role in leading the world and shaping its economy . . . . I was very much in favor of the Trade Expansion Act of 1962. I still desire an open, nondiscriminatory, and fair world economic system, but I am tired of the United States being the least favored nation in a world which is full of discrimination. We can no longer expose our markets, while the rest of the world hides behind variable levies, export subsidies, import equalization fees, border taxes, cartels, government procurement practices, dumping, import quotas, and a host of other practices which effectively bar our products . . . what I am saying is that trade legislation comes before the committee bearing a heavy burden.[1]

Precisely because of its heavy burden, and exactly because the framers of the Trade Act feared that the bill could be interpreted as a mandate for liberalization even to the detriment of domestic constituencies -- goring

---

[1]U.S. Congress, Senate Committee on Finance, The Trade Reform Act of 1973, "Hearings Before the Committee on Finance on H.R. 10710," 93rd Congress, 1st Session (Washington, D.C.: Government Printing Office 1974). p. 2.

as well as nicking oxes -- a series of provisions were included in the Act which were intended to protect these interests. So, while U.S. negotiators were given a broader mandate for negotiations than ever before -- "to obtain full reciprocity and equal competitive opportunities for U.S. commerce . . . in assaulting non-tariff trade barriers"[1] -- the framers of the law also sought to promote a cooperative and consultative relationship between U.S. negotiators and domestic interests. They created a situation which put serious constraints on the mandate by giving ". . . U.S. business-men the same access to the U.S. negotiating team that businessmen in other countries have to theirs,"[2] and by providing for a "constitutionally sound procedure for Congressional consideration of the resulting agreements."[3] So, with regard to the MTN, the Trade Act was a double-edged sword.

It is not surprising, however, that the Administration couched virtually all questions about trade policy in terms of what it meant for the MTN; U.S. policy

---

[1] 1974 Trade Act, P.L. 93-618.

[2] U.S. Congress, Senate Committee on Finance, Report of the Committee of Finance on the Trade Act of 1974, "Senate Finance Committee Report on H.R. 10710," 93rd Congress, 2d Session (Washington, D.C.: Government Printing Office 1974).

[3] Ibid.

officials had a mandate to fulfill:[1] As a major participant in the Tokyo Round of the MTN, the U.S. was committed to trade liberalization not only in the more conventional tariff cutting areas, but also in the less conventional, and much more difficult non-tariff barrier area.[2] While progressive liberalization of international trade in the tariff cutting area had been accomplished in the Dillon Round of 1960-61, and the Kennedy Round of 1964-67, the Tokyo Round had broken new and important negotiating ground. In the Kennedy Rounds the major countries were successful at reaching agreement on some of the non-tariff barrier issues, but the United States Congress failed to pass the necessary

---

[1]High level officials who have indicated this position on the public record: Ambassador Strauss, Assistant Ambassador Wolff, and General Counsel Rivers at the Special Trade Representative's office; Assistant Secretary Bergsten, Under Secretary Solomon, Assistant Secretary Erenhaft, and General Counsel Mundheim at Treasury; and Assistant Secretary Cooper at State.

[2]The Tokyo Round of the Multilateral Trade Negotiations of the GATT officially began when the Ministers of 104 nations adopted the Tokyo Declaration at a GATT Conference in Tokyo on September 14, 1973. However, the negotiations didn't officially start until February 5, 1975, and the more serious part of the negotiations didn't begin until the summer of 1977, after the Carter Administration took office. While 104 nations officially participate in the GATT negotiations of the Tokyo Round, less than thirty participate actively in all aspects of the negotiations. For a good analysis of the intended effects of the Tokyo Round see, William Cline, et. al., Trade Negotiations at the Tokyo Round: A Quantitative Assessment (Washington, D.C.: The Brookings Institution 1977).

implementing legislation. The U.S. negotiating team would want to be at least as successful as they had been in the Kennedy Round in tariff cutting, and avoid the unpleasant embarrassment of the non-tariff barrier experience.

But, it was also not surprising that domestic interests couched their demands in terms of the MTN, for it was the overriding concern of the Administration and a certain forum in which one could be heard. Steel was no exception. Ironically, it was the very Trade Act which gave the Administration its mandate to negotiate a Trade Agreement which also provided the institutional channels through which the steel lobby[1] could effectively press its demands. From the Administration's viewpoint, it always came down to saving the MTN, and the stronger lobbies, of which steel must be counted were therefore able to exercise strong leverage.

While the Trade Act committed the United States to a Multilateral Trade Agreement, there were provisions in it which set the stage for a political debate over what constituted liberalization. The MTN created the political climate in which the steel issue was absorbed,

---

[1]The term "steel lobby" will be used throughout this paper. Unless otherwise specified, it refers to the coalition of labor and industry which jointly lobbied the Administration. For a good history of the evolution of the "steel lobby," the internal relationship, and its relationship with the U.S. government, survey "Steel Labor," a weekly trade paper for the United Steelworkers of America.

and from which the policy developed; the Trade Act promoted this in two specific ways.

First, the advisory committee framework which provided the institutional network for communication between representatives from industry and labor, and the Administration.[1] Second, the Trade Act gave the President the authority to "negotiate by sectors" within the manufacturing sector -- i.e., ". . . the U.S. negotiators [are] to obtain, to the maximum extent feasible, equivalent competitive sectors . . . .[2]

A great deal of importance was attached to both provisions. As an illustration, consider the comprehensive analysis of the Trade Act by Ambassador Wolff where he pointed to the relationship between both provisions, and the degree to which the Trade Act recognized the need for U.S. negotiators to respond to domestic constituencies. Accordingly, he wrote that:

> The Special Trade Representative [was] instructed to consult with private and other

---

[1]Creation of the Advisory Sector Committees was provided by the Trade Act of 1974. Advisory Sector Committees were created for Industry, Labor and Agriculture to advise the American negotiators on the Multilateral Trade Agreements. It was felt by the framers of the Trade Act of 1974 that close consultation between the Administration negotiators and domestic interests would be absolutely critical since the final package of Trade Agreements would go before the Congress as one and all interests would therefore have to be satisfied during the negotiating process.

[2]"Summary of Provisions of the Trade Act of 1974," p. 7.

> advisory groups to define appropriate product sectors of manufacturing,

and also pointed to the President's responsibility;

> to include with each trade agreement submitted to Congress a sector-by-sector analysis of the extent to which the objective of obtaining substantially equivalent competitive opportunities had been achieved.[1]

Both provisions underscored the concern expressed by interest groups and Members of Congress that the Executive branch may fail to adequately protect their particular interests while conducting the nation's foreign trade policy at the international negotiating level. Let us examine both provisions to see how they contributed to the political climate of the MTN.

The Advisory Committees

The Advisory Committees are significant because for the first time in the history of GATT negotiations they provided a major advisory role for the private sector. In his annual report to the Congress on Trade Agreements, President Ford said of the Committees that they are establishing a system,

> . . . to represent, in connection with trade negotiations, the interests of the public at large as well as specific interests of industry, agriculture, and labor . . . . These advisory

---

[1]Alan Wolff, "The U.S. Mandate for Trade Negotiations."

> committees will evaluate the result of the trade agreements for both the Congress and the President.[1]

The evolution of the advisory committee structure from idea to law is interesting, since it supports the basic notion found in "bureaucratic politics decision-making theory" that constituencies match up with Executive branch bureaucratic agencies. The idea was originated by Forrest Abdul, senior trade policy specialist in the Department of Commerce, who had served in the bureaucracy since the early sixties, and so had participated in the Kennedy Round negotiations of the GATT. Having been through the unpleasant experience of the failure to win Congressional approval on the non-tariff barrier provision of the MTN agreement during the Kennedy Round, and having recognized a generally disagreeable relationship between industry and government during that period, Abdul understood the need, as he put it, "for a better mechanism . . . to get advice from industry on trade negotiations."[2]

During consideration of the 1974 Trade Bill, therefore, he orchestrated a series of letters between "his Secretary" (of Commerce) and the Special Trade Representative's office. Support at the staff levels of Commerce and STR led to support at the Secretary levels,

---

[1]*The Nineteenth Annual Report on the Trade Agreements Program: Message from the President of the United States*, May 15, 1975 (Washington, D.C.: Government Printing Office, May 1975). p. 7.

[2]Interview, November 9, 1978.

who, in turn, promoted it in the Congress. At the same time, Congressional leaders were lobbied by industry, and by labor as well, since the idea had come around that advisory sector groups would be established for "all manner of constituencies."[1]

Predictably, there was no opposition to the provision, since the only ones who might have been expected to oppose it -- the Administration, on the grounds that it might further complicate an already complicated negotiating process -- had already been lined up behind it by Abdul's office in Commerce and the STR's office.

Once consensus had formed around it in the Administration, and especially after it was written into law, each of the departments involved in the trade negotiations -- Treasury, STR, Commerce, State and Labor -- came to view the advisory sectors as a necessary and desirable element of the trade negotiating process. Indeed, each of the agencies used it to promote its particular interests. But, it was also a major vehicle by which domestic constituencies pressed for concessions from the MTN.

Both the industry and labor considered the advisory committees one of their great victories of the Trade Act. For example, Jack Sheehan, legislative director for the United Steelworkers of America, has since referred to the

---

[1]Interview, November 9, 1978.

provision as one which ensures ". . . a framework for discussion . . . [through which] the Administration responds to us, and we respond to them. It [the steel issue] was kept on the front boiler all the time through it . . ."[1] And, reflecting on the lack of consultation during the Kennedy Round, he remembered: "This time it [is] different."[2]

Once the MTN actually got underway in 1975, the advisory committees began to operate, and as indicated by Sheehan's comments, did so rather successfully. We shall see in later sections that they operated with the force of law, strengthened by the power of political support throughout the bureaucracy, in the private sector, and on the Hill.

The foundation for the steel industry's claims during the course of the MTN, and the beginning of the Administration's awareness of the industry's basic interests, were set forth in a March 11, 1975 American Iron and Steel Institute (AISI) letter to Ambassador Dent, then Secretary of Commerce. It was the product of an AISI "work group" established to work with government negotiators in the MTN process. It was submitted, in AISI's words "to conform to the time schedule set forth by the Department of Commerce and the Office of Special

---

[1]Interview with Jack Sheehan, legislative director for United Steelworkers of America, December 14, 1978.

[2]Ibid.

Trade Representative for Trade Negotiations for initial input from the private sector."[1] In basic outline, the letter read:

> Dear Mr. Secretary . . . Hopefully our confidential document submitted today will initiate constructive assessment and set the direction for vitally important sector trade negotiations affecting our industry and the nation.[2]

By way of the document industry set forth its platform:

> There may be sectoral negotiations for steel . . . an effective international safeguard system for steel . . . negotiations should focus in reducing disparities between the U.S. and other countries in total costs of entry resulting from tariff as well as non-tariff charges . . . tariff preferences for developing countries present special problems in the steel sector.[3]

Thus, the advisory committees served industry well. Inasmuch as the Administration relied on domestic constituencies for ultimate support of a Multilateral Trade Agreement there were benefits for the Administration also.

Sectoral Negotiations

The second element in the Trade Act which molded the MTN's political climate was the "sector negotiating objective." The Trade Act gives the President the authority for, and directed the U.S. negotiators to

---

[1]American Iron and Steel Institute, "Introductory Note to the Special Trade Representative and the Secretary of Commerce," 3/11/75 (xeroxed: on file with the Department of Commerce and STR's office).

[2]Ibid.

[3]Ibid.

negotiate, sector arrangements in the MTN.[1] Although it does not specify sectors for negotiation within the manufacturing sector -- Administration officials had persuaded the Congress that "[the] United States is only one party in the multilateral trade negotiating process . . . [so it therefore] doesn't make sense to mandate specific sectors for negotiations,"[2] -- there is legislative history which specifies industrial sectors. Responding to strong pressures, the Senate Finance Committee Report specified particular sectors which were to be given special consideration. According to the Report:

> The Committee feels that appropriate product sectors would include, among others, such industries as steel, aluminum, electronics, chemicals, and electrical machinery . . . [and the Committee Report went on to say] . . . the Special Representative for Trade Negotiations is expected to work with the sector advisory groups . . . .[3]

As it happened, the steel lobby was instrumental[4] in getting the "sectoral negotiations" language into law and specific reference to it in the Finance Committee Report. Obviously, this considerably strengthened their position. The steel lobby, represented by the American Iron and Steel Institute, stated its position at the time: "The

---

[1] <u>1974 Trade Act</u>, P.L. 93-618; especially see, Title I, Section 103.

[2] Interview, November 9, 1978.

[3] Senate Finance Committee Report, p. 79.

[4] Interview, 1/5/79.

negotiating authority in Title I should be amended to require sector negotiations for steel and other essential basic commodities."[1] Thus, the steel lobby had won a major victory of basic principles -- one that would, as much as any specific facet of the MTN, or any of the other conditions, shape the political debate about U.S. trade policy for steel during 1977-78.

In fact, the steel lobby, and Congressional pressures on the Administration, explicitly coalesced around the demand for steel sectoral negotiations in the GATT. "There must be sectoral negotiations for steel," the industry argued, "so that the many special issues which distort trade flows and prevent fair competition internationally can be surfaced, discussed, and, hopefully, resolved." In addition, they insisted, "Sector negotiations must include the developing countries emerging as significant steel producers."[2] The industry was hopeful that negotiating by sectors would increase the chances that the range of "steel-specific" trade distortions could be exposed -- a situation which they believed would greatly benefit those who were the victims of unfair trading practices, i.e., the American steelmaker. The American steel industry expected

---

[1]Senate Finance Committee Digest, p. 2.

[2]American Iron and Steel Institute Document, "Steel Sector Preliminary Report on Multilateral Trade Negotiations," February 14, 1979 (xeroxed: on file with Department of Commerce and STR's office).

that negotiating by sectors would begin the process of depoliticizing the steel issue; they wished the issue considered on the technical grounds of trade details and influenced less by the political atmosphere of international relations. The Europeans and the Japanese, as we shall see, opposed this. They wanted politics to continue as a major determinant of trade negotiation and opposed sectoral negotiations on the grounds that it would take politics out of the decisionmaking process.

In addition, the American steel industry was quite familiar with the machinations of multilateral trade negotiations, and so they knew that one sector, or group of sectors, might well be forced by the government's negotiators to give concessions in exchange for receiving concessions elsewhere. Negotiating by sectors, however, would substantially limit the chances that U.S. negotiators might lower the tariffs on imported steel in exchange for, let us say, increased access to the Japanese market for citrus fruit.

This view is supported by Susan Strange, a far more objective observer of trade policy. In an article for International Affairs Journal, she has written of the general value of negotiating by sectors: "The problems of sectoral management deserve serious attention . . . because these often technical problems are becoming ever more political with the integration of the world market economy."[1] So, it is understandable, then, why the steel lobby pursued sectoral negotiations at the MTN. They were able to exert considerable leverage because of the support which had been generated in the Congress and written into the legislative history of the Trade Act.

Their position was strengthened further by the fact that the Multilateral Trade Agreement required approval by the Congress, as a package; if one part of the package failed the whole of the Agreement was lost. The Administration knew that the support of critical lobbies like steel would be necessary if the MTN was ever to be approved by the Congress.

While this situation benefitted the steel lobby, others were not as pleased. In early 1976, for instance, the Economist wrote of this "crazy" American plural system:

> Congressional meddling in Trade negotiations is now firmly institutionalized in the Trade Act of 1974 . . . it gives the Congressional committees most involved with international trade issues -- the House Ways and Means and the Senate Finance Committees -- the right to choose five advisors each to the American negotiating team . . . and also giving the Congress the right to review, and to reject, American concessions.[2]

---

[1]Susan Strange, "Transnational Relations," International Affairs, volume 52, July 1976, p. 345.

[2]This is how the Europeans perceived it, as reported in The Economist March 20, 1976, "The Trade Act and Congress," p. 82.

As the steel industry pressed for steel sectoral negotiations in the MTN, they simultaneously used their power and influence to bring other sorts of demands to the surface, i.e., a safeguard code in the MTN, or lower levels of tariff concessions.[1] But, at the same time, the Administration was faced with "adamant opposition from its major trading partners to sectoral negotiations, steel or any others."[2]

The MTN, then, should be understood as the institutional embodiment, and practical application of, the Administration's commitment to trade liberalization. On that general principle, the Administration was not willing to budge. If a resolution had not been reached, and the steel lobby continued to pursue sectoral negotiations in the MTN as they had since early 1975,[3] the MTN process would have been damaged, and its outcome jeopardized. This was a circumstance which the Administration wished to avoid. The steel lobby persistently pressured the Administration on the sectoral negotiating issue. At the same time the Europeans and Japanese adamantly opposed it. From "below" -- domestic constituencies, and from "above" -- its trading partners in the international

---

[1]As of this writing, the negotiations at the MTN in Geneva on a Safeguard Code seem to have broken down.

[2]Interview, November 6, 1978.

[3]Interview, November 6, 1978.

system, the Administration was equally pressured. Hence, efforts to reconcile both positions, which at once seemed irreconcilable, defined for the Administration the narrow course which it would tread.

Let us look at the Japanese and European opposition to sectoral negotiations. According to a Japanese official for commercial relations and international trade:

> Sectoral negotiating . . . was never really defined . . . we didn't really know what it meant because no one ever really clarified it . . . but there were certain preconceived notions . . . sectoral negotiations meant a legalistic structure with certain rules and regulations . . . it's not relaxed or flexible enough . . . besides, your industry asked for it, and they want tariffs and quotas.[1]

Their unstated belief was that sectoral negotiations were a euphemism for "protection." The Japanese feared, probably correctly, that they would be hurt by protection. As we shall see in subsequent chapters, the Japanese maintained a highly competitive, efficient steel industry. But the growth of the industry in the post-World War II years, including its level of efficiency, grew dependent on foreign markets. While the Japanese steel industry earned its access to foreign markets -- in Europe and the United States, for instance -- by efficient, competitive productive capacity, this was made possible largely through a series of technical, sophisticated, and well-managed

---

[1]Interview, November 16, 1978.

government strategies for industrial development. The Japanese believed that a sectoral negotiating approach would focus on these technicalities which could lead to arrangements that would limit their foreign trade policies.

The Europeans, for somewhat different reasons, were also opposed to sectoral negotiations. Their argument may be separated into two propositions: 1) They began from the premise that steelmakers in the United States were fundamentally interested, at least during times of crises, in engaging in world market-sharing arrangements. It is a matter, one diplomat stated,

> where your interests lie . . . . Anyway, the Europeans are now net exporters, and the United States is a net importer. In that sense, it is in the interest of the United States to cut up the market . . . you would have the world industry calculized . . . because the United States industry is a net importer it is logical for them to want a defensive strategy . . . like market sharing, to ensure that their own domestic market doesn't get taken from them.[1]

2) The second point followed from the first: if there were to be negotiations to determine who would get what share of the global market, those negotiations would surely take place in the GATT. In fact, this had been the American proposal. They opposed it on two grounds: "First, this would set a precedent; surely other industries would ask, demand, and probably have the right to receive, similar kinds of dispensation at the GATT." Thus, they argued,

---

[1]Interview, November 16, 1978.

"the whole GATT negotiations . . . would explode . . . ." And secondly, they argued, "The EC is of the mind that the idea behind the GATT is to get an agreement in general terms, not so specific."[1] Going the sectoral route would surely have compromised that principle. Thus, Alan Wolff expressed the views of the Administration on sectoral negotiations. He said, they "could result in early stalemate . . . in many product sectors."[2]

Summary

In summary, then, the steel lobby had the power to wreck an MTN agreement, if not during the negotiating process by demanding sectoral negotiations for steel, which the Japanese and Europeans opposed unconditionally, then when the Administration sent it to the Congress for approval. Since the completion of a successful MTN -- which meant acceptance of the Agreement by the Congress, as well as international agreement among trading partners -- was the most important goal of the Administration in trade policy, all other trade matters were subordinated to it.

The steel lobby had made it clear that its most critical demand was "to negotiate by sectors." We shall see how the domestic political crisis, triggered by record levels of imports from Europe and Japan, prompted the

---

[1]Interview, November 16, 1978.

[2]Alan Wolff, "The U.S. Mandate for Trade Negotiations," p. 529.

domestic steel lobby to ask for other short-term government assistance. But until late 1977, when the domestic political crisis became paramount, the steel lobby pursued a strategy of sectoral negotiations in the MTN as a way to "get a handle on the long term structural crisis."[1] As they indicated in their "Steel Sector Preliminary Report on the MTN," February 14, 1979, "equity and reciprocity have not yet been reached for our sector."[2] Thus, even at that late date, after the Trigger Price Mechanism had been in effect, and in spite of the establishment of the OECD Steel Committee[3] -- the Administration's answer to sector negotiations -- there were serious misgivings about the effects of the MTN on the American steel industry.

Regardless of the outcome, the steel issue had been tagged to the MTN. On the one hand, this meant that the steel issue by itself was secondary, i.e., the Administration would give certain concessions to

---

[1]Interview, November 9, 1978.

[2]"Industrial Sector Advisory Committee Preliminary Report on the Multilateral Trade Negotiations -- the Non-Ferrous Metals," February 1979. (xeroxed: in personal files of author, and in the Senate Finance Committee Private Files.)

[3]Turn to Chapter 6 for a description of the OECD International Steel Committee.

its trading partners in order to keep the MTN going.[1] On the other hand, however, the resolution of the steel issue, as with a number of other key industrial sectors such as textiles, was imperative as they were made a condition of the MTN by the respective interest groups.

Throughout the entire negotiating period the Administration realized it was treading on very sensitive ground. As an illustration of the general state of uncertainty, consider this assessment in the National Journal: "The climate for the treaty isn't good anywhere . . . after more than four years of sputtering, the MTN may finally cough up a treaty, but will anyone support it?"[2] The negotiations could have unraveled at any time from any number of cross-cutting pressures in the international or domestic arenas. Administration officials approached the steel issue as one critical pressure threatening the breakup of the negotiations. The domestic lobby understood, accepted, and played on this. Therefore, it had to be resolved, but as one of several factors conditioned by the political climate of the MTN.

---

[1]As we shall see in Chapter 5, the Europeans seem to have benefitted most from the TPM. Thus, the TPM, as it will be argued later, was established not only to satisfy domestic pressures in the United States, but also to address negotiating problems we had been encountering with the Europeans.

[2]"There May Be A Treaty, But Will Anyone Support It?", National Journal (June 17, 1978) pp. 958-62.

III. Domestic Legal Framework for the Operation of International Trade -- The Legal Claims

The second element which defined the parameters for the development of a United States foreign trade policy toward steel was the domestic legal framework for trade, especially those aspects concerned with "antidumping." Its effects on the policy process were twofold. First, it was the legal claim available to the steel lobby against unfair competition from foreigners. Second, the process by which these claims were applied served to concentrate the collective mind of the Administration on the fundamental incompatibility between pressures from the domestic interest groups, and its international trading partners, and how each one felt about the broad principles of trade policy. Recognition of this incompatibility helped the Administration define for itself how it would approach particular questions like steel. As with the MTN, it become apparent both to the Administration, and to the steel lobby, what it could and could not do.

The Legal Framework

Antidumping laws have been on the books since 1921. They were then part of a coordinated effort by the United States government to protect infant industries, particularly the petrochemical industry, from the increasing competition of European industries seeking markets for the excess capacity they had developed during the First War.[1] The basic intent of the 1921 Antidumping Act was, and remains:

> [to] provide that articles imported into the United States will be subject to a special duty when such articles are being, or are likely to be, sold at less than fair value and an industry in the United States is being, or is likely to be, injured or is prevented from being established by reason of the importation into the United States of the articles.[2]

Typically, these laws were intended to protect infant industries; ironically, today they are used to protect older, and in some cases, dying industries. Still, the basic intent of the law -- to protect against unfair trading practices that cause injury to domestic producers -- has remained constant, though the statute was amended in 1953 and 1962, and still further refined in 1974. This author has not found anyone who argues that the antidumping laws themselves are protectionist. It is agreed by most trade experts that the antidumping laws are designed to nullify the unfair trade advantages accruing to the country engaged in dumping. Indeed, the International Trade Commission (ITC), allegedly an unbiased regulatory government agency, observed:

---

[1]John F. McDermid and F. David Foster, "The United States International Trade Commission's 30-day Inquiry Under the Antidumping Act: Section 201 (c)(2)," Mercer Law Review, volume 27, number 3, Spring 1976.

[2]Ibid., pp. 657, 8.

> The imposition of dumping duties provided in the Antidumping Act is consistent with liberal trade policy of the United States. When the sales at less than fair value have stopped, the dumping finding can be revoked. Thus, the domestic industry is not being protected against the ingenuity or natural advantage of the foreign producer. Rather, it is being protected from the effects of trade practices which Congress has found to be unfair and injurious.[1]

Several changes were made in the 1974 Trade Act which reflected both the general unease American industry had come to view international trade, and which, according to some experts "[could] have farreaching potential for limiting imports."[2]

The significant changes in the antidumping provisions which make it easier for industry to seek, and possibly obtain, relief are found in Titles II and III of the 1974 Trade Act. Since they are so important in understanding U.S. trade policy, we shall go into some detail.

In Title II -- the "import relief" section -- the 1974 Trade Act changed the degree to which increased imports

---

[1]32 Federal Register, 12928, Cast Iron Soil Pie from Poland (1967).

[2]Corrine Bell, "Interpretative History of the Escape Clause Under the Trade Act of 1974," The Journal of International Law and Economics, volume 12, number 3, 1978, pp. 532, 33; Walter Adams and Joel B. Dirlam, "Import Competition and the Trade Act of 1974: A Case Study of Section 201 and Its Interpretation by the International Trade Commission," Indiana Law Journal, volume 52, number 3, Spring 1977, p. 538. Note that injury is the key concept which, along with less than fair value (LTFV) determines whether a complainant is entitled to relief under the antidumping laws of the Trade Act of 1974.

must be a function of "trade agreement concession." Before 1974, increased imports must have been "in major part the result of trade agreement concessions before import relief measures were undertaken."[1] Under the 1974 Act, however, "no link to concessions" is required.[2] A potentially greater effect, however, occurs in the degree to which it must be proven that increased import penetration is a cause of serious injury to the industry which filed for relief. Under the 1974 Trade Act, "increased imports must only be a substantial cause of serious injury of threat thereof."[3] It is no longer necessary to establish a causal link between increased import penetration and injury to the degree that "increased imports [must be a] major factor of such injury."[4]

Indeed, the "eligibility requirements" under the "escape clause" had been decried by industry, labor, and government officials, during the debate over the trade bill in 1973 and 1974, as far too stringent. Frederick Dent, President Ford's Special Trade Representative during those years testified in support of reform: "More realistic eligibility criteria for safeguard relief are necessary under present conditions . . . to deal with disruptions

---

[1] 1974 Trade Act, P.L. 93-618.

[2] Ibid.

[3] Ibid.

[4] Ibid.

caused by changing patterns of international trade.[1]

Title III, "Relief from Unfair Trade Practices" also reflected apparent changes in government awareness of the increased imports problem in industrial sectors. The Trade Act of 1974 revised to a considerable extent Executive authority to respond to unfair trade practices including authorities under the Trade Expansion Act of 1962, the Antidumping Act of 1921, and the Tariff Act of 1930. Generally, its intention was to speed up the investigatory process, "[to] assure a swift and certain response to foreign import restrictions, export subsidies, and price discrimination (dumping) and other unfair trade practices . . .[2] Sections 301 and 321 are both relevant to these considerations.

Section 301 was specifically intended as a general section that may be used -- "against foreign practices and policies adversely affecting U.S. economy . . . in an international economic period characterized by widespread inflation . . .[3] A specific change made in the Trade Act of 1974, intended to facilitate use of this particular provision, was to:

> provide [for a] complaint procedure whereby interested parties can petition the Special

---

[1]Senate Finance Committee Digest of Testimony Received on H.R. 10710.

[2]Senate Finance Committee Digest

[3]Ibid.

> Trade Representative for Trade Negotiations to conduct a review, with public hearings of such alleged practices and policies [that may adversely affect the economy of the United States]. The Special Representative is required to report to the Congress on a semiannual basis concerning the status of the reviews . . .[1]

Finally, the Trade Act made changes in the antidumping duties, Title III, Section 321, "to improve the United States response to foreign price discrimination practices."[2] Here there were two changes: first, that:

> [Domestic] manufacturers, producers, or wholesalers of merchandise, as well as foreign manufacturers, exporters, and domestic importers [were to be given] an equal and automatic right to appear at hearings before the Secretary of the Treasury or the [International Trade] Commission in connection with less than fair value or injury determinations.[2]

Second, the Act reduced considerably the time period in which less than fair value and injury determinations were to be made.

So, the provisions relating to the antidumping laws and other import relief provisions were intended, under the Trade Act of 1974, to respond better to complaints by industry. The law, according to those who wished to use it, had never been very effective. By Ambassador Dent's reckoning, two-thirds of the petitioning industries since 1962 failed to meet the "qualifying test."[3] During the

---

[1]Ibid.

[2]<u>1974 Trade Act</u>, P.L. 93-618.

[3]Senate Finance Committee Report.

first three years of operation of the 1974 Trade Act,[1] 29 petitions were filed under the escape clause provisions. Only shoes and specialty steel received any sort of protection, while the others either received a negative determination from the International Trade Commission, dismissed by the Treasury as "unqualified," or denied relief by the President who makes the final decision in these matters.

The debate over the Trade Act, and the language which eventually made its way into law, highlighted the antidumping issue; indeed, it had become, as the New York Times pointed out, a principal element in the debate about United States foreign trade policy:

> The [American] industry has fought back hard in the last two years by filing a wide-ranging series of complaints in Washington under the 1974 Trade Act. Deciding how to deal with these cases will be one of the first tasks facing President-elect Jimmy Carter in the trade field.[2]

Thus, when faced with the steel issue -- couched as a problem of international trade in international products experiencing surplus capacity -- the Administration and the steel lobby, both, settled on the antidumping laws as "a new antidote for the steel blues."[3]

---

[1]Senate Finance Committee Digest of Testimony Received on H.R. 10710.

[2]"Steel Renews War on Imports," New York Times, November 26, 1976.

[3]"A New Antidote for the Steel Blues," National Journal, October 22, 1977.

By September 1977, a not altogether coincidental set of circumstances politicized the steel issue, forcing the Carter Administration to find a quick solution;[1] a solution that many hoped would get the government through a period of high political tension, and the industry through a period of economic difficulties.[2] With various alternatives facing them, one worse than the other, and each threatening the success of the Multilateral Trade Negotiations, the Administration advised the steel lobby to look for relief under the antidumping statute of the Trade Act of 1974.[3] According to a high level policy official at the Office of the Special Trade Representative, "the issue . . . from that time on . . . was dumping . . . . It was the turning point . . . we encouraged [steel executives] to use the antidumping statute, and to begin filing petitions with Treasury."[4]

And so it began: the steel industry, which had apparently done some preparation prior to September necessary to file the petitions, followed the course

---

[1]The "quick solution" was the Trigger Price Mechanism. Turn to Chapter 5 for an explanation of the Trigger Price Mechanism.

[2]There is predictable disagreement over how much the U.S. steel industry has actually suffered during this period. For an elaboration on this point see the introduction to Chapter 3, and the conclusion to Part II.

[3]Interview, November 6, 1978.

[4]Interview, November 9, 1978.

advised them by the Carter Administration trade policy officials. The industry, according to the Director of Special Projects Office in Treasury, filed twenty-three petitions against Britain, France, Italy, the Netherlands, Belgium, West Germany, Japan, India, and South Korea, in a host of product sectors;[1] all but one within a three month period. The system, as we shall see below, had been overloaded.

What at first seemed like a good solution -- derived from the trade laws recently modified to the relative comfort of industry; consistent with GATT law, and therefore within the legal bounds of free trade principles; and agreed to by all those concerned in the domestic political arena -- became an "unmitigated disaster."[2] Still the approach was tantalizing. An especially insightful article in the _National Journal_ attempted to explain the appeal of the solution in terms of "fair trade": "American producers agreed to compete," according to the _Journal_, "as long as foreign exporters agree to sell at fair prices. In turn, the Administration avoids both a bruising battle in Congress over steel imports restrictions and the discomfort of trying to negotiate with affected trading partners . . ."[3]

---

[1]"The Office of the Special Trade Representative's Computer Printout of Antidumping Cases, 1977-78" (xerox: on file with the STR's office).

[2]Interview, November 2, 1978.

[3]_The National Journal_ (October 22, 1977), p. 1636.

But, the article went on to assert "that the antidumping appeal may tarnish."[1]

Tarnish it did. But details on why and how this happened will come in a later chapter. For now it is enough to say that the "antidumping solution," while it did indeed define the parameters of the policy debate, turned out to be itself a non-solution. Simply stated, the dumping petitions from the steel industry were so widespread that it became impossible both as a matter of principle and practicality to implement, and in any event would have "virtually excluded the Europeans from our market." ". . . it would have killed them," according to one policy official.[2] Hence, an official in the Treasury Department, now charged with the responsibility for implementation of the enforcement of the Trigger Price Mechanism put it in very real terms. He said of the industry: "They wanted us to investigate the world, and stop the dumping . . . we just couldn't enforce the law, it's a damn hard law to enforce."[3]

The Treasury official was referring to how the system had been overloaded; 1) the impracticability of undertaking such a large task -- there simply weren't enough people to gather and analyze the data; and 2) the

---

[1]Ibid.

[2]Interview, November 9, 1978.

[3]Interview, November 14, 1978.

political and economic unacceptability of pursuing a course which would have virtually castrated the European steel industry.

Had the antidumping strategy been pursued exactly as the law stated, the two major objectives of the Administration's foreign trade policy would have come undone: the MTN would have failed, thereby wrecking any chance of further trade liberalization during this period; and the international economy would have been left unstable, at best, since it would have wreaked havoc first on the European steel industry, but then on other markets. Still, the Administration had committed itself publicly, as well as privately, to a very precise understanding of the steel issue; as one high level official in Ambassador Strauss's office admitted, "It was from this point a matter of dumping."[1] And from this, one of the major pillars of United States foreign trade policy for steel followed: The Trigger Price Mechanism (TPM), a method of implementing traditional antidumping remedies in expedited fashion. The trigger price system was never viewed as an alternative to a vigorous enforcement of the Antidumping Act. Instead, it was conceived as "a benchmark for quickly focusing Treasury resources on

---

[1]Interview, November 9, 1978. For a good discussion of the merits of a workable antidumping law see, Bart Fisher, "Dumping: Confronting the Paradox of Internal Weakness and External Demand" (xeroxed: 1978).

antidumping investigations of steel mill products when the situation warrants . . . . The trigger price system centers on Treasury's self-initiation of dumping investigations.[1] As we shall see in Chapter 5, it was conditioned on the domestic legal framework for trade.

Applicability of the Legal Claims in Conducting Trade Policy

The inapplicability of the antidumping laws, as originally intended, underscored a basic incompatibility between the American approach to international trade as understood by its major trading partners, and their own approach. Predictably, the perceptions of incompatibility were likely to be exacerbated during conditions of global oversupply and structural instability, of the sort that existed in the case of steel. In general terms, then, the difference in approach suggests a difference in conception of how to organize the international trading system, which understandably had a large effect on the way U.S. policy developed.

Both the sectoral approach in the GATT, referred to in part II of this chapter, and the antidumping provisions available for conducting trade policy, represent what the Europeans have characterized as a "very specific, legalistic, and very American prescription" for

---

[1]William A. Anawaty, "The United States Legal Response to Steel Dumping," September 30, 1978; speech at the University of Western Ontario, London, Canada.

policy.[1] The European and Japanese opposition to sectoral negotiations in the GATT stemmed as much from a philosophical distaste as from their fear of the damage it could do to their position in the world steel trade. Similarly, their opposition to United States antidumping laws was characterized in terms of how it was an "inappropriate" solution to the problem.

This point is best illustrated by Fernand Spaak, head of the Washington delegation of the European Commission to the United States. In an article obviously intended for American policymakers, he wrote:

> Now, it may be true that imports have played a part in the recent and present difficulties of some of our industries. But they are not the only, nor even the principal, factor involved. Very often they serve only to highlight much deeper and more serious problems in those industries. And trade laws designed to protect industries against injurious competition, whether fair or unfair, though they have a role to play, are not necessarily the most adequate, nor the only possible remedy. Solving the difficulties that some of our industries face at present requires dealing with the problem at its roots. It is not just a matter of greater enforcement of law and order in the international marketplace. We have to tackle the cause of the threatened breakdown.
>
> The political will that existed formerly and still exists towards free trade in general must now be accompanied by an additional commitment to deal with structural problems. And by structural problems I mean the overcapacity and lack of competitiveness that exist in such industries as steel, textiles, footwar, synthetic fibers, and shipbuilding . . .[2]

---

[1]Interview, November 16, 1978.

[2]Fernand Spaak, "The Disease of Protectionism," European Community, no. 208, July-August 1978, pp. 6, 7.

The Europeans argued rather forcefully that anti-dumping measures represent the wrong remedy for the wrong disease. Not only was it the wrong approach, but, they argued, the condition would only get worse by the "American propensity to put everything into writing."[1] In the end, Americans were charged with not quite understanding the notion of consensus and bargaining. Reflecting on the condition, a trade expert in the Washington office of the European Community remarked, "Rules can't solve the problems of international trade. You do need rules, but you also need discretion."[2]

Japanese attitudes about how to conduct trade policy are also different from the American propensity for legalisms: In his book on Japan's Public Policy Companies, Chalmers Johnson explains the distinction in Japanese attitudes between "principle" and "reality." Quoting Kato Eiichi of the Ministry of Home Affairs:

> The Japanese don't care if there is a gap between tatamae (a "principle," "a policy," "a rule") and reality. The Japanese are used to having foreign rules. They themselves are poor theorists, so they don't change the rules. Instead, they say, "Theory is so, but . . . (or) Tatamae is so, but . . . and thus make everything possible."

And, Johnson continues:

> When a citizen appealed to the government for relief from some crisis or burden and is told

---

[1]Interview, November 16, 1978.

[2]Interview, November 16, 1978.

> by the bureaucracy that the law does not cover his case, the citizen then appeals through the newspaper or politicians. They all cry Horitsu no kaishaku wa tomokaku (whatever the wording of the law may be), do something good for him. And the bureaucrats discover a new interpretation of the (usually very vague legal) definition.[1]

The difference is that they don't look for a new, or another law, but instead they are more flexible on the definition of existing law than in the United States.

The Europeans and Japanese both argue they allow a greater amount of discretionary powers to legal interpretations. That is, they afford a wider amount of flexibility to the political arm of government such that "[one is] not put under strict rules that will oblige you to do things you really don't want to do . . . ." They are proud of this difference. Accordingly, one European official phrased it like this:

> . . . a substantial part of United States trade is based on rules, leaving less and less discretion for the political leaders . . . trade policy should be conducted on grounds different from quasi-legal, quasi-judicial . . . terms.

And, he emphasized, "Dumping as an instrument of trade policy can get very clumsy . . ."[2]

"In contrast [to the U.S.]," Fernand Spaak wrote, "we use our trade laws sparingly because our philosophy

---

[1]Chalmers Johnson, Japan's Public Policy Companies (Washington, D.C.: The American Enterprise Institute for Public Policy Research 1978). p. 10.

[2]Interview, November 16, 1978.

in dealing with these problems stems directly from our experience in managing free trade within the Community . . ."[1] He implicitly distinguishes between outcome and process. Hence, while it may be true that few cases in the United States actually find their way into the category of protection -- quotas, duty imposition, and the like -- the mere process of investigation becomes a bothersome and complicating element in trade relations. Spaak went on to contrast the number of cases investigated in Europe with those in the United States: "From 1970 to mid-1977, the United States investigated more than 200 cases of alleged dumping and around seventy countervailing duty cases.[2] In the same period, he argued, the European Community investigated less than forty similar cases. Europeans are proud that their Commission turned down requests for investigations, because it felt that such investigations would have been more harm than help to international trade, i.e., the politics of international trade.

So, the dumping issue framed the tenor and direction of the debate about the United States foreign trade policy for steel. While dumping was thought at one critical stage in the policy development process to be a viable solution, it turned out to be untenable. It was

---

[1]Fernand Spaak, "The Disease of Protectionism," p. 7.

[2]Ibid.

untenable for reasons of a broader scope than just the mechanics of dumping, or the specifics of the steel case.

Many in the United States recognized that antidumping laws couldn't adequately cope with the problems posed by global surplus capacity in industrial sectors. Unlike the Europeans and the Japanese, however, such businessmen, Congressmen, and labor leaders in the United States focused on ways to make these laws effective by more explicit definition of its rules and regulations. During 1977 and 1978, Congressmen introduced a number of bills into the House and Senate, mostly intended to address procedural reforms by speeding up the investigatory process of the antidumping and countervailing duty petitions filed with Treasury. In part, they wanted to foreclose the option that Administration officials could excuse themselves from investigating dumping complaints because they didn't have the resources, i.e., time, money or staff. Upon introducing his bill, for example, Senator John Heinz (D.-Pa.) characterized it as "a bill to amend the Antidumping Act of 1921, the Trade Act of 1974, and the Tariff Act of 1930 to improve procedures relating to the determination of certain unfair trade practices."[1] Similarly when George Stinson, president of U.S. Steel, said of the

---

[1]For example, Senators Heinz and Danforth both introduced bills into the 95th Congress which would have amended the antidumping and countervailing duty laws of the Trade Act of 1974. Neither the Heinz "Trade Procedures

dumping laws: "There is the basic fact . . . the inadequacy of the antidumping laws which point to flaws . . . in laws and procedures,"[1] he implied the need for more, not less, regulation to ensure appropriate application and enforcement of the laws.

Thus, there was a basic incompatibility between domestic constituencies' understanding of how the import relief provisions of the Trade Act should be used, and

---

Reform Act," nor the Danforth "International Unfair Trade Laws Reform Act" became law. But, both provided important vehicles for Congressional discussion about trade policy. And, both were reintroduced into the 96th Congress, and have been considered in conjunction with the implementing legislation for the Multilateral Trade Agreement.

[1]Senate Steel Caucus Briefing, February 6, 1979; in his article on the antidumping laws in the United States, Mr. Bart Fisher points to the development of the Trigger Price Mechanism for steel in 1977, and the dismissal by the Treasury Department of the Automobile Case in 1975, as indicators that "the current antidumping laws may be inadequate to handle large-scale continuous dumping." Mr. Fisher goes on to argue that such instances of large-scale dumping are a result of other governments' national objectives to reach goals of employment, and reduce their balance of trade deficits: "The goals of unemployment, reduced balance of trade deficits, and use of overcapacity, are national objectives superimposed on the objectives of individual enterprises. While an individual firm may be willing to lay off workers, and idle capacity, the government is not willing to do so, for political reasons." Thus, Fisher concludes, that under the circumstances where "dumping policies are state-led or supported efforts to improve national economies," U.S. policy to control dumping is justified. See Bart Fisher, "Dumping: The Paradox of Internal Weakness and External Challenge," (unpublished), especially pp. 33, 40.

how the trading partners of the United States viewed it. In the middle stood an Administration which could neither accept nor reject either perspective. Trade policy officials were charged with the responsibility of balancing both.

IV. Market Sharing -- The Ideological Background

So, in developing a foreign trade policy for steel, the Administration was faced with two pressures, the MTN -- creating the overall political climate in which the steel issue was absorbed -- and a domestic legal framework for the operation of international trade. The concept of a "national policy" or the "Administration's goals and objectives" was further defined by increased legitimacy of trade limiting measures.

The U.S. government has increased its use of interventionist policies in international trade to protect domestic constituencies from distortion in trade. Many of these industries have already begun to question the axiomatic operating assumption of the post-war era -- that prosperity was synonymous with free trade. Recent trends in industries like steel, textiles, shoes, consumer electronics, have led the United States government to consider the use of protective measures. Many now argue, for example, that these arrangements are necessary to promote goals of national prosperity. The use of the Voluntary Restraint Agreements (VRA) and the Orderly Marketing Arrangements (OMA) to protect domestic producers from increased import penetration represents a change in the ideological background of how the United States conducts its foreign trade policy in these international industries. The U.S. foreign trade policy for steel developed amidst these ideas.

OMAs and VRAs are both voluntary mechanisms. Usually, but not necessarily, they are negotiated bilaterally to limit the amount of imports by sectors. As a practical matter, they are similar to quotas, but since they are voluntary, they are not subject to the international prohibitions of non-tariff barriers. In fact, the "Executive Branch GATT Study" prepared for the Senate Finance Committee, explicitly refers to these agreements as ways to avoid the use of Article XIX, the Import Relief Provision, of the GATT. The study concluded that:

> The use of export restraints has also reduced the need for countries to resort to Article XIX. Export restraints affect shipments of selected goods which are ordinarily free of import restriction but pose a threat to production in the importing country . . . controls are imposed at the request of the importing country that would be principally affected by the export restraints.[1]

While these arrangements are not embodied in international agreements, they are sometimes reflected in written

---

[1]U.S. Senate Committee on Finance, Executive Branch GATT Studies, 93rd Congress, 2d Session (Washington, D.C.: Government Printing Office, 1974). p. 127.

"understandings."[1]

Import control mechanisms for industrial sectors are not new inventions. For textiles they date to 1935, when the Administration of President Franklin D. Roosevelt entered into what was then called a "friendly and voluntary" agreement with Japan. Its purpose was to limit Japan's shipments to the United States of cotton products, then the principal textile category.[2] A subsequent arrangement for textiles in 1962, negotiated under the GATT, was heralded as "the most comprehensive example of an export control arrangement . . . ." It was supposed that this 1962 Long Term Agreement Regarding International Trade in Cotton Textiles would ". . . provide the mechanism that [would] enable exporting and importing countries to control the growth of trade in cotton textiles through a network of bilateral agreements . . ."[3]

The Long Term Cotton Agreement became, in effect, the Multifiber Arrangement, first negotiated in 1973 for five years, and then renewed in 1978 for an additional four years. The Multifiber Agreement, technically under

---

[1]Export controls are the subject of the "Safeguard Code" in the GATT under the MTN.

[2]An excellent analysis of this subject appeared in "Orderly Marketing Pact and Restrictions on Imports," New York Times, March 10, 1978.

[3]Finance Committee Executive Branch GATT Study, p. 126.

the jurisdiction of the GATT, provides the multilateral framework under which the United States negotiates separate bilateral OMAs for textiles with over fifty countries.

Thus, the OMA, and the VRA, are not new. Indeed, market sharing has been used regularly by the United States and its trading partners in the agricultural sector. But, the degree, and way in which U.S. policy has come to employ such tactics for industrial sector products, is new. Sharing markets provide policymakers with a middle course between outright protection and international liberalism; or, as Robert Keohane describes it, "defending liberalism through moderate protectionism."[1] It is indicative of what has been referred to above as "collective protection" -- a strategy used to address problems of surplus capacity that derive, in large part, from the political economic policies of intervention in the market. U.S. reaction to such policies has been to promote what Susan Strange describes as ". . . earnest and often heated discussions among governments and producers over the share-out of markets and rules, not of free

---

[1]Robert O. Keohane, "The International Politics of Inflation"; paper presented at the Brookings Institution Conference on "The Politics and Sociology of Global Inflation," Washington, D.C., December 6-8, 1978, p. 37.

trade, but of fair trade."[1] Accordingly, these arrangements have become familiar, acceptable, and even respectable elements of government policy. The federal bureaucracy which deals with foreign trade matters, Congressmen, and industry and labor all have learned to approach market-sharing arrangements as normal and viable policy alternatives. Simply put, it has become a popular and reasonable thing to ask for. As an illustration, consider the statement of Jacob Sheinkman, Secretary-Treasurer of the Amalgamated Clothing Workers Union, when he expressed concern over the plight of the domestic shoe industry -- an industry for which Sheinkman was not directly responsible. There evolved, however, a brotherhood among industries in the United States experiencing adjustment problems posed by international competition. Thus, Sheinkman said of his support for the American shoe industry: "We take this position because we see ourselves in the same position as workers in the shoe industry if we don't stand up and fight now . . ."[2]

Since the textile arrangements which by now have been institutionalized, the steel industry itself has

---

[1]Susan Strange, "The Management of Surplus Capacity: Or, How Does Theory Stand Up to Protectionism 1970s Style" (xerox). p. 4.

[2]"AFL-CIO Assails Trade Policy," Washington Post, November 22, 1977.

become quite familiar with market-sharing arrangements. By the early 1960s, the steel industries of Japan and Europe (especially West Germany) had expanded their capacity; by the mid-sixties steel was available for export, and the United States market had apparently become the most attractive.[1] As imports increased -- from ten million tons, or a market share of about ten percent of apparent domestic consumption, in 1965, to eighteen million tons by 1968, representing over sixteen percent of the market -- domestic political pressure gathered considerable momentum, and government responded by negotiating voluntary restraint agreements with the Japanese and Europeans in 1968. Conditions improved, but then got worse again; the government negotiated still another VRA for steel in 1972.[2]

Thus, over the last ten years, 1968-78, the steel sector has become quite familiar with market-sharing strategies. And, since the VRAs in 1968-72 for steel,

---

[1]For a good discussion of the politics of the Voluntary Restraint Agreements see, William T. Hogan, S.J. The 1970s: The Critical Years for Steel (Massachusetts: Lexington Books, 1972); especially Chapter 3. For a good discussion of the economics of steel imports from Japan to the United States see, Kiyoshi Kawahito, The Japanese Steel Industry (New York: Praeger, 1972); especially Part II. Also, see my introduction to Part I .

[2]For an elaboration, please turn to my introduction to Part I .

there has been an OMA with Korea and Taiwan for non-rubber footwear, and most recently another OMA with Japan for color television sets.

Each agreement proposed to limit the amount of product exported into the United States, effectively organizing trade by cutting up markets. These kinds of arrangements increasingly have covered the landscape of U.S. foreign trade policy and are justified as legitimate responses to others' policies of intervening in the market, i.e., a policy of national protection. Still, there are many who see market-sharing arrangements, voluntary or otherwise, as strategies for protection, rather than ones which "defend liberalism." Such concern over the willingness to intervene in the market was illustrated by a rather disparaging characterization in the *Washington Post*: "Call it organized free trade. Call it quotas. Call it cartelization. Call it orderly marketing arrangements. It amounts to the same thing."[1] And the *Post* concluded, ". . . this submission to protectionism is gained new surface dignity and acceptability."[2]

Evidence supports, therefore, that U.S. policy-makers have increasingly come to believe that economic liberalism in the 1970s and 1980s is best defended by

---

[1]"Foreign Trade: Is Its Future in Jeopardy?" *Washington Post*, December 18, 1977.

[2]Ibid.

policies of intervening in the market. Whether this approach is successful, or not, its acceptability and respectability has done much to shape the direction of United States foreign trade policy for the seventies and beyond. It set a pattern which would certainly apply in the case of steel.

V. Summary

This chapter set forth the policy parameters of the United States foreign trade policy process for steel. They are the points that define the terms in which policy was framed. They comprise what was referred to in the first chapter as the "National Policy," or "Administration Policy." That is not to say that the sum of these factors equaled the foreign trade policy for steel. They did not. But together they did provide the closest thing we have in the United States to a concept of the "national interest" -- a set of goals and objectives which comprised the irreducible minimum beyond which policy could not bend. In fact, there exists a body of trade policy officials -- the Trade Policy Staff Committee, the Trade Policy Review Group, or the Trade Policy Committee, each a different level of decisionmaking. Those who made up these groups thought about trade policy together. And so, it was they who together developed the Administration's position.[1] Hence, the three principles, or goals and objectives, with which the Administration entered into the policymaking process, were:

1) That trade liberalization and international economic stability were paramount -- i.e., the successful

---

[1]Interview, January 8, 1979.

completion of an MTN under the GATT was accorded top priority in all aspects of U.S. trade policy.

2) That the concept of "dumping" defined the terms of the "import problem." This was particularly attractive for the Administration since any action against dumping could be framed in terms consistent with GATT principles, codified in domestic trade law, and therefore fit rather comfortably with its commitment to trade liberalization. It was a free trader's way out since, as the GATT Study on international trade put it: "[One] cannot count as protection antidumping or countervailing measures which are, in principle, legitimate actions to protect fair competition."[1]

3) That the difficulties posed by surplus capacity in many of the other sectors led to the beginning of an acceptance of a set of operating principles which included mechanisms such as market-sharing arrangements designed to respond to the overall structural changes in the international economy. Rapidly, a U.S. policy of "intervention" in the market was becoming legitimate. But, only so long as one intervened according to broad principles of liberal trade.

---

[1]Richard Blackhurst, et. al., "Trade Liberalization, Protectionism, and Interdependence," GATT Studies in International Trade (Geneva: November 1977) p. 49.

From these points the Administration would begin a complex bargaining process to balance simultaneously the domestic and international levels. But first, let us examine the economic strategies, and foreign economic policies of its trading partners which were, or believed to be, largely responsible for the political economic conditions of steel in the United States.

CHAPTER 3

INTERNATIONAL POLITICAL ECONOMY

The United States has been a net importer of steel since about 1960. At first this caused no serious economic hardships for the domestic industry. As the import penetration level increased -- from 4.7 percent of apparent domestic consumption in 1960 to over 16 percent by 1977 -- strains in the relationship between the United States and the rest of the world steelmaking community developed.[1] The accompanying chart shows the increase in imports as a percentage of domestic consumption during the twenty years from 1958 to 1978. Significant increases have taken place

[1]In 1957, United States steel exports were 5.3 million tons, and imports only 1.2 million tons. It wasn't until 1959 that the United States became a net importer of steel; in 1959, imports of steel mill products were recorded at 4.4 million net tons, and accounted for 6.1 percent of apparent domestic consumption. The trend continued; in 1965, import tonnage exceeded ten million tons, and its market share rose above ten percent. In 1968, the corresponding figures surged to 18 million tons and 16.1 percent of apparent domestic consumption. Thus, the increasing penetration of steel became a national concern, and the government negotiated voluntary restraint agreements with Japan and the EEC to limit steel imports from those countries. The voluntary restraint agreements were terminated in 1972. In 1973, total imports were recorded at 15.1 million tons; by 1977, total imports had increased to a record high of 19.3 million tons, and in 1978 increased again to 21.1 million tons. These figures received from the United States Department of Commerce. (See my introduction to Part I for an elaboration.)

U.S. STEEL MILL PRODUCTS 1958-1978 (in thousands of tons)

	Domestic Shipments 1/	Exports 1/	Imports 1/	Apparent Domestic Consumption 1/	Imports as a % of Apparent Domestic Consumption
1958	59,914	2,823	1,707	58,798	2.9
1959	69,377	1,677	4,396	72,096	6.1
1960	71,149	2,977	3,359	71,531	4.7
1961	66,126	1,990	3,163	67,299	4.7
1962	70,552	2,013	4,100	72,639	5.6
1963	75,555	2,224	5,446	78,777	6.9
1964	84,945	3,442	6,440	87,943	7.3
1965	92,666	2,496	10,383	100,553	10.3
1966	89,995	1,724	10,753	99,024	10.9
1967	83,897	1,685	11,455	93,667	12.2
1968	91,856	2,170	17,960	107,646	16.7
1969	91,877	5,229	14,034	102,682	13.7
1970	90,798	7,062	13,364	97,100	13.8
1971	87,038	2,827	18,304	102,515	17.9
1972	91,805	2,873	17,681	106,613	16.6
1973	111,430	4,052	15,150	122,528	12.4
1974	109,472	5,833	15,970	119,609	13.4
1975	79,957	2,953	12,012	89,016	13.5
1976	89,447	2,654	14,285	101,078	14.1
1977	91,147	2,003	19,306	108,450	17.8
1978	97,935	2,422	21,135	116,648	18.1

1/ Apparent Domestic Consumption = Domestic Shipments - Exports + Imports

Source: Domestic shipments - American Iron and Steel Institute, Exports and Imports - U.S. Department of Commerce. All of these are as reported in the Survey of Current Business.

after 1964, leading to the voluntary restraint agreement in 1968, and after 1976, leading to the establishment of the Trigger Price Mechanism and the International Steel Committee in 1977-78.

Thus, the rising amount of steel imports caused political pressures, and led to a movement for some type of protection against foreign steel by United States producers and workers. This situation also resulted in a clash between the two motive forces in American foreign trade policy; two goals that coexisted until the mid-sixties: 1) The desire to build a connecting web of cooperative relationships which would lead to increased security for the United States and its allies, promote global prosperity, and support a stable international system; and 2) The desire to maintain a healthy and profitable domestic industrial base.

As United States policymakers tried to develop a foreign trade policy for steel that somehow met both goals, their policy options were constrained by the political economic conditions of its trading partners. In this chapter we shall examine the overall global[1] economic

---

[1]While we shall continue to refer to global steel production, this study only included "Free World" steel production. That is, the OECD countries with emphasis on the United States, Japan, and the European Community. Efforts will be made to include the more advanced developing countries where appropriate. The study does not include steel production in the USSR, or other "non-market" economies.

conditions which affected the U.S. policy-process, and then those conditions in the European Community, Japan, and to a lesser extent the Third World, which contributed in more specific ways the formation of U.S. policy.

I. The Global Political Economy of Steel

An Overview of the Structural Crisis

The single largest factor contributing to the politicization of the steel issue among the industrial trading countries is the "global" overcapacity of steel-making facilities which has led to a condition of oversupply of steel. The facts of this condition -- approximately 100 million metric tons a year -- are a matter of record.[1] In a May 1977 report, the Central Intelligence Agency began its pessimistic assessment with the argument that:

> The world steel industry is in trouble. Competition for markets is intensifying as the growth in steel demand slows, the global import market shrinks, and most producers contend with large underutilized capacity.[2]

Two related, but separable problems are signalled by the CIA report. First, the slowdown in the growth of steel demand, exacerbated by a generally slow growth period in the industrial economies; second, an excess capacity of

---

[1]United States Department of Commerce, February 10, 1979; also, "New OECD Steel Committee on Steel Seen Near," Journal of Commerce, June 12, 1978. As a frame of reference note that Japan produced 100.3 million tons of steel in 1977, approximately equal to the amount of estimated global oversupply during that period.

[2]"World Steel Market -- Continued Trouble Ahead," Central Intelligence Agency, May 1977, p. i.

steel worldwide. The two must be taken together to comprehend the global political economic atmosphere in which United States foreign trade policy for steel developed in the late seventies. In this first section we shall examine the structural problem and then take a look at the short term recessionary conditions which have complicated matters, especially for the United States.

Between the two conditions -- a sputtering economic growth among the industrial countries, and an excess capacity of steelmaking facilities -- the latter is the more serious; there is consensus among economists, political scientists, and government officials in all the industrial countries that excess capacity portends consequences of a basic, structural, and long term nature.[1] The nature of the problem in the United States is illustrated by the lack of growth in steel consumption since about 1968; aside from the extraordinary "boom" years of 1973-74, there has been no growth apparent in steel consumption despite overall growth in the United States economy.[2] The Commerce Department recorded steel consumption in the

---

[1]U.S. Congress, House of Representatives, Subcommittee on Trade of the House Ways and Means Committee, World Steel Trade: Current Trends and Structural Problems, 95th Congress, 1st Session (Washington, D.C.: Government Printing Office, 1977).

[2]A large proportion of the growth in the U.S. economy in recent years has been in the service sector, rather than the manufacturing sector of the economy. Source: Department of Commerce.

United States at about 104 million tons in 1977, three million tons less than 1968; by comparison, during the 1960-68 period, steel consumption increased by about fifty percent.[1]

Globally, the capacity-consumption rates underline the problem in even more dramatic terms: Capacity in the industrial world has grown steadily from slightly less than 400 million net tons in 1967 to about 550 million net tons in 1976. During the same period, however, consumption remained at about the same level, increasing only slightly from less than 300 million net tons to slightly above that.[2]

Quite apart from the numbers, however, there are a few ideas which explain the global structural dilemma of excess capacity of the late seventies. It is worth going into these points in some detail as excess capacity is allegedly a major cause of the present crisis in steel.

Economists agree that the rate of growth of industrial development increases at very high proportions at the beginning of industrial development, but then begins to fall off.[3] It has been true of the U.S. economy, for

---

[1]U.S. House Subcommittee on International Trade, World Steel Trade: Current Trends and Structural Problems, p. 110.

[2]Central Intelligence Agency, May 1977 Report; also, "The Implications of Foreign Steel Pricing Practices in the U.S. Market," Putnam, Hayes, and Bartlett, Inc. for the American Iron and Steel Institute (Newton, Massachusetts: Putnam, Hayes, and Bartlett, Inc., August 1978) p. 2.

[3]This point was first brought to the author's attention in this context by economists at the American Iron

example, that the rate of growth of industrial development in the late nineteenth and early twentieth century was very great. Other countries have exhibited this same phenomena at comparable periods of development.[1] One very important reason for such high rates of growth is the

---

and Steel Institute. In addition see, U.S. House of Representatives, World Steel Trade: Current Trends and Structural Problems, 95th Congress, 1st Session; William Hogan, Economic History of the Iron and Steel Industry in the United States, (Lexington, Massachusetts: Lexington Books, 1971); Raymond Vernon, "International Investment and International Trade in the Product Cycle," Quarterly Journal of Economics, volume 80, no. 2, May 1966, pp. 199-207; and Michael F. Elliott-Jones, and Robert M. Whelan, "Iron and Steel in the Eighties: The Crucial Decade," prepared for the Chase Econometrics Group (xerox: 1979).

[1]See, for example, Donald N. McCloskey, Economic Maturity and Enterprenurial Decline: British Iron and Steel 1870-1913 (Cambridge, Massachusetts: Harvard University Press, 1973); Raymond Vernon, Big Business and the State: Changing Relations in Western Europe (Cambridge, Massachusetts: Harvard University Press, 1974); especially where the authors discuss the increased government involvement as a result of the need to manage a decline in the rate of growth of consumption; International Iron and Steel Institute, Committee on Economic Studies Working Party on Capital Investment Financing, "Financing of Investment in Certain Major Steel Producing Countries, 1961-71" (Belgium: International Iron and Steel Institute, 1974).

In discussions with Lawrence Krause, Senior Fellow at the Brookings Institution, an important distinction was made between a decline in the rate of growth of consumption, and an actual decline in consumption. Dr. Krause makes the point that the "energy crisis" has had a real effect on steel consumption since large producers consume less steel in an attempt to conserve. For example, automobiles are now made with less steel; for example, automobile makers have replaced the use of heavy steel with lighter steel. The result may be that we will experience a decline in consumption in addition to a decline in the rate of growth of consumption. At the least, he suggests, there is a transfer of intensive steel consumption from the industrial world to the developing world where there seems to be less concern over conservation, and more emphasis on growth.

emphasis during these initial stages of development on capital intensive industries; as a country builds up its infrastructure, it also tends to build up its capital intensive industries; various industries tend to feed off this level of growth, and themselves grow.

The condition of the steel industry is especially sensitive to the stage of industrial development of a given economy. At the earlier stages, for example, it stands to reason that the construction, railroad, and shipbuilding industries -- all heavy consumers of steel -- will grow at high rates and therefore maintain a high level of steel demand and consumption. As a country's economic development progresses, however, it is likely that the steel industry will experience a concomitant slowdown in the rate of growth of consumption of steel.

Accordingly, one might expect that industrial economies will reach a level of growth where the rate of growth of steel consumption is likely to decline in a rather considerable measure. Since steel economists and industry leaders come to expect this process, more or less, it is natural that economists -- government as well as private -- plan for a decline in the rate of growth of steel consumption. In the United States, the steel industry claims to have figured in its projections for the seventies and eighties that such a slowdown in the rate of growth of consumption would in fact occur.[1] In other words, projections on steel demand took account of an inevitable decline in the consumption of the capital intensive industries; economists presumed that less steel would be consumed in the period from 1970 to 1980, than had been consumed in earlier periods.[2] One might argue that this is especially true for the United States since its steel industry made the decision in about 1960 to produce almost entirely for the home market, and therefore would not produce for export.

Thus, under optimal conditions one would find that the industry, in the United States or elsewhere, plans for a slowdown in the rate of growth of steel consumption as its economy ages. This rational model gets complicated, however, by government intervention to avoid unacceptable social and political costs such as high unemployment. Even under the best economic conditions, therefore, it is likely that political constraints would increase the chance for excess capacity of steel. As a country's level of demand decreases, for instance, the government might

---

[1]Interview, Donald Barnett and Jim Collins of the American Iron and Steel Institute, January 5, 1979; also, Interview, Father William Hogan of Fordham University's Industrial Economics Institute, May 1978.

[2]Admittedly, there is a disagreement over whether the steel industry made the right decisions, even accounting for a decline in the rate of growth of steel consumption in the domestic economy. We shall see in Chapter 4 that some economists, notably Robert Crandall of the Brookings

continue to promote production for export -- one way of absorbing production not consumed in the home market. The rational economic model suggests that the British steel industry, for example, should have substantially cut its capacity by the first period after World War II, rather than the government supporting inefficient, obsolete capacity through enormous subsidies, as they've done especially since 1967. We shall see throughout this chapter how government policies in Europe, Japan, and the Third World led to a situation where global excess capacity would have been rather hard to avoid, quite apart from the foreign trade strategies developed in the United States in the late seventies.

The present structural crisis of excess capacity has been further exacerbated by the "oil crisis" -- referred to by one steel economist as "a major event in world economic history."[1]

Simply, the oil crisis sped up the process described above: the decline in the rate of growth of capital intensive industries, which leads to a decline in the rate of growth of steel consumption, occurred at a

---

Institution, argue that the steel industry is in economic trouble largely because of its management decisions in the fifties and even early sixties not to modernize.

[1]Interview, Donald Barnett and Jim Collins of the American Iron and Steel Institute, January 5, 1979.

quicker rate than had been anticipated.[1] As an economist for the American Iron and Steel Institute put it: "It's pretty tough when you tried to plan ten years ahead . . . anticipating a one percent decline in consumption, but then you get a three to four percent decline in one year."[2] So, according to this explanation, the normal decline in the rate of growth of the capital intensive industries was sped up by the inordinate rise in oil prices; this extra, unexpected, and persistent expense made it even more difficult for capital intensive industries which consume steel to maintain the levels of growth which had been planned. Or, as Takashi Hosomi put it in an article for The World Economy: "The continuation of large-scale deficits on the part of the oil importing countries is enough to cause continuous leaks in effective demand, with the deflationary gap constricting economic growth." And referring to Japan as an example, "One of the main reasons why Japan has not yet completely recovered from the recession of two years ago (1975) is that managers have insufficient confidence in the future to make required

---

[1]Some economists have argued, however, that in the long term, the oil crisis may have an opposite effect. That is, it may have the effect of stimulating demand for steel as the capital intensive industries are forced to readjust their machinery to energy-saving devices and the like. In this case, the oil crisis will have had the effect of increasing the rate of steel consumption.

[2]Interview, Barnett, Collins, January 5, 1979.

capital outlays. Business psychology itself has undergone a profound "structural change."[1]

These two factors -- political pressures on governments to maintain older steel mills at what many argued were unwarranted levels of capacity, and the effects of the oil crisis on the normal structural decline in the rate of growth of the capital intensive industries -- combined with the unusually rapid rate of growth of Japan and to a lesser extent West Germany, came together after 1973 to leave the world steel industry with especially high levels of excess capacity. We shall see later in this chapter how the Japanese' extraordinary rate of growth, and then decline -- telescoping 100 years into 20 -- had a precipitous affect on the rest of the world steelmaking community. Its rapid growth rate, especially in modern, efficient, and competitive steelmaking capacity created a situation where the older facilities in Europe and the United States grew obsolete at a relatively quicker pace than had been anticipated. As we shall see in the next section of this chapter, this was especially true for Europe. First, let us continue to explore in an introductory fashion, the overall global conditions of the world steel trade as it was seen by U.S. policymakers in the late seventies.

---

[1]Takashi Hosomi, "Japan's Changing Role," The World Economy, volume 1, number 2, January 1978 (London: Elsevier, for the Trade Policy Research Center) p. 138.

All serious projections of world steel demand point to the persistence of excess capacity. By CIA reckoning, for example:

> World demand for steel will grow only about four percent annually through 1980 . . . about one percentage point below the industry's long term growth rate . . . at this rate, world steel demand will total about 540 million tons in 1980, only seven percent more than 1973 . . . there is about 600 million tons worth of installed steelmaking capacity.[1]

Putting this in an even more stark perspective, the American Iron and Steel Institute in its May 1977 study indicated that by 1980 free world capacity will grow by at least 10.3 percent over the 1976 total to a level of 763 million tons. They projected that this capacity will far exceed consumption forecasts by at least sixteen percent, and possibly as high as twenty-three percent.[2] This condition (set forth in the accompanying chart) has affected the entire industrial world. To a large degree, the effects on the United States stemmed from conditions in the other OECD countries. In fact, the changing international economy should be seen as the major explanatory variable in the equation which led to the changing U.S. trade policy.

---

[1]Central Intelligence Agency, May 1977 Report.

[2]"Economics of International Steel Trade: Policy Implications for the U.S.," An analysis and forecast for American Iron and Steel Institute (Newton, Massachusetts: Putnam, Hayes, and Bartlett, Inc., May 1977).

Free World Steel: Supply/Demand Scenarios

Year	Capacity Yearly Average (million tons)	Demand (million tons)		Capacity Utilization Rate (percent)	
		Scenario 1[1]	Scenario 2[2]	Scenario 1	Scenario 2
1978	613	474	474	77.0	77.0
1980	637	503	503	79.0	79.0
1985	730	529	583	72.0	80.0

1. 3 percent growth 1978-80, 1 percent growth 1981-85.
2. 3 percent growth 1978-85.

It is important to recognize that the economic problems of the American steel industry were paled by those in the other industrial economies. For U.S. foreign trade policy, however, the link between the two has been essential. Indeed, there is a direct and fundamental connection between the economic policies and foreign trade strategies of other countries and the economic conditions of the steel industry in the United States. The importance of this relationship was emphasized by the GATT study on "Liberalization, Protectionism, and Interdependence" prepared as a background paper for the Multilateral Trade Negotiations in Geneva. It admitted that "the sudden increase in protectionist pressures in the last few years is clearly related to the inadequate recovery from the 1974-75 recession" -- the slow and uneven growth among the industrial countries. But the study goes on to point out, the "roots of the malaise" date back to the late sixties when "long-established growth trends began to change and a general difficulty of adjustment began to be felt in the advanced industrial economies"[1] -- the structural dilemma which led to global excess capacity.

Complicating the Structural Crisis -- Governmental Policies, the Recession and Uneven Growth

---

[1]Richard Blackhurst, et. al., "Trade Liberalization, Protectionism, and Interdependence," GATT Studies in International Trade (Geneva: GATT, November 1977).

While the most vexing combination of problems -- high rates of inflation and unemployment -- date from about the late sixties, the most significant development affecting the political economy of international trade has been the fact that "production subsidies as a proportion of gross domestic product show a more or less pronounced rise"[1] since that time.

Also focusing on the long term problem of excess capacity, and on the political implications of the economic condition, John Marshall, in testimony before the House Subcommittee Hearings on World Steel Trade, pointed to what he termed "government involvement" in Japan and Europe as a factor which "will seriously aggravate the problem of excess capacity . . . ." He went on to explain the crux of the problem as one where:

> Steel producers in Japan and Europe entered 1977 with considerably more capacity than they needed at current levels of domestic consumption and export demand. This situation was brought about in part by the unusual severity of the decline in worldwide steel demand beginning in 1975. The situation was compounded by government involvement in steel operations of these countries at the peak of the cycle and slower cutbacks when demand turned down than market forces would have dictated.[2]

This led, as Susan Strange in her essay on "surplus capacity"

---

[1]Ibid.

[2]U.S. House Subcommittee on International Trade, World Steel Trade: Current Trends and Structural Problems, p. 182.

characterized it, to a situation where "bóth producers in Japan and Europe, in order to manage their end of the constricted market, have had to intensify output regulation arrangements among themselves."[1]

It is precisely this relationship between the economic facts and the resultant political reality -- the Europeans and Japanese intensifying regulations among themselves -- which has made it difficult for advanced industrial societies in the West to adjust to either unemployment or inflation, and especially to both. In response to the economic pressures which had been building since the early sixties, governments and producers might have opted for one of two general courses: on the one hand, they might have depended on traditional mechanisms of competition such as market reactions to prices, actual consumption, or output and investment; on the other hand, they might have resorted to cartelization policies, national protection, or price discrimination practices between the home and the export markets. During the period under discussion, 1976-78, the perceived social and political costs of the first option led governments of the European countries, Japan, and the United States to choose the latter option -- i.e., one or more forms of protection in varying

[1]Susan Strange, "The Management of Surplus Capacity: Or, How Does Theory Stand Up to Protectionism 1970s Style?" (xerox: 1978) p. 2. Also see my section in Chapter 4 on the "301 complaint."

degrees. In each case there was an unwillingness, and to some degree an inability, to adjust to both the short term problem of slow growth and decline in demand, as well as the longer term structural problem symbolized by excess capacity. Absorbing unemployment or risking higher rates of inflation -- two probable results of adjusting to bad economic conditions -- might have eased the immediate crisis in the world steel market, but it would surely have brought about political and social consequences that many of the governments involved were unwilling, and probably unable, to withstand. Each had a political rationale for acting as it did. In the end, there would be a form of "collective" protectionism as the alternative to straightforward "national" protection.

For the United States there was an additional, more complicating factor associated with the immediate circumstances, but one that would have a rather large impact on the longer term consequences as well. It so happened that the United States recovered from the 1974-75 recession more quickly and with greater economic strength than its trading partners were able to do. Thus, United States market growth attracted goods from countries where the economies were still suffering from the "doldrums of the recession." Europe, in particular, has still not recovered. Economic growth in Europe for 1979 has been projected at the low rate of 2.7 percent, nearly 40 percent lower than the growth projections for the whole of the OECD, which itself is considerably less than the 4.5 percent rate economists say is needed to sustain present employment levels.[1] The effects of unequal growth between Europe and the United States has had repercussions in international trade.

Thus, the unheralded level of manufactured products exported into the United States from about 1975, may in part be attributed to the different rates of recovery between the U.S. and the other OECD countries. Predictably, this condition generated powerful political pressures on the U.S. government to stem the import surge.

Scolding Germany and Japan, in particular, the OECD 1977 Report argued the point directly: "In the short run reduction in [U.S.] deficit will depend largely on changing the present differentials between rates of recovery in the United States and other important trading partners."[2] And the OECD Report also pointed to the dangerous political implications of a low, or no, growth period:

> Low growth means low levels of productive investment that could prejudice job opportunities for years to come . . . and brings the risk of a widening net of overt and covert

---

[1]"The Bonn Summit," The European Community, no. 208, July-August 1978, p. 3.

[2]Reported in "The OECD Cautions," New York Times, December 28, 1978.

> subsidies to help particular sectors of the population or industry. Those difficulties which at present result from cyclical conditions would gradually get built into the structure of the OECD economies.[1]

The slow rate of recovery outside the United States, where indeed there was recovery at all, was complicated for the older industries burdened with excess capacity. This was especially true for steel, as has been asserted by the President's Council on Economic Advisors:

> Current forecasts of steel demand point to the persistence of a substantial margin of unused world steel capacity at least until 1980, and very likely well into the next decade. Thus steel is likely to remain a problem industry.[2]

Arguing this point in more general terms President Carter in the Fall of 1977 characterized the world steel problem as a "chronic one." In a press briefing at the height of the political tensions over steel in the United States, the President stated:

> The worldwide economic structure is not growing as rapidly as it has in the past . . . there are just not so many orders for steel . . . we believe that the problems are chronic . . . .[3]

The United Steelworkers agreed with this assessment and underscored their concern with the growing obsolescence of steelmaking facilities:

---

[1]Ibid.

[2]House Subcommittee on International Trade, <u>World Steel Trade: Current Trends and Structural Crisis</u>, p. 104.

[3]Quoted in "President Carter's Press Conference," <u>New York Times</u>, September 30, 1977.

> The American steel industry is saddled with a number of weak, marginal facilities. Unless major efforts are taken by the industry to modernize these facilities, the workers in these plants will remain highly exposed to permanent job loss.[1]

Faced with excess capacity, governments are also confronted with labor movements which saw it in their interests to promote "nationalization," modernization of existing facilities rather than "rationalization," thereby further complicating the equation. As we shall see, it was difficult if not politically impossible for government to promote rationalization of its country's steelmaking facilities when highly concentrated and powerful groups like labor unions were opposed.

So the economic recession of the mid to late seventies has had a particularly exacerbating effect on the situation of the world steel industry. William Nordhaus of the Council on Economic Advisors cited the immediate cause of the "present crisis in the steel industry as the general depression of economic activity of the world around." Confirming this assessment, the United Steelworkers Union pointed to a "stagnant economy" as the first priority for government in considering how to cope with the problems in steel. At a Conference on Basic Steel, the Executive Council stated: "The most

---

[1]"Unemployment in the Steel Industry," Basic Steel Conference, Washington Hilton Hotel, December 2, 1977, p. 3.

basic problem is the fact that the general economy is depressed, leaving the steel industry and other sectors in a weakened state."[1]

Summary

Each of these conditions have contributed to the problem in world steel since about 1975. As we shall see throughout this chapter, governments responded to the condition in a variety of ways. In some cases governments cooperated -- as in the case of the European Community and Japan -- effectively organizing their own markets. They claimed to have acted to avoid pernicious forms of national protection. In other cases, governments provided further subsidies for their industries in an effort to satisfy domestic social and political pressure.

In both cases, however, the effect on the United States has been to further erode its competitive position. United States dominance in the world steel industry in 1950 -- accounting for 47 percent of total world output, and 57 percent of free world production -- has given way to a position in which Japan and the countries of the European Community have grown to a point roughly equivalent to U.S. production levels. As the following charts illustrate, production grew more rapidly outside the United States after 1950, so that by 1976, the United States

---

[1]Ibid., p. 1.

World Production of Raw Steel: 1950-78
(in millions of net tons)

	Raw Steel Production		
Year	United States	World	U.S. Percentage of World Production
1950	97	207	46.9
1951	105	232	45.3
1952	93	234	39.7
1953	112	259	43.2
1954	88	246	35.8
1955	117	298	39.3
1956	115	313	36.7
1957	113	322	35.1
1958	85	299	28.4
1959	93	337	27.6
1960	99	382	25.9
1961	98	390	25.1
1962	98	395	24.8
1963	109	422	25.8
1964	127	479	26.5
1965	131	503	26.0
1966	134	519	25.8
1967	127	548	23.2
1968	131	583	22.5
1969	141	632	22.3
1970	132	654	20.2
1971	121	633	19.1
1972	133	692	19.2
1973	151	767	19.7
1974	146	783	18.6
1975	117	712	16.4
1976	128	746	17.0
1977	125	742	16.8
1978	136	784	17.3

Source: American Iron and Steel Institute, *Annual Statistical Report*, various issues.

Trends in Raw Steel Production by Major Non-Communist Steel Producing Countries: 1960 and 1974

Country	Production (million metric tons) 1960	1974	Percent Change	Average Annual Rate of Growth (percent)
United States	93.3	132.2	41.7	2.52
Japan	21.8	117.2	437.6	12.76
West Germany	32.9	53.2	61.7	3.49
Italy	8.1	23.9	195.1	8.03
France	17.2	27.0	57.0	3.27
United Kingdom	24.7	22.4	-9.3	-.70
Belgium	6.9	16.2	134.8	6.28
Luxembourg	4.0	6.5	62.5	3.52

Source: International Iron and Steel Institute.

Steel Production
(millions of tons)

Country	1977	1978
United States	125.3	136.7
Japan	112.9	112.6
West Germany	43.0	45.5
Italy	25.7	26.7
France	24.4	25.2
United Kingdom	22.6	22.3
Belgium/Luxembourg	17.2	19.2

Source: American Iron and Steel Institute, March 1979

produced only about one-fourth of free world steel. Accompanying the rapid growth in the productive capacities of Japan and the European Community has been a concomitant increase in the amount of steel which is traded; 22 percent was traded in 1975, or in absolute terms, the amount rose from 18 million tons to over 102 million tons during the 1950-74 period.[1] Clearly, this shift in who produces what amount, as well as the total amount of steel which makes its way into international trade, has had a rather marked effect on the realignment of power relations in the world steel market.

The major world steel producers, and their governments, were faced by the mid-seventies with a situation of excess capacity resulting in part from the short-term slow growth of the industrial economies, and in part from the longer-term buildup of the failure to adjust to the "emergence of more efficient, competing productive facilities."[2] The structural problem was exacerbated by the oil crisis to the degree that it constricted steel demand in many of the capital intensive industries quicker than expected. In the face of this situation, three alternatives were available to the governments (and steel

---

[1]"Economics of International Steel Trade: Policy Implications for the United States," American Iron and Steel Institute, iv.

[2]GATT Study on "Trade Liberalization, Protectionism, and Interdependence," p. 55.

producers) of the OECD countries: 1) Address the short term problem by stimulating growth in all the industrial countries, and in particular, to try to narrow the gap in economic recovery among them; 2) To respond in a serious and basic way to the structural problem characterized here as excess capacity, by rationalizing existing capacity and take other acute measures which, however, could lead to political and social adjustment problems; and 3) To look for other markets outside their particular domestic economic marketplace which might help absorb the excess steel each produced nationally, both from the excess capacity and from the slack demand.

In reality, all three were pursued. Some were pursued more seriously and with greater vigor than others, largely because they met with the least amount of opposition in the short term. It would have been hard, for example, for those countries which, ironically, needed it the most to act on the analysis of a study prepared for the American Iron and Steel Institute that "it is unlikely that world-wide demand will be sufficient to support world capacity in the near term and possibly not until 1980,"[1] by simply rationalizing or cutting back production accordingly. Politics are simply not that rational.

---

[1]"Economics of International Steel Trade: Policy Implications for the United States," American Iron and Steel Institute, iv.

So, beyond the economic crisis of steel -- the structural crisis symbolized by excess capacity and low demand -- there developed a political crisis. Contributing significantly to the political crisis of the world steel market, and rebounding to further exacerbate the economic crisis, was the difference in state-society relations among the major industrial trading partners. Roughly speaking, the stronger the society, the less likely it is that this relationship will ensue. Among the United States, the European countries, and Japan, United States industry operates most independently from either state involvement or intervention; the Japanese government, on the other hand, is commonly understood to "play a very active role in all phases of economic life."[1]

This difference in relations between industry and government among the OECD countries has been a source of friction in their foreign relations with one another. In matters of international trade it has been especially troublesome. The United States foreign trade policy process has been largely influenced, since about the mid-sixties, by the perception that government involvement in the other OECD countries has worked to the disadvantage of the United States. This view is clearly and succinctly

---

[1]Chalmers Johnson, Japan's Public Policy Companies (Washington, D.C.: The American Enterprise Institute for Public Policy Research 1978) p. 14.

illustrated by Lloyd McBride, president of the United Steelworkers of America, when he said:

> Foreign nations have been exporting their unemployment to the United States by means of government guaranteed loans, subsidies, and tax concessions that enable their steel mills to keep producing and selling to American consumers regardless of whether they make a profit or break even.[1]

The rest of this chapter, therefore, will look at the political-economic choices made by the Europeans, the Japanese, and the Third World, which had a direct effect on the development of the United States foreign trade policy for steel, 1976-78.

---

[1]Quoted in "Chicago Businessmen Seek International Trade Policy," Journal of Commerce, April 11, 1978.

II. Europe

The establishment of the European Coal and Steel Community (ECSC) in 1951 was a clear statement by the member countries of their deep and serious commitment to a healthy, prosperous, and powerful steel industry. Title I, Article 2 of the Treaty states that commitment:

> The European Coal and Steel Community shall have as its task to contribute, in harmony with the general economy of the Member States and through the establishment of a common market as provided in Article 4, to economic expansion, growth of employment and a rising standard of living in the Member States.
>
> The Community shall progressively bring about conditions which will of themselves ensure the most rational distribution of products at the highest possible level of productivity which safeguarding continuity of employment and taking care not to provide fundamental and persistent disturbances in the economies of the Member States.[1]

The willingness to enter into a community-wide agreement covering coal and steel signified an interest among the governments of Western Europe in the production and marketing of steel. Indeed, there are those who will argue that the ECSC was a post-war attempt to revitalize the International Steel Cartel that was set up in

---

[1]"Treaty Establishing the European Coal and Steel Community, Paris, April 18, 1951" (Dublin: Stationary Office, 1951).

1926,[1] and only disbanded in 1939 as World War II broke out. In either circumstance, the ECSC represented a clear commitment to the iron and steel industry, and the propensity toward government supervision and intervention in the market.

Although each European nation responded in a variety of particular ways to the steel crisis of the mid-seventies, a steel strategy for the whole of the ECSC was also developed. With the ECSC in place, and all of the European countries (with some qualifications for West Germany) suffering from roughly the same conditions, it

---

[1]Interestingly, the reason for the establishment of the International Steel Cartel in 1926 (Entente Internationale de l'Acier) was "over production," or excess supply. According to a study done for the United States Department of Commerce by John Palmer in 1927, the Cartel was necessary because "consumption in home markets [at low level] pushed the steel producing industries of Europe [into] a price war in which profits had to be sacrificed in an effort to keep up plant activity, and in which each was underselling the other, both in home markets and in other markets where steel either was not produced at all or where steel either was not produced at all or where production was insufficient to meet local demands." John Palmer, "The International Steel Cartel," _United States Department of Commerce Reports_ (Washington, D.C.: Government Printing Office 1927) p. 2; also see, Louis Lister, _Europe's Coal and Steel Community: An Experiment in Economic Union_ (New York: Twentieth Century Fund 1960); especially pp. 183-97; Ervin Hexner, _The International Steel Cartel_ (Chapel Hill: The University of North Carolina Press, 1943); George W. Stocking, and Myron W. Watkins, _Cartels in Action: Case Studies in International Business Diplomacy_ (New York: Twentieth Century Fund 1946); especially Chapter 5; Walter S. Tower, "The New Steel Cartel," _Foreign Affairs_, January 1927, pp. 249-67.

was both natural and practical that a "European policy" apply. As a United States International Trade Commission economist who went to Europe on a "steel data collecting mission" put it:

> The basic premise on which the Europeans proceed is that the steel industry for Europe and in each country individually is inseparable from national defense, and as such must be propped up. The Europeans are not only not afraid to have an industrial steel policy, but find it necessary.[1]

Thus, national government participation in steel operations was supported, both directly and indirectly, by a series of measures from the European Commission -- all with the idea in common that the European steel industry must be kept afloat, and that this be accomplished without further instability to the international system.

It is legally and politically proper, therefore, to think of the European response to the steel crisis in terms of one policy which tried to take account of national peculiarities. This view is supported by many, including Gerard Depayre, top staff official of the European Community office based in Washington. Depayre remarked:

> It is valid to consider the European Community as talking with one voice when it comes to steel. This is so because of the impact on all the industries from the recession . . . which made things so bad that they needed to join together . . . even Germany, which was not hurt as bad, came around to this view.

---

[1]"United States International Trade Commission Briefing for Congressional Staff," February 10, 1978.

> Another reason beyond the one of the conditions of the recession which imposed itself on all of the European countries, is that the institutional framework -- the ECSC -- was already in place and functioning. They already exchange information and have something of a legal framework from which to work.
>
> It is the case as well that the area of steel is special because the problem is so pervasive and because there existed an institutional framework . . . Article 13 of the [Common Market] Treaty recognized the special field of Trade Policy. And as the Community took the responsibility and acted upon it, many of the differences which might have seemed unapproachable in the beginning began to wane.[1]

Let us proceed, then, to examine the steel crisis in Europe at the Community level. For it was at that level that policy developed which had its most direct affect on U.S. policy. While each country's national policies -- the British, French, Belgium, and Italian subsidization policies through nationalization -- imposed great burdens on the U.S. market, it will be argued that Community Policy promoted arrangements within and outside the Community which channeled pressures onto the American market.

Europe's Steel Crisis and a Community-wide Policy

While the United States recovered from the 1974-75 recession, the Europeans in late 1975 were still, according to the *Official Journal of the European Community* "experiencing the most severe and prolonged economic recession of their recent history." In particular, the *Journal* went on

---

[1]Interview, November 16, 1978.

to record, "Steel demand was more drastically affected by this recession than most other sectors of the economy."[1] A high level European official drew a qualitative distinction between these conditions, and previous ones: "[European Steel] has had many cyclical ups and downs in the past few years. None of them constitute a crisis like the one we are going through now."[2] Even by late 1978, when a good part of the world steel industry had begun to emerge from "the disastrous slump of 1975-77," the Economist was still describing the situation of the European steel industry in rather grim terms: "Steel industries in the richest countries, especially in Western Europe, are still plunged in gloom, still trying to come to terms with a shrinking market."[3]

The European steel industry's depressed performance was officially attributed to four factors: 1) the rundown of stocks by consumers in order to adjust their stock levels; 2) the depressed state of other industries such as the construction, shipbuilding and machine industries that normally consume large quantities of steel;[4] 3) the fact

---

[1]"Official Journal of the European Community," October 10, 1975; all European Community documents are on file with the author.

[2]"European Steel in Crisis," Journal of Commerce, December 17, 1976, p. 1.

[3]"Quietly Steel is Booming, But Not In the West," The Economist, December 16, 1978.

[4]According to the European Community office in Washington, these three industries normally account for two-thirds of total steel demand.

that producers had reached the limits of their financial and/or physical capacity; and 4) an especially tight contraction on exports because of the worldwide recessionary conditions.[1]

As conditions got worse throughout 1975 and the Community attempted to rely even more heavily on export markets, the ability to do so became less easy. Competition was getting more fierce, not only because of real economic conditions, but also because of the particular set of political conditions associated with the recession. The unique position of the European steel industry -- one which depends on exports as well as imports -- caused it to suffer even more than the other industrial countries. Both Japan as a net exporter, and the United States as a net importer, had, at least, somewhere to turn. By contrast, the Europeans were squeezed at both ends. As an illustration of this "squeeze," consider that the first quarter of 1976 showed exports down 42 percent from the fourth quarter of 1974, the latter representing the height of the global recession.[2] During the same two periods, however, imports remained about the same, roughly 1.7 million metric tons.[3] Imports were to go up, but exports continued to decrease. Something had to be done. Thus,

---

[1]"European Journal," October 10, 1975.

[2]"European Journal," December 31, 1975.

[3]"European Journal," December 31, 1975.

the Community sought to develop a Community-wide steel program to deal with what it called "crisis conditions."

By December 1975, the ECSC believed conditions had become serious enough to establish a system of Community-wide surveillance over "imports into the Community of iron and steel products . . ."[1] This would have an impact both on the amount of imports going into the U.S. markets, and on the development of a U.S. steel policy. We shall see in the next chapter, for example, that a major claim by U.S. steelmakers against the European Community and Japan was "diversion of Japanese steel from Europe to the U.S. market."[2]

The "Commission Decision" was based on the fact that increased imports into the Community "cause[d] serious injury to Community production."[3] So, it provided for the Member States to notify the Commission at a specified time each month such that "the quantities imported during the last month are reported . . . [and] the prices of the imported products are reports."[4]

---

[1]"European Journal," December 10, 1975; and attachment, Document L7/15.

[2]See the section on the 301 petition in Chapter 4. As we shall see, the American steel industry alleged that the European Community and the Japanese government entered into an agreement where Japanese steel normally exported to Europe was diverted to the American market.

[3]"European Journal," December 10, 1975 and attachment, Document L7/15.

[4]Ibid.

In a subsequent, clarifying note of the "Community Steel Policy Explanatory Annex" the goals of the year-end 1975 decision were set forth:

> The aim is to be able to ascertain rapidly, and predict, fluctuations on the steel market . . . . Statistics on production, consumption, external trade, and utilization of capacity have to be assessed in advance so as to detect cyclical movements at an early stage instead of merely recording them after the event. A notification system will also provide information . . . .[1]

As stated, the purpose of the "common steel policy" was to establish some degree of control over short term supply and demand, expansion of capacity, and long term development of supply and demand. In addition, the consultative process in the Community would establish a basis, and framework, for the development of "some kind of worldwide orderly marketing agreement or an international steel charter."[2] The Community policy also sought to "adapt the levels of imports to internal demand" by providing information which would first of all monitor the import penetration and project estimated penetration, but secondly, "prevent duplication of effort and overcapacity and would thereby contribute toward a better balance between world supply and demand."[3]

---

[1]"European Journal," October 1976, and attachment "Community Steel Policy Explantory Annex," Brussels, October 1976, Document Sec. (76) 3467 Final.

[2]Ibid.

[3]"European Journal," December 1976, and "Cable from

To do this, the Europeans devised a special Community-wide crisis plan known as the Simonet Plan, which went into effect on January 1, 1977. It was expected to deal with a situation which "the most recent figures [had] indicate[d] that the steel industry ha[d] entered a critical phase."[1] The Simonet Plan consisted of measures designed to arrest a particular and immediate crisis. Its mandate, known as the "Community Decision," contained four provisions -- to monitor production levels, prices, export shipments within the Community, and imports.[2] In fact, the Simonet plan only began by monitoring these factors; monitoring provided the information from which the Community could limit imports, control prices within the Community, and control prices of imports. In the words of an official at the European Community "the idea was to try to avoid cutthroat competition among the Europeans themselves . . . so no one is hurt more than any other in the process of [closing down] unused

---

Europe to the United States State Department, December 3, 1976, No. 2106 New Series, p. 9; also see, "European Journal," "Commission of the European Community Com (76) 543 Final," Brussels, October 8, 1976, "Common Steel Policy."

[1]"European Journal," attachment document, "Crisis Measures on the Steel Market," Brussels, December 1976.

[2]"European Journal," attachment, "Commission Decision," No. 3017/76/ECSC of December 8, 1976.

capacity."[1] But, as with most efforts at "supranational" governance, there is little that the supranational body can do to ensure compliance with its guidelines. Predictably, there was minimal compliance with the "restructuring effort" -- that part of the simonet plan which sought to cut back excess capacity which was obsolete and/or inefficient, but from the American steelmaker's perspective too much compliance in limiting imports into the Community -- that part of the European plan which sought to ensure European producers a significant share of their own market oftentimes in spite of an uncompetitive position.

Conditions continued to get worse for Europe. By the following summer, July 1977, the European Paliament said of the Simonet Plan that "it was not effective in combatting the steady decline in the iron and steel industry."[2] Even before summer, however, the Europeans had already begun to develop still another plan; one that would be tougher in its economic goals and stricter on the Member States. The European Consultative Committee had resolved in March of the year:

> . . . to bring those [Member States] who have not yet committed themselves to a voluntary limit on deliveries to do so as quickly as possible . . . to give effect to quantitative measures in areas where they have so far had

---

[1]Interview, November 16, 1978.

[2]"Official Journal," attachment, "European Parliament Working Document," July 1977.

> no results . . . to reduce the volume of Community imports of iron and steel products from third countries . . . in this connection the reintroduction of automatic import licenses is stringently to be urged . . . to ensure that the restructuring plans in various steelmaking areas are compatible with general objects.[1]

This constituted the "second stage," developed by Commissioner Davignon, Simonet's successor as industrial Commissioner for the Community. "It didn't change very much [in its specific] from the Simonet Plan," according to a European official, "but evolved from it." Its underlying drive as a "grave concern at the continuing deterioration in the situation of the Community's iron and steel industry and the serious threats this poses to employment, regional balance, and the future of this vital industrial sector."[2]

The Community Plan and National Policies

Both the Simonet and Davignon Plans, actually two parts of the same effort, were developed under the auspices of the ECSC acting for the "Committee on Economic and Monetary Affairs" in the European Parliament. Two series of events led to both: 1) the worsening condition of

---

[1]"Official Journal," attachment "Resolution of the European Coal and Steel Community Consultative Committee," 182d Session, March 17, 1977, Doc. No. C 86/7.

[2]"European Journal," attachment "European Communities Documents: European Parliament Working Document 1977-78," July 4, 1977, Document 198/7, p. 5.

the European steel industry; and 2) the need to organize on a "Community-wide" basis the somewhat disparate, and sometimes countervailing, national responses to these deteriorating economic conditions.

By mid-1977, roughly six months after the Simonet anti-crisis plan had gone into effect, and about a year and a half after the crisis had been officially recognized by the European Community, the European steel industries were still operating at about sixty percent capacity -- quite a low figure for an industry which depends on high rates of capacity utilization for profits. Large deficits, which led to more serious threats of unemployment, had already reached what most of the governments viewed as unacceptable levels both from a financial, and a social-political standpoint. The Belgium steel industries were operating a $2 billion deficit and had begun serious plans to nationalize; Britain already had run up a $5 billion deficit in its nationalized steel corporation; and France's deficit had reached a wopping $10 billion before they too would turn to nationalization.[1] The political costs which would have followed, or were recommended to follow, had these countries followed a rationalization plan where they complied with the "restructuring" program

---

[1]"We Don't Really Like Protectionism, But It's Working," The Economist, May 13, 1978, pp. 63, 64.

of the European Community were in many instances too high to accept.

As an illustration consider Belgium where a private consulting firm hired by the government had recommended that the Belgium steel industries cut about one-fourth of the country's 46,000 steelworkers. Similarly, projections for British Steel job losses were (conservatively) figured by the *Economist* at "38,000 of the industry's present work force of 168,000 to go over the five years into 1982."[1] And the British White Paper on the control of nationalized industries pointed to the fact that stringent austerity measures were being seriously contemplated. According to the White Paper "the government intends to take powers to give nationalized industries specific directions to do things that their boards will not do willingly."[2] France was also planning to cut back employment; its goal was to cut approximately 16,500 workers of the 153,000 steelworkers in the country.[3] Even

---

[1]Ibid.

[2]"European Steel," *The Economist*, April 8, 1978, p. 103.

[3]This amount is expected to increase by another 20,000, since the government nationalized its steel industry in the summer of 1978. But it is unclear whether the political costs won't prove too great, and the government won't have to reconsider this policy. For example, there have been a number of bloody strikes in February-March 1979, in response to attempted increases in unemployment. For example, see "France to Soften on Steel Industry Cutbacks," *New York Times*, March 10, 1979.

Germany, the only European country which operated any kind of acceptable debt-to equity ratio during the 1975-77 period, planned to cut back 36,000 jobs out of 342,000 during this period.[1] Threats of such high levels of unemployment throughout Europe were bound to cause political tensions. Each government had to ask whether it could withstand the social and political tensions that would have surely followed from massive layoffs in a basic industry which was geographically concentrated in some of the older more depressed regions of the countries. As a result, governments hesitated to force employment cuts. Predictably, various economic and political arrangements made it more or less difficult in the Member States. Let us look at some of these factors.

One critical factor was the different political arrangements in the Member States, as between labor unions and government, for example. The amount of unemployment a country can withstand is partly due to the underlying economic vitality of the society, but is also a function of the power and influence wielded by particular domestic constituencies -- the political stability of its institutional structure. Mancur Olsen has argued this point when he asserted that the older industrial nations are likely to encounter greater difficulties in dealing with

---

[1]"We Don't Really Like Protectionism, But It's Working," The Economist, May 13, 1978, p. 64.

problems like unemployment and inflation. Olsen argues that the institutionalization of political arrangements -- i.e., the degree to which the labor movement is embedded in the governmental process of a country, for example, tend to decrease the chances that a government will be able to satisfactorily deal with its unemployment problems.[1]

In Britain, for example, the Trades Union Council (TUC) largely influences the political choices made with regard to plant shutdowns and capacity rationalization, which were both part of the restructuring plan proposed by the ECSC Plan.[2] The TUC's influence is widely recognized in Britain; a British businessman was recently quoted as saying, "The TUC has become the only effective opposition party to the government. The Tories can criticize, but the TUC can wreck a government."[3] TUC leaders have used their power to promote basic objectives -- full employment, through more government spending, nationalization, if necessary, and import controls to protect

---

[1]Adopted from remarks by Mancur Olsen at the Brookings Institution Conference on "The Politics and Sociology of Global Inflation," December 6-8, 1978.

[2]Many in the European Community argue that the European Davignon Plan, as well as the International Steel Committee, will make it easier for national governments to follow policies of rationalization, since they can blame these policies on the European policy and/or the OECD policy.

[3]"Britain's True Shadow of Government," Wall Street Journal, November 23, 1977. It will be interesting to see whether the Conservatives under Margaret Thatcher will take

British jobs against foreign competition -- not dissimilar from labor's objective in the United States. Partly as a consequence of this, recent labor governments have advocated interventionist policies for selective industries, steel among them.[1] Under labor governments, and with the growing power of the TUC, market intervention in Britain -- through government grants and loans, nationalization, or the use of the National Enterprise Board -- has led to a condition where "job support" seems to take precedence over "adjustment."[2] Thus, intervention in Britain has come, in large part, from the influences of labor which has "increased the capacity" as John Zysman points out, "to resist adjustment."[3]

Indeed, the British have come to look more like the French who for a long time have chosen national industries as champions,[4] and promoted them accordingly.

---

with regard to labor cutbacks and plant shutdowns that her predecessors in both Labor and Conservative governments have been unable to accomplish.

[1]John Zysman, "Inflation and Industrial Adjustment: The Politics of Supply," presented at the Brookings Institution Conference on the Politics and Sociology of Global Inflation, December 6-8, 1978 (Washington, D.C.: Brookings xerox); p. 47; also see, "France to Soften on Steel Industry Cutbacks," New York Times, March 10, 1979.

[2]John Zysman, "Inflation and Industrial Adjustment: The Politics of Supply," p. 48.

[3]Ibid.

[4]John H. McArthur and Bruce R. Scott, Industrial Planning in France (Boston: Harvard University, 1969); especially Part IV.

Like France -- where "layoffs are not simply expensive, but may formally require labor department permission"[1] -- institutional arrangements in Britain between government and labor have provided a natural nexus for the politicization of the issue. Under these circumstances one could well understand if production quotas and restructuring plans set by the European Community fall by the wayside. In fact, the economic situation in many of the European countries where the steel industry has been nationalized -- most notably Britain and France -- has developed to a point where the governments view labor as a fixed cost. This point is well illustrated by a revealing comment to an American's question about dumping wire steel. French leaders and steelmakers remarked, "We can't stop dumping wire steel . . . we have to keep people employed."[2] They admit they dump, but also admit that they can't stop because of the high political costs involved.

The second factor which resulted in different kinds of responses by national governments was the economic conditions of its particular industries. Varying degrees of debt, low levels of capacity utilization, internal steel demand, reliance on exports, and age of steel facilities all played a part in the degree to which they could respond.

---

[1]John Zysman, "Inflation and Industrial Adjustment: The Politics of Supply," p. 41.

[2]Interview, February 18, 1979.

A third interrelated factor was the difference in government-business relations. The German government, on the one hand, has closely followed the principles of free enterprise, "[by] not telling its privately owned industry what to do."[1] On the other hand, the British government (leaving aside for the moment the political complications of the unions on its decision) was telling its British Steel Corporation, accounting for 86 percent of the steelmaking capacity in the United Kingdom, what it should do.[2] At the same time, Finsider, the Italian controlled steel firm accounting for about 60 percent of Italy's steelmaking facilities, was not planning any major cutbacks in employment during the 1976-78 period. The point here is that steelmakers in Germany, where industry operates largely independent of direct government intervention, are free to make decisions about worker layoffs and plant shutdowns if they decide those decisions to be in their companies' interests. By contrast, the steelmakers in countries like Italy, France, and Britain are pushed to maintain inefficient and oftentimes obsolete facilities by government involvement on behalf of labor.

---

[1]"We Don't Really Like Protectionism, But It's Working," The Economist, May 13, 1978, p. 64.

[2]"Staff Report on the U.S. Steel Industry and Its International Rivals: Trends and Factors Determining International Competitiveness," The Federal Trade Commission, Bureau of Economics (Washington, D.C.: Government Printing Office, November 1977) p. 350.

Thus, despite pressures from the European Commission different governments responded differently. Whether their reason was unyielding political pressures from labor against adjustment, as in the case of Britain and France, or, the force of a country's economic strategy based on "export oriented growth" as in the case of West Germany,[1] each of the European countries had institutionalized attitudes and policies which made it difficult for a Community-wide plan to succeed. Or rather, it could succeed only to the degree that each country used it to promote their own interests.

Typically, governments whose industries were in the more deteriorated condition tended to respond with greater amounts of government intervention -- nationalization in the cases of Britain, France, and Italy; semi-nationalization in the case of Belgium; and subsidization in the largest amounts in the cases of the British Steel Corporation, Italy's Finsider, and the French industry.[2] By contrast, according to the rather exhaustive United States Federal Trade Commission Report, "subsidies to major steel industries in the United States . . . is negligible or zero."[3] Thus,

---

[1]Michael Kreile, "West Germany: The Dynamics of Expansion," in Between Power and Plenty, ed. Peter J. Katzenstein (Madison, Wisconsin: University of Wisconsin Press 1978), pp. 191-225.

[2]Federal Trade Commission Report on "The United States Steel Industry and Its International Rivals," p. 367.

[3]Ibid.

as we shall see, accepted social-economic arrangements in Europe were considered unfair by Americans, and believed to have contributed to the world steel crisis especially harsh in the period after 1975.

The Community Plan and Transnational Responses

In addition to the particular national responses by the European governments the European steelmakers also organized in response to the crisis. For purposes of U.S. policy, however, the steelmakers' responses should also be seen in the context of the European Community policy. As steelmakers got together the Community feared that smaller cartels within the Community might develop, and that these cartels could be especially disruptive. Thus, these "alarming and dangerous developments," to use the words of the official European Journal, also prompted the ECSC to organize a "Community-wide" response.[1] From the point of view of the European Commission, a "Community-wide" response leading to what we shall call "collective protection" was perceived as less harmful in the long run to world steel market stability than national protection or transnational cartels.

The particular arrangements which the Community wished to avoid were those organized by the iron and

---

[1]"European Journal," attachment, European Parliament Document, July 4, 1977, Working Document, pp. 8-9.

steel companies of West Germany and the Denelux countries. In February 1976, the two formed an international economic group called Denelux "aimed at promoting cooperation . . . with regard to supplies, transport and production, increasing specialization."[1] Denelux caused a good deal of concern among the other European governments. According to a debate in the European Parliament the other countries were especially afraid that Denelux could "introduce production restraints," but they also expressed alarm over "the danger of the formation of new cartels and of the disruption to market unity"[2] which could follow. Variant levels of national steelmaking facilities as we referred to above would inevitably lead to different perceptions of one's interest. Predictably, therefore, competition among the European steelmakers led to "frightening infighting," as one official described it.[3] One might have expected, for example, a situation described by the Financial Times of London: "Surplus steel coming from West Germany, France, and Belgium [was] sold at lower prices whenever it found customers . . . both Britain and the United States [were] under particularly heavy pressure

---

[1]"No Silver Lining Seen in Clouds Confronting Steel Industry," Journal of Commerce, December 17, 1976, p. 1.

[2]Ibid.

[3]Ibid.

from steel from the Continent."[1] So in résponse to Denelux, and other cartel-type arrangements which "seemed to be cropping up everywhere," the European steelmakers formed Eurofer -- a grouping of European Community steelmakers with a full time staff and headquarters in Luxembourg,[2] and with the authority to set production targets for individual members and minimum prices for the steel shipped.

Understandably, the non-Denelux producers believed they could maintain more control over a "cartel" they belonged to, than one they didn't. Eurofer was also welcomed by the European Commission since it included all of the European countries, and was therefore thought to be less dangerous than cutting up the European market itself.[3] As bad as conditions were, commercial wars within Europe, as Commissioner Davignon called them, would make them even worse.

Apparently, the European steelmakers were convinced that "individual action" was necessary to overcome "the shortcomings of the Davignon plan."[4] They knew a Community-wide plan was necessary, but didn't entirely trust the

---

[1]"European Steel," Financial Times of London, September 15, 1978.

[2]"Japan Infighting Faces The Music," The Times of London, October 25, 1976, p. 18.

[3]"EEC Steel Group Seeks Solution to Financial Losses," Financial Times of London, August 21, 1978, p. 1.

[4]Journal of Commerce, August 2, 1978, p. 1.

European Commission to take complete control over stabilizing market conditions. Hence, Eurofer legitimized for producers many of the protective measures which had already been proposed by the European Community -- first under Commissioner Simonet, and then by Commissioner Davignon. For its part, the European Community preferred a Community-wide producer organization to a series of producer organizations competing among themselves. As the Economist put it, "The Commission in Brussels buried its instinctive preference for free(ish) trade and allowed the EEC's steel industry to set up the Eurofer cartel."[1] And it gave as the underlying reason the inability for certain of the Member States to accept the political and social consequences:

> A rapid rundown of [Europe's steel industry] . . . would create social straint in areas like Lorraine, Charleroi, the Saarland and parts of Britain (South Wales, the Northeast and Scotland) already suffering from high unemployment.[2]

Understandably, the member governments were more interested in cartelization policies in which their market shares were protected, than in emphasizing rationalization which meant employment cuts and plant closedowns.

As it happened Eurofer was a catalyst for Community-wide action by the ECSC. In the event, it worked closely

---

[1]"The Crisis in World Steel," The Economist, February 12, 1977, p. 83.

[2]Ibid.

with the Community as a partner, but also as a pressure on it. In an article on EEC lobbying, it was argued that Eurofer operated as a "powerful industrial lobby," in part because "the EEC steel directorate, which has been understaffed to cope with the post-1974 European steel crisis badly needs its help to run the Davignon plan for steel."[1] The article did point out, however, that another important reason for the political clout of Eurofer was its official lobbying status conferred upon it by the ECSC Treaty. The Treaty states that "undertakings, workers, consumers, and dealers and their association shall be entitled to present any suggestions or comments to the higher authority (Commission) on questions affecting them."[2] Eurofer therefore could legally and politically answer for the European steel industry. In that sense, the Davignon Plan was responsive to it. Eurofer worked on the one hand to undercut the effectiveness of the Plan, but paradoxically it also gave it more clout in those areas where producers and governments agreed action needed to be taken anyway. Indeed, there was a "tug-of-war" between Eurofer and the European Commission over which one was best qualified to administer production quotas. In the end they complemented one another, although neither

---

[1]"How Industry Can Put More Clout Into EEC Lobbying," Financial Times of London, August 2, 1978, p. 4.

[2]Ibid.

one was very successful since the European governments were not ready to absorb the social and political costs of adjustment which would have come from strict "rationalization" of the various industries. Producers might have agreed to cut back production if they could be assured certain profit levels, but governments as agents for labor, could not. There was little prospect of any short term political solution to the economic crisis.

Consensus for the Davignon Plan

Both Eurofer and the European Commission had realized that an international solution to the steel issue was necessary. Jaques Ferry, the president of Eurofer, for example, acknowledged that a mechanism was needed to moderate international competition, and control penetration of imports into national markets.[1] And the Community working paper also emphasized the need for an international framework:

> The crisis being worldwise, we should . . . with our main trading partners in the international steel market . . . coordinate . . . and calculate not to clash with efforts being made internally to tackle the present difficulties.[2]

It went on to set forth what needed to be done to protect export markets, and its own market from imports:

---

[1]"How Industry Can Put More Clout Into EEC Lobbying," Financial Times of London, August 2, 1978, p. 4.

[2]"European Journal," attachment, "European Community Working Document": Working Paper, December 5-6, 1977.

> *For exports*, everything must be done to prevent the introduction of further antidumping measures which inhibit international trade and instead reach understandings, particularly with the United States and Japan whereby normal trade flows can be continued.
>
> *For imports*, we should take care (i) by establishing the right contractual basis, and (ii) by adopting attitudes . . . to ensure that our trade with our partners does not further worsen the state of our own market.[1]

So, by the end of 1977, the ECSC, acting under the directives from the European Community and responding to the political pressures of, first, Denelux, but then Eurofer, put forth a rather comprehensive Davignon Plan. The cutting edge of the plan was to limit imports; in certain respects it should be understood as a Community-wide effort to prevent individual countries, or clusters of countries, from opting for tougher more protectionist unilateral measures. For, even the Germans, "the staunchest free traders agreed that imports had to be limited,"[2] and even the European Community, a body with an institutional network that considered itself fundamentally internationalist, also understood their "protectionist measures" had to be undertaken. In addition to limiting imports the plans also set forth a twofold restructuring policy "to adopt capacities to the long term trend in demand, and to improve

---

[1]Ibid.

[2]"A Protectionist Christmas Parcel," *The Economist*, December 24, 1977, p. 41.

competitiveness by reducing production costs."[1]

The Davignon Plan had four stages; each had an effect on the course of U.S. policy. They were:

First, and most important, were a series of bilateral talks between the European Community and its main exporters -- Japan, Eastern Europe, South Africa, Brazil, Korea, and Sweden. It was established under this provision that the EC would enter into Agreements on volumes and prices of imports from each of those countries. American steelmakers feared, probably correctly, that each bilateral arrangement could well have the effect of diverting steel to third markets like the United States. Take, for example, the situation in Spain. According to a Journal of Commerce article six weeks after the Davignon Plan was announced: "It is now taken for granted that the [Spanish steel] industry, reeling under a marked decrease in domestic demand and European Community curbs on imports, will get a massive injection of government aid."[2] Limiting Spanish imports in an already overburdened with capacity Spanish steel industry would lead the Spaniards to look for other markets

---

[1]"European Journal," attachment "Commission of the European Communities," Com (UU) 688, Final, Brussels, December 9, 1977, "Restructuring of the Steel Industry: Methods and Organizations."

[2]"Spain Expected to Aid Steel Firm," Journal of Commerce, April 5, 1978, pp. 13, 33.

to "unload" their excess steel. Hence, U.S. officials, as well as steel leaders, feared that these arrangements were likely from the start to lead to trade distortions, and adversely affect the U.S. steel industry's access to its own market.

The second part of the Davignon Plan was the establishment of a minimum price system designed to limit the amount of imports into the European Community. Obviously, this provision was blatantly protectionist, but we shall see in Chapter 5 how the Europeans were able to hide behind the American Trigger Price System as a legitimizer of these kinds of actions.

Third, the plan undertook to make it easier for Member Countries or producers to seek relief from the Community's antidumping laws. A fourth provision, but related to the second and third, was the cancellation of all existing import licenses as of December 20, 1977, in order to preempt potential exporters into the Community from dumping steel before the other provisions took effect.

And finally, the Plan sought to address the problem of excess capacity -- productive capacity greater than demand in the Community. The minister of signatories had agreed that they would strengthen the EEC's internal steel policy to rationalize older, less efficient plants by enforcing tougher rules on documentation; they sought a crackdown on the widespread evasion of the rules with regard to the restructuring policy under the Simonet Plan.[1]

U.S. Reactions

The U.S. reaction to the Davignon Plan was skeptical, at best. Peter Erenheft, Deputy Secretary of the Department of Treasury for Tariff Affairs, said of the European Plan: "We have no intentions of interfering in other governments' internal affairs, but we feel that it is our duty to point out certain dangers."[2]

The United States had two major difficulties with the European steel plan: first, a basic objection to the bilateral discussions. The United States, as will be shown in subsequent chapters, tried to avoid "bilateralism," under the assumption that the solution to structural problems in international industries lie in a multilateral framework approach. The second major difficulty was signalled by the basic difference between the Davignon Plan and the Solomon Reference Price System.[3] While the latter set reference prices to determine dumping

---

[1]"A Protectionist Christmas Parcel," The Economist, December 24, 1977, p. 42.

[2]"U.S. Warns Europe on Steel Aid Plan," New York Times, October 21, 1978, p. D-1.

[3]For a detailed discussion of the Solomon Reference price plan see Chapter 5.

in the U.S. market, the former set minimum as well as reference prices. In fact, the European Community planned to assist bankrupt producers raise prices by fifteen percent by restricting the volume of low priced imports. From the American perspective, however, an increase in the domestic market price along those lines should have resulted in a concomitant increase in the prices of their exports to the United States. If there was not a concomitant increase in export prices, then the Europeans would be subject to dumping under the American antidumping laws.

For the development of United States foreign trade policy the most important conclusion to be drawn from the response of the European Community during the period 1975-77 is that the Community was serious about a problem which it characterized as structural in nature and global in scope. In its effort to organize a Community-wide policy, however, certain of the aspects would have a detrimental impact on steelmakers in the United States. While restructuring the steel industry to bring capacity in line with demand -- an altogether welcome and responsible plan for the long term -- it resulted in a short term dilemma which effectively closed or limited the access of their markets to imports, and further stimulated their exports to other markets. While the Community was rather successful in organizing its

Member States to avoid the most harmful of the national responses among themselves, the fact remained that a surplus amount of steel which normally would have gone to the European markets from outside, could no longer, by arrangement among the Europeans, go there. This developed in part from the bilateral deals between the European Community and some of the countries listed above. In particular, the Europeans had already arranged market shares with the Japanese -- an allegation we shall address in some detail in the next chapter -- and the new Davignon Plan gave them legitimate channels to maintain similar arrangements. Rather than serious "restructuring" the Europeans promoted policies which exacerbated the structural crisis in steel. Governments increased nationalization policies and continued to sell in other markets quite often at "dumped prices." In part this was a defensive strategy intended to avoid the rationalization of their own facilities which had lost a competitive position on a purely "free market" basis. We shall see in the next section how the European crisis itself was in large part precipitated by the unusual Japanese growth, and how this in its turn led to the world steel crisis.

III. Japan

As we saw in the last section in the case of most of the European countries, especially Britain, France, Belgium and Italy, the relationship between government and the steel industry is a direct one -- nationalized industries benefitting from government support and subsidies. For Japan the relationship is less clear. According to the Federal Trade Commission Report, for example, Japanese government subsidies to major steel industries during the period 1950-75, were considerably below those enjoyed by Britain, France, Belgium, and even West Germany.[1] But in other more subtle, and by by some reckoning more successful ways, the Japanese government has played an integral part in the affairs of its steel industry. As we shall see below, its corporate financial structure -- which not only allows but in some respects encourages a high level of debt in relation to equity -- provided very real mechanisms from which the steel industry could continue to grow. Consider for example Chalmers Johnson's characterization of Japanese government-industry relations, a view which is representative

---

[1]United States Federal Trade Commission Study on the "United States Steel Industry and Its International Rivals," p. 369.

of those who have studied the Japanese economy in a serious way:

> The Japanese government helped to create the financial conditions which enabled steel producers to carry out greenfield[1] projects of unprecedented size and, by outdistancing their foreign rivals in both capital and labor productivity, to underbid them in international competition.[2]

Johnson goes on to sum up the role of government as "plainly, then, the government's role in the Japanese economy is a complex and pervasive one."[3] Japanese industrial development since World War II -- "telescoping one hundred years into twenty,"[4] in the words of one steel economist -- has had a precipitous effect on the long term structural problems of the liberal trading order. Its unusually rapid growth, associated with a powerful export economy, combined with the effects of the 1973 oil crisis and the recession of 1974-75, contributed significantly to the unstable trading system the industrial nations now face.

---

[1]Greenfield Steel Plants are a new, modern, and efficient style of plant. See, for example, "Is the Steel Industry Getting Out of the Woods?" Iron Age, May 22, 1978.

[2]United States Federal Trade Commission Study on the United States Steel Industry and Its International Rivals," p. 369.

[3]Chalmers Johnson, Japan's Public Policy Companies, p. 223.

[4]Interview, Donald Barnett from the American Iron and Steel Institute, January 5, 1979.

As bad as the overall trade picture seemed during the mid-seventies -- and the condition of the liberal trading system looked worse in the face of an inability to reach agreement on major issues at the GATT negotiations in Geneva -- the crisis in steel (along with a handful of the other industries) was even more treacherous. And Japan got the "blame" for steel in even harsher terms. In early 1977, no doubt responding to a condition which already had become "unbearable in certain countries of the European Community," the Economist wrote of the "deep recession in world steel" which it said was more serious than many wished to admit because "the short term crisis hides a secular change in steel production" which would have long term structural affects on the industry.[1] In characteristically stark, but admittedly "simplified" terms, the Economist placed the largest share of the burden for the world steel crisis on Japan:

> In a word, the reason this recession is hurting the world's steelmakers worse than previous ones -- and probably why the next one will hurt even more -- is Japan.[2]

An Overview of Japanese Steel

Growth in Japan's steel trade -- its exports of steel grew fourteen-fold from 1955 to 1974, making it the

---

[1]"The Crisis in World Steel," The Economist, February 12, 1977, p. 31.

[2]Ibid.

largest exporter by a considerable margin since world steel trade grew only five-fold during the same period[1] -- was listed as the single largest factor leading to structural changes in the world steel industry. Japan now ranks number three in world steel production, ahead of West Germany, and second only to the United States among the OECD countries.[2] As indicated by the accompanying chart, Japan also has the world's largest steel company, Nippon Steel, three of the six runners up, and fifteen of the world's twenty-three largest blast furnaces. Indeed, Japan's unusually rapid rate of development has contributed significantly to the global excess capacity of steel in the seventies. Since 1972 alone, the Japanese steel industry has had a fifty percent rise in capacity, with virtually no change in demand.[3] As we shall see below, a goodly part of that increased capacity came as a result of the special corporate financial structure which tends to allow investment in spite of short term recessionary fluctuations in world steel market conditions. The fifty percent rise in capacity from 1972 -- from 100 million tons to about 150 million tons of steel produced annually -- has yielded an increase in output from 96 million

---

[1]Ibid.

[2]The USSR is the leading producer. See "World Steel Crisis," The Economist, February 12, 1977, p. 81.

[3]Chase Econometric Associates, "Iron and Steel in the 1980s: The Crucial Decade."

Largest Steel Producing Companies by Size: 1976

Rank	Company	Country	1976 Output (million metric tons)
1	Nippon Steel	Japan	33.97
2	U.S. Steel	USA	25.67
3	British Steel Corporation	United Kingdom	19.07
4	Bethlehem	USA	17.14
5	Nippon Kolan a/	Japan	15.67
6	Finsider group	Italy	13.43
7	Sumitomo	Japan	13.30
8	Kawasaki	Japan	13.30
9	ATH	Germany	12.82
10	Estel b/	Germany-Netherlands	10.40
11	National	USA	9.77
12	Arbed group c/	Luxembourg	9.72
13	Usinor d/	France	8.90
14	Republic	USA	8.73
15	Kobe Steel	Japan	7.81
16	BHP	Australia	7.78
17	Inland	USA	7.17
18	Armco	USA	6.80
19	Sacilor group e/	France	6.60
20	Jones & Laughlin	USA	6.32

a/ Includes 1.01 million metric tons from subsidiaries.

b/ Hoesch 5.6 million metric tons, Hoogovens 4.8 million metric tons.

c/ Includes 5.7 million metric tons from subsidiaries.

d/ Includes subsidiaries - Alpa, share in Solmer, etc.

e/ Includes share in Solmer.

Source: "Annual Review," Metal Bulletin Monthly, March 1977.

tons in 1972 to approximately 102 million-tons in 1978.[1] Since demand hasn't experienced an increase concomitant with the increase in either capacity or supply, it follows that the Japanese steel industry has contributed both to the condition of excess capacity, as well as an actual surplus of steel, in the global market. As we shall see in Part II, this situation was partly responsible for the political arrangements between the Japanese and the Europeans which resulted in increased tonnages of steel exported to the U.S. market.[2] For purposes of this section, however, it is enough to point out that the Japanese steel industry grew at a rate disproportionate to the level of demand in its home market.

Of all these statistics cited above, however, a description by a group of economists from the United States International Trade Commission upon their return from a visit to Japan's steel industry, is even more illustrative:

> The entire layout of steel is exceptional. There are larger complexes than in the United States . . . in all the steel works there is room for expansion, which means, if we ever get out of this mess, the Japanese will be in a far better position to benefit from a condition of increased demand and higher growth than we . . . they have computerized plants where

---

[1] Ibid.

[2] See Chapter 4, section 3.

> we were able to walk for a half mile without seeing a person, and the plants are incredibly clean.[1]

It is no accident that the Japanese steel industry and its position in the international market became so strong so quickly. Concerted and directed economic policies by the government combined with a unique corporate financial structure promoted the development of its steel industry. In a study prepared by the Japanese government for the OECD, its intentions in these matters were set forth:

> The Ministry of International Trade and Industry decided to establish in Japan industries which require intensive employment of capital and technology, industries that in consideration of comparative cost of production should be most inappropriate for Japan, industries such as steel . . .[2]

The Report went on to say how industries like steel, on purely rational economic grounds, would be those industries accorded a lower priority, but that the overriding goal of industrial development and technological growth led to the exaltation of steel:

> From a short run, static viewpoint encouragement of such industries would seem to conflict with economic rationalism. But from a long range viewpoint, these are precisely the industries where income elasticity of demand is high, technological progress is rapid,

---

[1]"United States International Trade Commission Congressional Briefing," February 10, 1978.

[2]The Industrial Policy of Japan (Paris: The OECD 1972) p. 15.

> and labor productivity rises fast. It was clear that without these industries it would be difficult to employ a population of one hundred million and raise their standard of living to that of Europe and America with light industries alone; whether right or wrong, Japan had to have these heavy and chemical industries.[1]

This was the rationale for its extraordinary growth in many respects contrary to accepted principles of economic development along the lines of competitive advantage. It led to a situation where:

> [The Japanese government] refused to concede the country's limited natural resources and indadequate capital supply and take advantage of its ample well-trained labor supply to concentrate on production of toys, textiles, and Christmas tree ornaments.[2]

From this kind of strategy Japan was able to "concentrate its scant capital in strategic industries."[3] Indeed, this was a strategy supported by the West until the late sixties when growth began to slow, recessionary cycles became longer and more severe, and the heavy industries in the West began to show signs of old age.

It is important to underscore that U.S. policy not only supported the growth of the Japanese industrial economy, but actively promoted it as an integral part of

---

[1]Ibid.

[2]T.J. Pempel, "Japanese Foreign Economic Policy: The Domestic Basis for International Behavior"; in Peter J. Katzenstein ed. Between Power and Plenty (The University of Wisconsin Press 1978), p. 158.

[3]The Industrial Policy of Japan, p. 15.

its own security arrangements in the post-World War II period. Japan was viewed by U.S. policymakers at the time as a key edifice in the post-World War II alliance system intended to contain the spread of communism. From the United States perspective, therefore, promoting Japan's economic development in basic industries like steel was considered necessary if those security arrangements were to be effective. While the tools used by American foreign policy to reconstruct the war torn economies of Western Europe may be more well-known, most notably the European Recovery Program (or the Marshall Plan), equally deliberate and effective efforts were made toward Japan. For example, Japan was granted privileged access to the U.S. home market starting in the early 1950s for a wide variety of industrial exports.[1] Thus, there were external stimuli in real economic terms as well as hard political incentives for the Japanese industrial economy to grow more rapidly than the economics of demand and consumption in its home market might have dictated. Indeed, one might argue that Japan, not unlike West Germany, was

---

[1]For a good discussion of relationships between U.S. foreign policy and the economic development of Japan and West Europe, see, Robert Gilpin, "The Politics of International Economic Relations" in Transnational Relations and World Politics ed. by Robert O. Keohane and Joseph S. Nye, Sr. (Cambridge: Harvard University Press 1973) pp. 48-69; Benjamin J. Cohen, "The Revolution in Atlantic Economic Relations: A Bargain Comes Unstuck," in Wolfram F. Hanrieder, The United States and Western Europe (Cambridge: Winthrop Publishers 1974) pp. 106-133; also see, William

encouraged to develop an "export-oriented" industrial economy.

Nonetheless, the Japanese industrial development success had begun, by the late sixties, to strain the liberal trading order from which it benefitted. And the effects of the strains were reflected in growing tensions between United States and Japanese foreign trade policies. Japan's overall trade with the United States expanded rapidly in particular sectors during the sixties; by 1969, a major dispute developed between Japan and the United States over textiles -- one glaring sector where Japanese exports to the United States increased disproportionately from the 1950s level, and where U.S. domestic producers pressured Washington for assistance from the increased level of import penetration.[1] In 1971, the United States signed an agreement with the Japanese where they agreed to limit cotton textile exports into the United States. As we indicated in Chapter 2, growing imports in the steel sector by the late sixties also led to strains between the sort of Japanese/U.S. relationship which prevailed in the first two decades after World War II.

Diebold, Jr., The United States and the Industrial World (New York: Praeger 1972)

[1]For a good discussion of the U.S./Japanese Textile Dispute of the late sixties and early seventies, see, I.M. Destler, et. al., Managing An Alliance: The Politics of U.S.-Japanese Relations (Washington, D.C.: Brookings Institution 1976), especially pp. 35-45.

Ironically, it was the success of the U.S. foreign policy objective to promote Japanese industrial development, combined with the ability of the Japanese to creatively and effectively use that relationship with the United States to ensure the rapid development of efficient and competitive industries, which eventually placed unacceptable burdens both on the liberal trading system as well as on U.S. foreign policy goals associated with that system. This situation had substantial effects on basic industries like steel, i.e., those industries where the Japanese proved most successful in establishing efficient and competitive industries, even according to highest international standards. More specifically, it contributed to the global crisis of excess capacity in a number of sectors like steel and thereby forced the United States to reassess its foreign trade policy for those sectors.

In the case of steel, there were two different kinds of effects that Japanese economic strategies and foreign economic policies had on the U.S. market. Let us distinguish between them: First, is the kind of exports: Japanese steel products essentially have undermined all competition in certain markets. For example, Japan has gained "forty percent of the market in some products in America."[1] Thus, pressure on American policymakers from

---

[1]"The Crisis in World Steel," The Economist, February 12, 1977, p. 81.

import-affected steel industries has been widespread, but it has also been highly concentrated with unrelenting attacks in particular product areas such as some of the specialty steels.[1]

Secondly, the Japanese have included in their major expansion plans over the years "a margin of capacity for export. And it has sold aggressively at marginal cost."[2] By any standards -- absolute or comparative -- Japanese steel exports have risen a dramatic 28.9 percent since 1966 alone, considerably higher than West Germany's 16.2 percent rise, the country which comes closest to Japan in "export power." Japan's increase in exports is even more astounding when one considers that it has increased its imports by only 0.1 percent during the same period, while West Germany did so by 8.9 percent.[3] While West Germany is a net exporter, like Japan, it has increased its imports to a larger extent than Japan, and to that extent contributes more to an overall balance in international steel trade. In fact, the Japanese were accused as early as 1967 of contributing to an unstable condition in international trade, not so much because of their "export policy," but because of its "no-import"

---

[1]See my section on "Specialty Steel" in Chapter 4.

[2]"The Crisis in World Steel," The Economist, February 12, 1977, p. 81

[3]Ibid.

policy.[1] Both policies have contributed to an economic strategy which effectively insulated the Japanese economy and its industrial development from impediments of the free market system -- i.e., it restricted goods from flowing freely into Japan, and it promoted Japanese goods in other markets quite often in spite of a natural competitive disadvantage. The U.S. domestic political economy could no longer withstand these pressures. Therefore, the international system suffered also. Let us now look at the Japanese policies which led to these tensions.

Economic Strategies

Emphasis on exports in Japan is not new. The Japanese government developed a number of export incentives for its steel industry beginning in 1953, when export earnings were exempt from the income tax.[2] Heavily criticized by the GATT and the International Monetary Fund, however, this fiscal device was abandoned in 1964. But it was quickly replaced by other, equally effective devices -- effective in promoting Japan's "export policy," and contributing to the overall perception of Japan's

---

[1]Norman Macrae, "The Risen Sun," The Economist, June 3, 1967, p. IX.

[2]The United States Federal Trade Commission Study on "The United States Steel Industry and Its International Rivals," p. 385.

foreign trade policy as problematic for a balanced world market. Consider, for instance, the New York Times' characterization of Japan as "the piece . . . in the jigsaw puzzle of world trade . . . that doesn't fit."[1]

Other devices have been used by the Japanese government to promote exports, some still operating, while others, largely because of pressure from its major trading partners, have been discontinued. For example, until March 1972, the government promoted an increased depreciation program which "permitted companies involved in exporting to increase normal depreciation charges on plant and equipment."[2] Its purpose, according to the U.S. FTC Report "was to reward companies which had won recognition by MITI for having made an outstanding contribution to exports."[3]

Three other programs, also established in the early sixties to support Japan's "export policy," and which were used by the steel industry to establish a firm overseas market base, include:

1) A Reserve for Overseas Market Development;

2) Tax exemption of earnings from Service Exports;

---

[1]Clyde Farnsworth, "Japan, The Piece That Doesn't Fit," New York Times, April 30, 1978, p. D-1.

[2]United States Federal Trade Commission Study on "United States Steel Industry and Its International Rivals," p. 385.

[3]Ibid.

3) Financial assistance to exports "which provides long term credit to exporters at lower rates than those charged by private lenders for loans of similar risk and duration."[1]

Japan's approach toward exports is summed up by one Japanese business executive's description of his government's attitude toward companies which have been successful in export promotion. It is "our equivalent of knighthood," he said.[2]

But in addition to the very attractive "export-promotion" devices listed above, the steel industry in Japan has benefitted from special attention according it as "the backbone of the national economy."[3]

The steel industry was declared, along with a few other industries, a "priority sector," which meant that steel firms in Japan were eligible for loans and other special financial arrangements from the government and private lending institutions to a degree unknown in most of the other OECD countries. In particular, the steel industry enjoyed the support of the Bank of Japan which

---

[1]Ibid., pp. 386-88.

[2]"How the Japanese Mount That Export Blitz," Fortune, September 1970, p. 129.

[3]"Report of the Industrial Structure Council (An Advisory Committee of the Ministry of International Trade and Industry)," Japan's Industrial Structure -- A Long Range Vision (Tokyo: Japan External Trade Organization, June 1975) p. 46.

helped to promote the expansionary boom in Japan. Its priority status provided an encouragement to the commercial banks to make large volumes of loans to steel firms. Clear indications from MITI, and other ministries in the government, as to their economic priorities served also to encourage private banks to favor such industries and firms in their lending policies.[1] In this way government policy contributed as much to strengthen a foundation that existed in the cultural and historical experience of the Japanese,[2] as to help build the post-war economy.

Japan's industrial policy -- developed under a "Plan-oriented Market Economy,"[3] and of which the steel industry has been a large beneficiary -- was made possible largely through special financial mechanisms. One such device is the Fiscal Investment and Loan Plan, popularly known as the second budget since it is almost fifty percent of the size of the national budget. Its funds have been used to finance national policy companies and public corporations of Japan.[4] Such financial arrangements -- which include government-backed credits at low interest rates,

---

[1]Chalmers Johnson, Japan's Public Policy Companies, p. 27.

[2]Ibid.; also see, John G. Roberts, Mitsui: Three Centuries of Japanese Business (New York: Weatherhill, 1973).

[3]Japan's Industrial Structure -- A Long Range Vision, p. 9.

[4]Chalmers Johnson, Japan's Public Policy Companies, p.26.

access to generous lending facilities of the Japan Development Bank, export incentives, and industrial development policy generally[1] -- are part of the overall industrial policy which Chalmers Johnson describes as "a matter of Japanese national policy, even national defense, to maintain [its] healthy and growing industries."[2] In a very real sense, according to Business Week Magazine, Japan's steel industry is "backed by an interlocked apparatus of banks and trading companies, closely linked with the government."[3] Hence, Japan has been able to define its national political agenda, and set forth a coherent economic strategy, largely because of the close alliance among key sectors. "Most prominent in this coalition," according to T.J. Pempel, "are the organs of the national bureaucracy, the peak federations and the trade associations of big business, the major financial institutions, particularly the government dominated banks, and finally, the ruling conservative political party."[4] This had led as well to a strong

---

[1]Richard Caves and Masu Uekusa, Industrial Organization in Japan (Washington, D.C.: Brookings Institution 1976); especially Chapter 8; also see, Hugh Patrick and Henry Rosovsky, Asia's New Giant: How the Japanese Economy Works (Washington, D.C.: Brookings Institution 1976); especially Chapters 1, 4, 11, 14.

[2]Chalmers Johnson, Japan's Public Policy Companies, p. 26.

[3]"Steel's Sea of Troubles," Business Week, September 19, 1977, p. 74.

[4]T.J. Pempel, "Japanese Foreign Economic Policy:

foreign economic strategy.

The interlocked apparatus works in still another way which is important to understand for the student of U.S. foreign trade policy. Japanese manufacturers form "export cartels" which are officially sanctioned and protected by MITI. What they are supposed to do, and do quite successfully, is to help Japanese outcompete foreigners in the home and in the foreign markets. As an illustration of how this works in the home market, let us quote from a rather frank statement by Masafumi Goto, a director general of MITI's Trade and Development Bureaus. Goto explained the practical purpose of the export cartel concept: "When an outsider, a company that's not a member of the [export] association rushes into the market at a lower price, MITI under law can order the outsider to stop."[1]

The Domestic Basis for International Behavior," Power and Plenty, ed. Peter J. Katzenstein, p. 144.

[1]"How the Japanese Mount That Export Blitz," Fortune, September 1970, p. 131. Note that the trade controversy between Japan and the United States had not yet reached the level of tensions in 1970 that we have been accustomed to since about 1975. There was of course the textile controversy, but most of the other industrial sectors were not experiencing the same levels of tension, as has been true since 1975. Apparently the Japanese were more willing then to discuss these kinds of subjects. Today, by contrast, the Japanese try very hard to hide or brush over these kinds of activities since they are precisely the activities which lead to the greatest amount of friction between Japan and the rest of the OECD countries, including the United States. For a good discussion of the 1969-70 "Textile Dispute," see I.M. Destler, et. al., Managing An Alliance: The Politics of U.S.-Japanese Relations (Washington, D.C.: Brookings

In the foreign market the export cartels have also worked quite well. One practical example of its benefits is illustrated by the effort launched in 1969 by three Japanese steelmakers which joined together to obtain orders for the $100 million worth of pipe for the Trans-Alaska Pipeline System. An executive from Sumitomo Shoji Kaisha Ltd., the Japanese trading company which negotiated the deal for the steelmakers, said of the attitude which promotes such enterprises: "In this kind of epoch-making huge project, cooperation among all our companies gives us a better chance against European mills."[1] He went on to argue the position which has by now been firmly institutionalized in Japan; an arrangement that might well be prosecuted under antitrust provisions in the United States. In an unusually frank statement, the executive said, "If we compete against each other overseas, it's no use; some foreign companies may get the job. We have to present a joint front against the overseas competitors."[2]

To a considerable degree, these financial and industrial arrangements have been organized through the "Japanese Soogoo Shoosa," or general trading companies. They thrive on traditional forms of Japanese economic

---

Institution, 1971); especially pp. 35-45.

[1]"How the Japanese Mount That Export Blitz," Fortune, September 1970, p. 131.

[2]Ibid.

arrangements -- an historical and cultural experience peculiar to Japan. In many cases the trading companies work as an integral part of the Zaibatsu, or large integrated industrial groups that go back in some cases a few hundred years.[1] Within this structure, supported not only by a remarkable success in the post-World War II period, but also by the larger forces of history, the Japanese trading companies can "mobilize the combined forces of manufacturers, banks, and government"; they are what many in the West perceive as "the day-to-day leaders in Japan's assault on world markets"[2]; an "assault" in many respects necessary for the implementation of Japan's unique corporate financial structure. Probably the most important single element of its corporate financial structure is the high debt-to-equity relationships. Since it is so important, let us look at this aspect of Japan's industrial organization.

It is clear that the Japanese government has taken a very active interest in industrial organization and economic growth; and it is equally apparent that the steel industry -- along with a handful of other priority sectors like shipbuilding, coal, power and fertilization --

---

[1]Norman Macrae, "The Risen Sun," The Economist, May 27, and June 3, Parts I and II.

[2]"How the Japanese Mount That Export Blitz," Fortune, September 1970, p. 130.

have been the recipients of special government assistance. As indicated in the first part of this section, however, the assistance provided by the Japanese government to its basic industries is far more subtle than outright subsidies leading to effective government ownership. Indeed, an especially important feature of Japan's current industrial organization is its exceptionally highly leveraged capital structure.[1]

Japanese industrial economic planning since the end of World War II has depended on a system where basic industries like steel maintain high levels of debt in relation to their equity positions. In an article on banking and finance in Japan, written for Patrick and Rosovsky's Asia's New Giant, Henry and Mable Wallich assert: "Among the principal characteristics of Japan's corporate finance are a heavy reliance on debt -- referred to in Japan as 'overborrowing' -- a low proportion of bond financing and a corresponding high level of bank financing, and a heavy reliance on trade credit." And as evidence of this situation, they write, "The sample of principal enterprises shows a ratio of equity to total capitalization in 1972 of about eighteen percent, compared with fifty-one

---

[1]"Report To The President On Prices and Costs in the United States Steel Industry," Council on Wage and Price Stability (U.S. Government Printing Office: Washington, D.C., October 1977), p. 95.

percent of all manufacturing and utilities in the United States."[1] While it may be argued that this ratio of equity to total capitalization has risen considerably -- the Council on Wage and Price Stability study puts it at forty percent[2] -- it is still quite low by U.S. standards. Thus, the system of financing which allows companies to maintain high levels of debt in relation to their equity positions, has been an important contributing factor to the condition of worldwide surplus capacity in industries like steel. According to the Report to the President from the Council on Wage and Price Stability, "The benefit to the [Japanese Steel] industry is in the form of assured availability of financing . . . allowing Japanese steel firms to continue investment projects without regard to short-term fluctuations in world steel market conditions."[3]

U.S. Reactions

The Japanese government's support for the steel industry -- particularly when it is different from and dissonant with U.S. government-industry relations -- has been the source of much of the tension between the two

---

[1]Henry C. and Mable I. Wallich, "Banking and Finance," in Hugh Patrick and Henry Rosovsky ed. Asia's New Giant: How the Japanese Economy Works," (Brookings Institution: Washington, D.C. 1976), p. 267.

[2]"Report to the President on Prices and Costs in the United States Steel Industry," October 1977, p. 95.

[3]Ibid., p. 96.

countries' foreign trade policies. The tensions in this most recent period come from two related premises that lead to the belief that the Japanese must bear the largest share of the burden for the structural problems in many of the industrial sectors. First as the pie of benefits appears to get smaller and Americans become more aware of the effects of Japanese economic strategies on the world, it does appear that their growth has caused the pie to dwindle. Second is the unwillingness to overburden the Europeans as it is felt that they might not withstand the pressures, especially in the steel sector. Or as a lobbyist for the American steel industry put it, "It has become politically popular to take on Japan."[1]

The political tensions caused by the perceptions of how Japan's economic strategies and foreign economic policies affect the United States are dramatized by the remarkably tough statement by Senator Kennedy -- one who is usually quick to support the liberal "free traders" position. In a speech before the Foreign Correspondents Club of Japan, Kennedy told them:

> It is extremely unlikely that the [U.S.] Congress would continue to support an open trading policy on the part of America when a variety of restrictive policies continue to be practiced on the part of Japan . . . . Now the tables are turned. Japan has the surplus and it is the United States that is concerned. The role of Japan has also changed. As a

---

[1]Interview, steel lobbyist, March 10, 1979.

> leading economic power in the modern world, Japan is now being asked to share the responsibilities, as well as the benefits, of creating and maintaining a healthy global economy.[1]

Like Senator Kennedy, other Congressmen from both ends of the American political spectrum have been rather quick to publicly criticize Japan. Congressman Jim Jones, a Democrat from Oklahoma and chairman of the House Ad Hoc Committee on Trade with Japan, accurately characterized "America's perception of Japan" as one which sees it as "a closed market because of bureaucratic red tape and other non-tariff barriers to American products."[2] Blame to Japan for America's international trade difficulties came also from Senator Hayakawa, Republic from California, and one who on most issues espouses very different political views than Senator Kennedy. It was interesting, therefore, that Hayakawa expressed roughly the same views as Kennedy on the U.S.-Japan trade situation:

> Japan's trade surplus . . . strikes you right in the face. I'm a free trader, but you can maintain an anti-protectionist position only so long as there's a mutuality of liberalism in trade . . .
>
> It's time that Japan faced up to its responsibilities as an adult nation and

---

[1]"U.S. and Japan Open Two Way Discussions on Trade Problems," New York Times, January 13, 1978, p. D-1.

[2]"U.S. and Japan Press for Accord in Trade Dispute," New York Times, January 10, 1978, pp. 45, 49.

> became willing to trade, bargain, and negotiate on adult terms.[1]

So in the United States and in Europe, Japan has been marked the villain in the mid-late seventies round of the international trade controversy. Among the major American newspapers -- a fair indication of either where public sentiment is, or where it is likely to go -- the U.S.-Japanese trade difficulties probably constituted one of the most written about topics since 1976.

Writing at the peak of the public controversy over steel in the United States, the Wall Street Journal -- a paper which usually supports the "free traders" position as a necessary condition for free enterprise -- presented a clear and rather insightful editorial which purported to explain the root of the "Japanese trade difficulties." The article addressed the general problems in the industrial sectors, but it applies in the specific case to steel also. It is worth quoting.

> In the first place, Japan is overstocked with high-priced inventories of industrial materials . . . .
>
> The second blunder was committed in 1975 and 1976. Japanese industry not only kept on producing when world demand turned down; it actually stepped up production in many cases. The need to maintain employment was responsible only in part, and probably in lesser part. The main reason was miscalculation . . . . The final blunder was the Japanese response to their predicament, partly by consensus among

---

[1] "U.S. Delegate Ease Hard-line Position on Japanese Trade," New York Times, January 11, 1978.

> government, businessmen, and labor unions, which are far more closely knit than in any other industrialized nation, and partly because of the politics of the situation, the Japanese decided to keep domestic production high and push exports . . .[1]

The *Journal* sought to do more than describe Japan's troubles, which it suggested was an inevitable outgrowth of its industrial policy. It also argued that a trade war between Japan and other industrial countries could develop. For many this seemed an inevitable conclusion since Japanese exports were effectively exporting adjustment costs of unemployment and inflation to the other industrialized nations -- a situation which many believed would cause Japan to "face a protectionist backlash of major proportions."[2]

It is something of an irony that the great economic success story of the post-World War II era would be a major cause of serious structural dilemmas in international industries like steel. Indeed, Japan's growth came about through the use of the free enterprise system which, at first, amazed the West, then confounded it, and in these times of economic instability threatens it. For the United States the political tensions have been mounting. For Europe the economic conditions have been deteriorating,

---

[1]"The Troubled Japanese Juggernaut," *The Wall Street Journal*, November 22, 1977, editorial page.

[2]Ibid.

contributing in a basic way to the political tensions in Europe and the United States.

As Japan pursued its industrial policy of expansion -- promoting the twin goals of rapid technological progress and higher levels of productive employment -- the overall pie of benefits among the industrial nations decreased. Having built its industrial base on a close industry-government relationship, Japan was in a much better position than its trading partners to grab quickly whatever benefits seemed still to be available. Referring to this relationship between government and industry in Japan and Europe, Business Week put it in perspective: "Both the Japanese and Europeans have ties with government and with other industries that make it easier to raise money for investment even when profits are disappointing."[1] By contrast, the article continued, "in the U.S. industry must raise its expansion money out of earnings or from private investors."[2]

One concludes, therefore, that investment decisions in Japan, as well as most of the European countries, are a function more of national policy than of the market. Lacking a national industrial policy the situation in the United States is more or less reversed. Thus, economic

---

[1]"Steel's Sea of Troubles," Business Week, September 19, 1977, p. 78.

[2]Ibid.

strategies and foreign economic policies which intervene to control the market have tended to work to the disadvantage of American producers. In response, U.S. foreign trade policy for steel sought to advance the competitive position of its domestic industry by intervening in the market also.

IV. Third World

An Overview

For United States foreign trade policy, the economics of steel in the Third World is more symbolic and of future concern than one which contributed in the 1970s in any large measure to the development of its policy. It of course has been a factor, but relative to Europe and Japan it has been only peripheral. This insignificance is because the developing countries represent a low proportion of world steel production, and are involved little in the international trade of steel -- all told, the developing world contributes eight percent of total production, a fraction of the international trade, and about ten to thirteen percent of world steel consumption. As of 1975, only nine countries in the whole of the developing world accounted for over 90 percent of the total LDC steel output: Brazil, India, Mexico, Argentina, South Korea, Venezuela, Iran, Chile and Taiwan.[1] Of these nine most productive, none are expected to become steel self-sufficient in the short term. But the Third World has been a factor in the equation which explains

[1]"Free World Steel Market: Supply/Demand Prospects Through 1985" (Washington, D.C.: Central Intelligence Agency, xerox).

the politicization of the steel issue globally. More important than the numbers, however, is the degree to which Third World steel production highlights some of the more difficult structural problems of industrial sectors which U.S. foreign trade policy faces.

Understandably, Third World countries seek to increase their steelmaking capacity. They are encouraged to do so by political factors of the world economic power structure, as well as by the technology of steel. Let us look at these factors.

The first, and most compelling motive for Third World countries to seek "steel self-sufficiency" is their self-image. The ability to produce steel carries with it the prestige value of symbolizing one's entrance into the industrial world -- a mantle to which all countries aspire. As an official of one of the leading American steel companies put it, "Every country that wants to industralize has to have steel. And the developing countries are doing just that -- starting their industrial base with steel."[1] Even beyond the symbol, however, there is evidence in both economic models and historical examples that one's national security, and internal economic prosperity will be enhanced by the capability to produce steel.

Second, the technology of steel is such that the last country to get it will most likely possess the most

---

[1]"World Steel Race," <u>Industry Week</u>, May 15, 1978, p. 76.

competitive facilities, immediately giving that country an advantage over the older steel industries. Thus, even in a period of slow growth, depressed demand, and excess capacity, the newer, modern, and more efficient steel producing countries will be encouraged by this objective condition of steel making. They also see that their competitive position is further enhanced by the generally low labor costs, and in some cases, low energy costs.[1] LDC's competitiveness in export markets, including the United States, is enhanced by governments' propensity to maintain productive facilities once it is in place.

The third factor which encourages Third World countries to enter the steelmaking business is easy financing; it has been made relatively easy and cheap for them to finance their own facilities through any number of global financial institutions like the World Bank or the Export-Import Bank.[2] National governments make it even easier through a variety of economic strategies which promote financial and political arrangements beneficial to developing a steel industry. It is cheaper for them because a good many possess the natural

---

[1]Interview with United States International Trade Commission economists, November 19, 1978.

[2]U.S. Congress, House of Representatives, Subcommittee of the Committee on Appropriations, United States Subsidy of Foreign Steel Producers, 95th Congress, 2d Session (Washington, D.C.: Government Printing Office 1978) pp. 16-32.

materials necessary for producing steel, and/or can purchase them through government sponsored programs. These countries benefit not only from relatively low wage scales and in many instances from convenience of raw material, but also from low export financing provided by their respective governments.

A final impetus is a condition which seems almost too simple, but applies in a unique way to steel: steel production tends to feed on itself, boosting demand internally at greater rates in the short term, than in the long term. To build steel mills one needs steel, and so there is an immediate and inflated demand for steel. During the initial steps of building steel capacity in a country, it is easy for policymakers, blinded by the goal of steel self-sufficiency, to get lulled into a sense of false demand -- a demand which may have been more a function of building steel mills, and other necessary bases for industrial development, than truly reflecting steel consumption in a broader economy. Thus, this principle also operates in a more general way as well. For countries at lower levels of development, the demand for steel -- for purposes of building an industrial infrastructure -- may appear greater in the planning stages than when the economy actually begins to develop. A variety of factors -- such as the oil crisis -- may depress the rate of growth of steel demand from what had been anticipated.[1]

These four elements lead to a desire, and produce support, for Third World countries to build considerable steelmaking capacities. The nine countries listed above all have begun this process. For example, they expect to increase their 1976 output of 43.6 million tons to 106 million tons by 1985.[2] They view it as the spearhead of a broader development process -- to build an infrastructure of capital intensive industries, leapfrogging, as it were, agricultural and transportation systems and light manufacturing, much as the Japanese.

Steel has played a central role in Third World development planning. At the Second General Conference for the United Nations Industrial Development Organization (UNIDO) in March 1975, for example, the "Lima Declaration on Industrial Development and Cooperation" set goals for the future industrialization of the developing countries. In general, the Lima Declaration sought to promote industrial production from "seven percent to at least 25

---

[1]See, for example, the discussion in the first section of this chapter. Some of the ideas on this particular point were sparked by a discussion with Philip Trezise at the Brookings Institution.

[2]William T. Hogan, "Future Plans in the Third World," Iron and Steel Engineer, November 19, 1977, p. 3.

percent of world total production by the year 2000 . . . distributed among the developing countries as equally as possible."[1] Recognizing the difficulties in achieving these goals in all industries, however, it was recommended at the Conference that certain key industries attain a higher level of production than 25 percent, so an average of twenty-five percent could be met. In steel, for example, it was suggested that the developing countries should produce thirty percent of world steel output. U.S. policymakers, along with Europeans and Japanese, fear that such a large increase, even over a twenty year period, could have a destabilizing effect on the correlation of forces in the world steel market.[2]

Effects on U.S. Policy

Whether such a change contributes to the political tensions among steel producing nations depends, in large part, on how much of the new steel capacity is used to meet what one would hope to be a concomitant increase in demand in those countries, and how much goes for export. For, one begins with a premise of the economics of steel: once capacity is created it must operate at a high level.

---

[1]Ibid.

[2]Central Intelligence Agency Paper on "Free World Steel Market: Supply/Demand Prospects Through 1985."

Capacity cannot be turned on and off. Would a large increase in the steelmaking capacity of Third World countries contribute to the condition of global excess capacity, or would it be consumed by their own expanding economies? Planning agencies in the U.S. government, especially those concerned with its "national defense," have developed several scenarios.

Most U.S. policy projections are pessimistic about the effects of increased steel capacity in Third World countries on U.S. steel producing operations. CIA scenarios, for example, assume that steel demand will grow at rates of one or three percent depending on average annual growth rates for the economy as a whole of 1.5 or 3.5 percent annually. These rates are themselves based on the rates of growth of steel demand over the two decades prior to 1973, which grew at an average rate of five percent annually.[1] As indicated earlier, one assumes a natural decrease in the rate of growth of steel consumption in industrial economies as the economy ages. They therefore assume that a large amount of Third World steel will be exported to the industrial world and further exacerbate the political tensions of the seventies caused largely by excess capacity.

Another CIA study also argued that LDC steel production will lead to substantial increases in LDC exports.

---

[1]Ibid.

Based on this assumption, the report goes on to conclude that the "emergence of some LDC producers as steel exporters . . . will be a disruptive factor in the world steel market. These countries will compete with industrial exporters in their regional markets as well as in some non-LDC import markets." In particular, "Latin American exports . . . are expected to take advantage of their proximity to North America."[1]

The political consequences for the United States are troublesome to some policymakers in the United States government; they are even more worrisome to U.S. producers. As it was put by a steel economist for the AISI:

> Once LDCs have invested massive amounts of capital in steel production, they will have to operate their facilities at a high rate to defray their annual interest costs on debt. Moreover, to retain the industrial jobs created in steel will require them to produce and ship into export markets, at whatever price it takes to move the steel.[2]

Take India as an illustration:

> In the 1970s international raw material and labor skyrocketed while Indian rates remained relatively stable. At the same time capacity utilization improved as the work force acquired more technical skills . . . . The new environment of the 1970s made India a major steel exporter.[3]

---

[1]Ibid.

[2]United States House of Representatives, Subcommittee on Appropriations, "United States Subsidy of Foreign Steel Producers," p. 115.

[3]"Quietly Steel is Booming, But Not in the West,"

Even if in the long run demand and consumption grow proportionately with steelmaking capacity in the Third World countries, it may be that the short term program will be to export to the established advanced industrial markets in North America, Europe, and Japan. Increased exports to these markets may well have a debilitating effect on the profit picture of steel producers in the United States, which may limit their ability to reinvest capital so that their operations will be able to compete with the newer facilities in the Third World if and when a rate of growth of consumption does begin to increase.

Still another scenario -- developed by economists from American steel industries -- envisions growth, not only in the developing world, but in the United States as well. Mr. Monnet, of U.S. Steel has suggested an interesting and rather hopeful circumstance based on what he refers to as a new kind of growth in the American industrial structure: "Our economy is the only advanced economy in the world that has not had its infrastructure destroyed by war. We haven't had to rebuild. But it does

---

The Economist, December 16, 1978, p. 98. India was expected to be a net importer in 1978 because of increased demand domestically. But, additional plans for expansion are also planned, and so the Central Intelligence Agency estimates that she will quickly revert to a net exporter position.

wear out. Does there come a time when our advanced economy must go through reconstruction?"[1]

Therefore, one may be optimistic, and assume that world demand and consumption of steel will grow sufficiently to absorb the growth in the new steel capacity of the Third World, whether that demand comes primarily from the Third World itself, or from a renaissance in the American infrastructure -- railroads, plants, bridges. Even under those conditions, however, U.S. policy makers and steel makers still worry about the short term where very competitive Third World producers will export to meet their capacity utilization needs, and may thereby undercut the producers' ability in the West to modernize their own facilities.

The question then becomes why we shouldn't encourage growth in steel producing facilities in the United States? Mr. Jim Collins, representing AISI, also espoused the belief that the United States is the world's prime growth area for steel: "We have the market, raw materials, a reservoir of skilled workers, and energy."[2] But, he says, "The government is not encouraging capital formation. We're living off our inventory of plants."[3]

---

[1]Ibid.

[2]Interview, January 5, 1979.

[3]Ibid.

Industry officials emphasize that the American steel industry has not added "one pound of capacity since 1965."[1] In more specific terms, F.G. Jaiks of Inland Steel Company notes that "capital spending for all purposes in the seventeen years from 1960 to 1976 totaled $30 billion."[2] An amount, most agree, which has not been enough to keep portions of the industry from declining into obsolescence. Conditions may get worse when one considers that the annual capital requirement is escalating rapidly.[3] By most industry executives' estimates, the industry should be spending about $12 billion by the mid-1980s, or roughly $1.5 billion per year, not including the cost of modernization and antipollution facilities which is estimated at about $5.5 billion.[4] But the range of tax policies, for example, makes it difficult for the industry to accumulate the kind of capital, and imprudent to seek it elsewhere, which is needed for expansion.

The prime concern among U.S. officials and industry executives is that U.S. government policy may not take account of long term prospects. In particular, that

---

[1]Comments from the Senate Steel Caucus Meeting, February 6, 1979, on file in personal notes of author.

[2]"Is the Steel Industry Out of the Goods?" Iron Age, May 22, 1978, p. 49.

[3]Ibid.

[4]Ibid.

imports will undercut profit potential and further erode the foundation necessary for capital formation[1] to prepare for 1980 and beyond.

In the short term, there is little disagreement that the industrial world will be burdened with excess capacity for steel. Notwithstanding, Third World countries have continued to build steel facilities in their countries, hoping to reach self-sufficiency. As with the industrial world, the plans of Third World countries have been altered several times during the seventies because of the recessionary conditions. However, the chart below shows that less developed country projections have been proportionately much higher than the industrial countries, and that their plans are roughly consistent with their proposals set forth in the Lima Declaration. This is understandable in light of the distance they must go to produce any significant amount of steel. But their increased capacity remains a source of tension in the face of excess capacity, slow growth and low demand for steel.

Hence there are four key factors in the equation which may lead to heightening political tensions among the world steel producing community, and which are considered by U.S. policymakers when they develop a foreign trade policy for steel.

---

[1]For further discussion of this point, see my Chapter 4.

Free World Steelmaking Capacity, Yearend
(millions of tons)

	1976 Actual	1980 Announced Beginning 1977	1985 Announced Beginning 1977	1980 Announced November 1977	1985 Announced November 1977
TOTAL	595.0	686.0	818.0	643.0	740.0
Major Developed	466.4	524.0	562.0	495.0	531.0
United States	147.0	168.0	175.0	155.0	165.0
Japan	140.0	165.0	173.0	155.0	165.0
West Germany	63.3	65.0	70.0	64.0	65.0
France	35.5	37.0	40.0	35.0	37.0
Italy	34.0	36.0	40.0	36.0	40.0
United Kingdom	30.0	34.0	37.0	32.0	34.0
Canada	16.5	19.0	25.0	18.0	25.0
Other Developed	85.0	91.0	116.0	88.0	103.0
Belgium	18.6	20.5	25.0	19.0	21.0
Spain	13.5	15.0	18.0	15.0	18.0
Sweden	8.0	8.2	12.0	8.0	10.0
Australia	9.4	10.3	14.0	10.0	14.0
Other	35.5	37.0	47.0	36.0	40.0
Less Developed	43.6	71.0	140.0	60.0	106.0
Brazil	11.2	18.0	35.0	15.0	25.0
Mexico	7.1	12.0	15.0	9.0	12.0
India	10.2	16.0	20.0	12.4	14.0
South Korea	2.8	5.0	8.0	3.8	6.0
Other	12.3	20.0	62.0	19.8	49.0

1) In spite of the long term structural problems of excess capacity, complicated by short term recessionary conditions, Third World countries will continue to build more steelmaking capacity. 2) The overall growth in LDC domestic economies, particularly in the short term, will more than likely not be capable of consuming the level of the capacity which is built. 3) Steelmaking capacity in Third World countries is likely to be very competitive since the operations will be new, modern, and efficient. In addition to labor costs which tend to be much lower than in the industrial world, energy and other raw material costs can be kept down by state supported subsidies. 4) If growth remains low, relative to expanding capacity, Third World countries will look for developed industrial markets like the United States to export that capacity.

Whether the developing world should continue building steelmaking capacity begs the central question of this study. From their own long term economic and political interests there is little doubt that they should, and will, expand their capabilities. The potential demand is overwhelming. As an example, Father Hogan -- steel economist and chairman at Fordham University's Industrial Economics Department -- has pointed to the fact that in China only 24 million tons of steel are consumed by 800 million people annually. According to Hogan, "If everyone in India and China used one tin can per week, that would be more than all the steel which is consumed in the United States at the present . . ."[1] But the problem in the short term is the difference between "demand" and "need," where demand is the need plus the ability to pay for it. While Third World countries may possess the need, their economies have not yet produced the demand.

As a net importer, with domestic steelmaking facilities vulnerable to the more competitive industries around the globe, United States interests are primarily those of protecting its own industry's share of the U.S. market from the threats posed by others.
In one sense, United States policymakers are in less of a dilemma than their counterparts in Europe and Japan:
in the case of Japan, Third World producers threaten the foundation on which the Japanese steel industry prospers and survives -- a powerful export capability; in the case of Europe, the Third World producers challenge European producers in export markets such as the United States, as well as cutting into Europe's own domestic markets.

The United States may learn to live with a condition in which imports comprise eighteen to twenty percent of apparent domestic consumption rather than the ten to fifteen percent level reached in the last half of the

---

[1]Interview with William Hogan of the Fordham University Industrial Development Department, May 1978.

sixties. In that case, the more serious political tensions would be between Third World producers such as Brazil, Mexico, and India, and the Europeans and the Japanese who will compete for a share of the American market. That is, in the short term. Beyond that, there is little reason to doubt that conditions in Europe and Japan won't reverberate across the oceans, in steel and other areas of the international economy. So the goal of U.S. policymakers will be to ensure that imports constitute a small enough share of domestic consumption such that U.S. domestic producers can maintain profits, jobs won't be threatened, and the disturbing political and social tensions can be held in check.

When the Economist blamed the Japanese for the severity of the global recession in the seventies, it implied an unwillingness on the part of the Japanese government to accept slower growth in a less technologically advanced economy. It is reasonable to assume that a number of the countries in the Third World will puruse similar policies that may lead to global adjustment problems in the eighties and beyond. If that is the case, we can expect that surplus capacity in international industries like steel will become a steady feature of the world economy.

Indeed, as many of the problems have been exacerbated by the "export-oriented" economies of Japan and

Germany, so the Third World seems destined to emphasize exports in its economic strategies as well. Over the past decade, LDC manufactured exports grew about ten times, now totaling $44 billion.[1] According to IBRD estimates, LDC exports in manufactured products are expected to grow by 1985 to between 100 and 145 billion dollars.[2] The increases between two recent periods are dramatic: from 1973 to 1977, for example, exports grew by $20 billion; from 1976 to 1977, alone, exported jumped $10.6 billion.[3] Because of the special attractiveness to developing economies of promoting a steel industry -- as Japan in the fifties and sixties -- one can expect that steel exports will constitute sizable proportions of LDC export growth.

If this situation develops, the political tensions caused by structural dilemmas of excess capacity, may become a permanent part of the international trading system. The lessons of the seventies, taken largely from its relationship with Japan and Europe, may encourage the United States steelmakers to look at industrial development in the Third World as a threat, and may lead U.S. policymakers to look at it with grave suspicion. Indeed,

---

[1]John Zysman, "Inflation and Industrial Adjustment: The Politics of Supply," p. 6.

[2]Ibid.

[3]Ibid.

the experience of the period under study, 1976-78, certainly suggests such a conclusion.

V. Summary

In each case we have seen how governments intervene in their domestic markets to promote certain economic strategies for political goals. As a key industry, the Japanese were willing to promote the development of its steel industry through a series of economic strategies and foreign economic policies even at the expense of adverse effects on its trading partners -- i.e., its industry produced to maintain high levels of capacity and exported it to the United States and Europe if consumption in the home market fell.[1] The Europeans, for their part, were not willing to let their steel industry adjust to the illness of old age -- a condition exacerbated by foreign economic policies of the Japanese and the short term hardships of the recession. Combined with associated events in the international economic system, such as the oil crisis, the steel crisis in Europe overflowed to the United States -- i.e., the Europeans tried to push their domestic adjustment costs onto the United States. We shall see in the next chapter how the political economic conditions of steel in Europe and Japan prompted them to

---

[1]Ibid., p. 17. As the United States and Europe have responded to crisis conditions in the global steel market, the Japanese have suffered. For example, their Capacity Utilization Rate has been under seventy percent for most of 1978.

enter into arrangements which aggravated the condition of instability already present in the international trade of steel. As domestic tensions in the United States bubbled to the surface, policymakers began to recognize that they too would be forced to intervene in the international trade of steel.

INTRODUCTION TO PART II

In Part II we shall look at the political circumstances which led to the development of the U.S. foreign trade policy for steel. As we shall see, domestic and international political factors converged to produce an "interventionist-type" policy. As a result of the conditions described in Part I, U.S. policymakers were constrained by pressures coming from domestic constituencies and from its trading partners in the international arena. In order to balance these two forces U.S. policymakers developed two programs which could be accepted by both and at least appear to satisfy the pressures imposed by the global economic steel conditions. Policymakers avoided strict protectionist measures such as quotas or increased tariffs, but were unable to avoid the tendency away from a strictly liberal trade policy. Chapter 4 will set forth the political development of the steel issue as it evolved in the United States during the 1976-78 period. In Chapters 5 and 6 we shall go into the actual development and analysis of the two programs for steel -- the Trigger Price Mechanism and the International Steel Committee. We shall conclude this section with an assessment of both programs, and their policy implications for the future. In this concluding section, we shall also point to the relationship between the U.S. foreign trade policy for steel, and a more comprehensive industrial policy for steel.

CHAPTER 4

DEVELOPING A FOREIGN TRADE POLICY FOR STEEL

I. Introduction

By 1976, it had become evident to U.S. policymakers that the steel issue would not resolve itself. If anything, the economic conditions were becoming more problematic; and the other international trade issue areas, most notably the MTN, provided a convenient context in which the steel lobby was able to keep the issue very much alive. While the tensions caused by developments in the world steel market, manifested in its international trade, were not the whole of the United States domestic steel industry's problems, they were by far the largest. Lewis Foy, in his capacity as chairman of the American Iron and Steel Institute, wrote in a letter to the Washington Post:

> I have always explained that the high level of steel imports has been one of a number of contributing factors, albeit an important one. What distinguishes the import situation from the other problems is, first, it came about because of "government's derogation of duty" (President Carter's words) and, second, it can be remedied by conscientious enforcement of existing laws . . .[1]

---

[1]"A Much Maligned Industry," Washington Post, August 1, 1978, editorial page.

The steel industry had a compelling case; it was supported by the global crisis especially manifest in Europe, and a general sympathy for protection in other industrial sectors in the United States. Referring to the protectionist sentiment in the country, Tom Wicker wrote in an editorial for the New York Times:

> . . . there are about 22 Senators and numerous House members that represent states with textile interests; about fifteen or twenty more Senators plus many Congressmen are from "shoe states" of the Northeast. And virtually every member of Congress represents some interests -- mushrooms, or shrimp, or footwear, or color TVs -- that is or may be threatened by imports.[1]

Partly because of the general support for protectionist measures in an atmosphere created by other industries affected by global surplus capacity, the resolution of the steel issue came, for the United States, to a matter of foreign trade policy. Advocates for the steel industry, as well as opponents, listed a host of other factors: the steel lobby pointed to enforcement of environmental laws which cost them over $2 billion,[2] unattractive tax laws, unusually long depreciation schedules, and high labor and energy costs. As an illustration consider the statement by the steel lobby to the newly formed Congressional steel caucuses in September 1977:

---

[1]"Halting the System," New York Times, July 25, 1978.

[2]"Testimony by Lewis Foy Before the Senate Steel Caucus," February 6, 1979.

> The caucus must impress upon the EPA the need for realistic recognition and consideration of economic factors in the promulgation of enforcement of standards and regulation.

In the area of tax reform, they urged:

> Guideline lives for the depreciation of production equipment can be reduced twenty percent . . . and legislation this year for the rapid write-off of pollution control expenditures.[1]

But the critics of the steel industry pointed to poor management decisions with regard to plant expansion, modernization, and price escalation. In the words of one critic:

> The U.S. steel industry has been mismanaged to the point of being unable to compete for even domestic customers with powerful, efficient exporters in Japan and elsewhere.[2]

As is evident from the Solomon Report to the President, none of these points were entirely ignored. But, for the U.S. government to develop policy which seriously addressed the substance associated with each -- energy, taxes, environment -- there would have had to have been a willingness on the part of government and industry to alter both the atmosphere and the details of the relationship between

---

[1]Quoted on a letter from National Steel Corporation to Senators, September 26, 1977, "Points for Consideration by the Steel Caucus." On file with the author.

[2]Robert Crandall, Challenge, July-August 1978, "Competition and Dumping in the United States Market, p. 1.

them. Neither the willingness, nor the ability, existed. It would have to come to an "industrial policy"[1] -- a course which was unworkable for elemental reasons and therefore never undertaken. On the one hand the industry remains cautious about government "mucking around its affairs."[2] On the other hand, however, government has been reticent to take such measures as lowering the tax rate on capital gains, or provide relief from the double taxation of corporate dividends. As W.J. DeLancey, president of Republic Steel put it:

> On the one hand our government says to us: "You're on your own in the competitive fray." On the other hand foreign governments say to their steelmakers: "We're with you."[3]

Washington has not been in the habit of choosing "key industries," like the Japanese, for which it develops economic strategies. Nor does it develop economic policies around specific sectors, like the French.

What developed instead was a two-pronged foreign trade policy -- one, a variation on the traditional forms of protection available to countries operating under the liberal trade principles expressed in the GATT; the other, a new version of protectionism in which all countries

---

[1]For a discussion of industrial policies, see, Lawrence G. Franco, "Industrial Policies in Western Europe," The World Economy, volume 2, number 1, January 1979.

[2]Interview with executives at the American Iron and Steel Institute, January 5, 1979.

[3]"Rising Demand Stirs Hopes for a Steel Turnaround," Iron Age, May 22, 1978, p. 55.

participate in what the French have called "organized free trade,"[1] or what might be called "collective protection." This is probably less inimical than "national protection" because the major trading partners work out the protective arrangements on commonly acceptable grounds, but it is protection nonetheless. For United States policymakers, there were three stages in the development of its foreign trade policy for steel.

1) Defining the problem as a foreign trade issue; this happened rather quickly since no one in the Administration during this period seriously contemplated a full-blown industrial policy where foreign trade strategies would be incorporated as part of a larger economic strategy to promote the steel sector.

2) Once the issue area had been clarified as one of foreign trade, government officials were still not clear how far they wanted to go, or how far they might be forced to go, in trying to resolve it. They were confronted with two related, but different, conditions: on the one hand there was the fact of a large number of imports penetrating the American market, and, arguably causing injury to American producers. As suggested by Lewis Foy in his letter quoted above, this particular condition could

---

[1]See, for example, The Economist, July 16, 1977, p. 83, "Don't Ditch Free Trade": "The French Voice in the EEC has been the loudest calling for what amounts to a rich man's version of a new economic order. The key phrase is organized free trade.

be resolved rather simply by keeping the imports at a low level by enforcing domestic trade laws.

At the same time, however, the nature of the global crisis shed doubt on this alternative. Mostly as a result of the interaction with its major trading partners, U.S. government officials recognized a subtle, but critical, difference between the import problem as a condition affecting the United States proper, and the global steel crisis which actually produced the domestic import problem. That is, the import problem was but a symptom of the global crisis. While quotas would keep the imports at a lower level, and thereby protect American producers, they might also exacerbate the global crisis, and possibly even the American situation in the long term. Recognition of this distinction -- between the domestic import problem creating a domestic political crisis, and the global economic crisis caused by excess capacity -- led to fundamentally different policy solutions, since it meant even a "conscientious enforcement of existing laws" would not redress the long term global structural crisis.

3) Recognition of this distinction -- that the high level of import penetration into the American market was a symptom of a more difficult problem -- made it no less urgent that U.S. policymakers address the immediate domestic crisis once it erupted. While the import problem might have been put in perspective by U.S. policymakers, it still remained a source of gnawing political tensions.

Thus, the final stage in the policy process was precipitated by an immediate domestic crisis caused by "the damaging surge of imports" into the American market, which "contributed importantly" to unemployment and plant closings."[1]

At each stage, U.S. policy for steel was more clearly defined. While the Administration continued to espouse a commitment to liberal trade -- emphasizing the completion of the MTN as a symbol of that commitment -- as the details of its foreign trade policy for steel began to unfold, it became more and more evident that what was emerging would not fit so easily into the traditional free trader's paradigm. The next pages will follow the policy process along the three broad developments listed above.

---

[1] Unemployment in the Steel Industry, Basic Steel Conference, Washington Hilton Hotel, December 2, 1977, United Steelworkers of America, p. 2., also see the Department of Labor study quoted in the New York Times, September 29, 1977, "5,000 From Youngstown Certified Because of Import Competition."

II. A Matter of Foreign Trade Policy

As early as mid-1975, representatives for the United States steel industry had begun to lobby the Ford Administration. While industry officials, from the first, had couched their problems mainly in terms of foreign trade, the Administration had considered other policy arenas. As late as the summer of 1977, President Carter's ad hoc Economic Policy Group was still quite open, according to an official from the Office of the Special Trade Representative, about their belief that the problems in the steel industry were more than a matter of international trade. Ambassador Strauss's office also sounded this theme, which was viewed as part of the "search for an agency"; Strauss apparently realized, that "if STR took it, it would have been an admission that the main problem was trade . . . [and] no one felt this was the case."[1]

Even the Trigger Price Mechanism -- the central feature in a system designed to initiate immediate investigations of possible steel dumping -- was part of the larger "Solomon Plan" which also contained non-foreign

---

[1]Interview, November 4, 1978.

trade elements. The Solomon Task Force, named for Under Secretary of the Treasury Anthony M. Solomon, who headed the Interagency Group which developed the plan, made seven other recommendations which are, somewhat optimistically, seen by the industry as "an attempt to formulate an industrial sector policy for steel."[1]

Notwithstanding all of the efforts to use policy arenas other than foreign trade, an official in the STR's office who had been part of an interagency task force studying the steel issue since about mid-1975, candidly admitted that "while trade may have been 20 to 25 percent of the problem, it had become clear that it would be 80 to 85 percent of solution."[2] Ironically, the process which defined the solution in terms not entirely appropriate to the problem tended to redefine the problem in terms of the solution.

The fact that there was some debate within the federal bureaucracy as to whether the resolution of the steel issue would come primarily under the jurisdiction of foreign policy, or domestic policy, underscores the complexity of the policymaking process for international trade. Unlike defense, or welfare issues, for instance,

---

[1]After a series of interviews, it has become clear that the American Iron and Steel Institute, as well as many industry executives, are hopeful that the United States government will work to develop an "Industrial Policy." See my conclusion to Part II.

[2]Interview, November 9, 1978.

policy jurisdiction is not so readily compartmentalized for industrial sector issues. And since many believed steel might well become a precedent-setting case for other industrial sectors, policymakers were especially cautious. Three factors led to the ultimate, and probably inevitable, decision that it would be addressed as a foreign trade issue.

First, it became apparent that the existing institutional framework for foreign trade policy issues provided a more coherent structure in which to deal with the steel industry's problems, than its counterpart in domestic policy. However ad hoc and fragmented the foreign trade institutional arrangements seemed to be, "domestic policy," according to one high level bureaucrat in charge of industry affairs "is ill-equipped to solve the burdens . . . we would need at once to address capital formation, government loan programs, and tax reform."[1] Quite apart from the question of whether necessary reforms would have come to pass in any or all of these categories, trade policy offered the advantage that the Special Trade Representative's Office already functioned as a coordinating body for trade policy. While this didn't eliminate all of the confusion one would expect to encounter in an issue for which so many parts of the bureaucracy claimed

---

[1]Interview, November 9, 1978.

responsibility, STR's presence tended to minimize it. STR's coordinating capabilities were enhanced during this period by the existence of the MTN. As major multilateral trade negotiations were underway, and the STR's Office was clearly the lead agency in this effort, it was easier for STR to take the lead in other trade matters also.

Coordinating a trade policy was made even easier in light of the advisory sector groups which had been created by the 1974 Trade Act.

These groups acted as a catch-all for industry and labor complaints -- trade or otherwise -- because their purpose was to advise U.S. negotiators at the MTN. It also provided an incentive for industry and labor to couch their complaints in the form of a trade issue.

If it were decided that the steel issue was to be addressed as a domestic problem, it is more than likely that the Commerce Department would have claimed coordinating jurisdiction. However, this would have presented several problems. In the first place, it was readily admitted that "Commerce is not in a position to coordinate an industrial policy."[1] While Commerce tends to offer the closest government institution at present the United States has to an agency for business and commerce, and

---

[1]Interview, November 9, 1978.

is most often the agency which "protects" the business community's interests in intra-agency disputes, it does not have responsibility for tax or environmental policy, both essential parts of the domestic reform package the steel industry wanted. So, while Commerce might have tried to coordinate a domestic policy, it would have been less capable of organizing the disparate elements than the STR's Office could do for foreign trade policy.

Therefore, lacking a coherent institutional framework to develop a domestic policy for industry, the Administration found it easier to "take action in the area of trade."[1]

A second factor which resulted in the steel issue being resolved by foreign trade policy was the perception that "trade policy is less painful than other (domestic) policy solutions."[2] "Less painful," in bureaucratic parlance, typically means "costs less." And so it was in this case as well. Under any circumstances, a domestic policy would have included "policy tools" that would cost money. Officials wished to avoid the budget process, and in particular, a struggle with the Office of Management and Budget which they surely expected in the event of a proposed domestic policy solution. Not only would trade policy avoid budget outlays, and with it, the delicate

---

[1]Interview, November 9, 1978.

[2]Interview, November 9, 1978.

budget process, but it could generate revenue for the Treasury, unlike domestic policy strategies which would appear as expenses.

In addition to direct expenditures, and the bureaucratic fights which surely would have followed, spending money on the steel industry, especially during a period of high inflation, would have been inconsistent with what increasingly became the Administration's primary economic objective -- to decrease levels of inflation. By mid-1977, anything which was thought to be "inflationary" was summarily dismissed as contrary to the national interest. For steel, it would have been particularly difficult since its public image was not a very attractive one -- big business, oligopoly, which in any event, had created its own problems through a series of poor management decisions in the post-World War II years.

Thirdly, the bulk of the pressures, first from industry, and then from Congress, were framed as international trade issues. As indicated in point one, this was the case in large part because of the MTN. But, there is more to it which should be examined. As an illustration, consider the statement delivered by George A. Stinson, chairman of National Steel Corporation, in which he emphasized that it was "the impact of foreign pricing practices . . . namely the loss of income in 1976 and 1977 aggregating $4.1 billion . . . [which had] a profound negative impact on our industry."[1] Chairman Stinson went on to point out that the industry's long term debt had grown from $4.7 billion in 1974 to $7.9 billion by the end of 1977, raising the industry's debt to equity ratio from 32 percent to 44 percent during that period.[2] Stinson's point, echoed by the other leaders of the industry, was that their "struggle to maintain or expand needed investment"[3] was due to declining profits resulting from unfair foreign trade practices.

Industry and labor both had realized that their greatest leverage was in the area of foreign trade since they could threaten the MTN. There was no parallel linkage in the domestic policy arena.

Hence, combined with the internal bureaucratic process described above, the Administration had little choice but to seek the inevitable -- foreign trade policy solutions.

As early as 1975, the industry had developed a "plan of action" which was formally presented to Ambassador Strauss's office. The program, coordinated and implemented by the AISI, was organized with four types of fora in

---

[1]"American Iron and Steel Institute Press Conference Release," May 23, 1978.

[2]Ibid.

[3]Ibid.

mind: the Executive branch, the Congress, at the community level especially where steel production was an implicit part of the local economic, and administrative, actions.[1] Their efforts at each level flowed from the three part plan submitted to the STR's Office in 1975.

The program submitted to the STR's Office, also developed by the official coordinating organization for the steel industry -- the American Iron and Steel Institute (AISI) located in Washington, D.C. just a few blocks from the White House -- consisted of three elements: (a) to establish an international framework similar to the Multi-fiber Arrangement for textiles;[2] (b) to persuade other countries to eliminate their duties on steel so that diversion of steel to markets such as the United States where duties were less stringent, would be minimized; (c) and, to do something through the MTN process about foreign government subsidization of steel, which, they argued, caused serious trade distortions to the detriment of steelmakers in the United States and elsewhere not enjoying similar subsidies.[3] The basic objective of the plan, according to an industry spokesman, was "to get the government to respond to market distortions whether that condition

---

[1]Interview, May 4, 1979.

[2]Interview, November 9, 1978.

[3]Interview, November 9, 1978.

came from fair or unfair trade."[1] In the end, they were rather successful at accomplishing the latter -- to respond to market distortions from unfair trade practices -- but not to the former.

While STR claimed it was "sympathetic to the overall objectives of the plan," it was clear from the first that the plan would serve mostly to raise the consciousness of policymakers in government, and to indicate industry's objectives -- to negotiate a multilateral steel sector, and to equalize government intervention in world steel markets. The second and third part of the plan became topics for discussion, partly through the multilateral trade negotiating process, and partly through an extra-MTN forum which was formed to respond specifically to the steel issue. However, STR raised several basic objections to the MFA approach for steel, and that part of the industry's plan never got very far. It should be noted that the industry still claims that the "Administration never really understood what we wanted, but opposed it on ideological grounds."[2]

In fact, the most serious objection to the "MFA approach" was that it assumed a series of bilateral arrangements between, and among, the major steel trading partners. Bilateralism, according to an Administration

---

[1]Interview, January 5, 1979.

[2]Interview, January 5, 1979.

spokesman "is the root of [national] protection . . . it lends itself to under the table deals, and doesn't take account of the overall global situation." Besides, Ambassador Strauss's office argued:

> We are already committed philosophically and legally to the Tokyo Round, and bilaterals would be in contradistinction to the underlying principles and spirit of the GATT.[1]

Even though policy officials continued to entertain non-trade aspects of the steel issue, it received serious attention only as a trade matter.

---

[1]Interview, November 9, 1979

III. The Structural Crisis and an Import Problem

Once consensus formed around seeking a foreign trade policy solution to the steel issue, a predictable "bureaucratic momentum" picked up. Even while consensus was forming, however, the second stage of the policy development process had gotten underway. Whether they clearly realized it at the time, the U.S. government's foreign policy approach to the steel issue was developing in two different directions: as an import problem, and as part of the world steel crisis. In fact they existed symbiotically, though policy-wise they were addressed separately.

The Wolff Trade Mission -- U.S. Becomes Part of the World Steel Crisis

Throughout 1975-76, the Europeans had called informal meeting on steel to which they invited representatives from the United States and Japan. As indicated in the last chapter, the European situation had reached crisis proportions by 1975, and it was in that context that U.S. government officials first indicated that they were aware of the seriousness of the world steel situation. As early as May 1975, Jacques Ferry, the president of the French Steel Federation had requested that the European Commission formally recognize a "manifest crisis." His intentions, along with those of other steelmakers in Europe, were to get the European Commission to take "remedial actions" by applying some kind of "production quotas, minimum prices, or import restrictions against steel coming from Japan, Spain, and Eastern Europe."[1]

Rejecting such measures at that time, the EC asked instead, in October 1975, for a meeting on the steel issue in the OECD. The Commission then issued a statement which emphasized the global nature of the steel problem:

> Although the problems that have to be faced by the Community's steel industry are in certain respects even more acute than those faced by other countries, they stem from the same root and should not therefore be treated in isolation. That is why the Commission considers that there is need for international measures . . .[2]

It wasn't until late in 1976, however, that U.S. policy officials began to take the initiative with regard to establishing international guidelines for dealing with the steel issue. In December 1976, a high level trade policy mission headed by Ambassador Wolff went to Tokyo and Brussels to begin separate bilateral discussions with the Japanese and the European Community respectively. The purpose of the mission, according to an official from the STR's Office who accompanied Wolff, was "to convey the

---

[1]See my Chapter 3, section on the European Community plan.

[2]_The European Community_, No. 209, June/July 1976, "The Steel Blues," p. 18.

message that the pressure on the United States steel industry from imports should be alleviated."[1] If that was its purpose, however, it was surely a failure; "Nobody paid a damn bit of attention," as one member of Wolff's staff put it some time later. Indeed, the facts support this judgment; imports in 1977 into the United States reached an all-time high.

From this rather unsuccessful attempt at negotiating what might have been a voluntary restraint agreement or orderly marketing arrangement with the Japanese and the Europeans, some good did come: the basis for the framework in which the three major trading partners could talk about steel. We shall see during the course of this chapter, and in Chapter 6, how these discussions among the United States, the European Community and Japan, which began with the Wolff Mission, led to a serious discussion framework from which the OECD International Steel Committee grew. Officials in Treasury, the STR's office, and State all agree that the International Ad Hoc Steel Committee set up in April 1977, was a result of the Wolff trade mission. And, it was this Ad Hoc Committee which met throughout the remainder of 1977, and all of 1978, until October 21, 1978 when the International Steel Committee was officially established.[2]

---

[1]Interview, November 9, 1979.

[2]See my Chapter 6, International Steel Agreement.

Even before Ambassador Wolff's mission in December 1976, two sets of actions were undertaken by the American steel industry which began to focus trade policy officials in the bureaucracy on the problems in the steel sector. On the one hand there was the "301" complaint petition filed by the American steel industry; it addressed the subtle and complex questions of trade distortions which they argued were a result of the economic strategies and foreign economic policies of its trading partners. Indeed, there is little doubt that the 301 petition was a major impetus for the Wolff trade mission in the first place. On the other hand, there was the Specialty Steel Case, which directly addressed the import penetration problem; it didn't frontally assault the complex problems of international trade in a sector experiencing surplus capacity as the 301 complaint, though the implications were certainly present. Let us begin, then, with the 301 complaint.

The 301 complaint petition

The autumn before the Carter Administration took office, the steel industry filed a "301 petition," which emphasized the international politics side of the foreign trade policy equation. As much as anything else, the 301 petition prodded the foreign trade policy bureaucracy to think about the global crisis aspect of the steel issue. In a letter to Ambassador Strauss, the American Iron and

Steel Institute presented the two "factual issues" of the 301 complaint as they understood them; the issue was clearly framed as an international one:

> (1) . . . an understanding reached whereby steel exports from Japan to Europe were curtailed; (2) if so, were Japanese shipments destined for Europe diverted to the United States.[1]

Though stated in the interrogative, both points were asserted as facts. Indeed, the precise argument was that negotiations between the Europeans and the Japanese led to an arrangement which restricted the quantity of shipments from Japan to Europe, and led to "the artificial diversion of substantial tonnages of steel to the United States constitut[ing] a severe burden on and restriction of United States commerce."[2]

While the specialty steel case, as we shall see, directly addressed the level of imports, in the 301 complaint the industry was asking for effective quotas to correct trade distortions caused by Japanese and European practices: "Compensation," the complaint argued, "can be made in the form of reduced steel shipments from Japan that

---

[1]"Letter to Ambassador Strauss from Edgar Spear, as chairman of the American Iron and Steel Institute," in personal files of author.

[2]"Brief in Support of Complaint Filed by the American Iron and Steel Institute Under Section 301 of the Trade Act of 1974, Against the Bilateral Agreement Between the European Coal and Steel Community and the Japanese Ministry of International Trade and Industry, Limiting Exports of Japanese Steel to Europe," in personal files of author.

would be roughly equivalent to the harm caused by the breach of its most favored nation obligation." American industry officials had calculated that the excess shipment amounted to "8,700,000 tons of steel . . . since the inception of the [Japanese-European Cartel] in August of 1975 through July 1977."[1] They suggested, therefore, that a "three year reduction of 2,900,000 tons per year of steel from the 1976 level of export from Japan to the United States."[2] The result, they had estimated, would be that Japan would be limited to "5,000,000 tons per year as the maximum allowable."[3] Since the basis for these quotas was a bilateral deal to which the alleged parties would not admit, it was a much broader, highly sophisticated, and terribly dangerous concept for the future of the liberal trade system. It pointed to inconsistencies in the practices among the major trading partners, to the structural flaws in the world steel market, and argued compensation accordingly. The 301 case relates more directly to the Wolff Trade Mission since they were both motivated by the belief that American steel producers suffered from a condition imposed on them by political control of the world steel market which resulted in the

---

[1]Ibid.

[2]Ibid.

[3]"Letter from the American Iron and Steel Institute to Ambassador Strauss," June 30, 1977, in personal files of author.

special diversion of Japanese steel to American markets. Accordingly, the industry complaint argued that "the bilateral pact discriminates against United States commerce by denying the U.S. equal treatment."[1]

And, it alleged, therefore:

> The secret accord between the ECSC and MITI is clearly actionable under Section 301 of the Trade Act of 1974. Section 301 was intended to provide relief from unfair trade practices which violate international law or international obligations, and which burden, restrict or discriminate against U.S. commerce. There can be no doubt that the government level agreement transgresses the dictates of the General Agreement on Trade and Tariffs (GATT).[2]

"It is a matter of record," the industry argued even through 1977, "that the European-Japanese Cartel was prompted, and indeed perhaps coerced, by the European Commission. Europe must not be allowed to profit from its participation in such an arrangement."[3] Hence, in addition to the limits on Japanese exports, the American Iron and Steel industry had proposed that:

> So long as the cartel continues to exist, the Common Market exports of steel to this country must be maintained at the level of the 1975-76 average. Furthermore, during the three year period of compensatory relief obtained from Japan the Common Market must not be able to obtain unjust enrichment by their exports supplanting the reduced Japanese exports.[4]

---

[1]"301 Brief Against the ECSC and Japan's MITI."

[2]Ibid.

[3]Ibid.

[4]Ibid.

It has always proved difficult to get the Europeans or the Japanese to admit publicly that they had ever entered into an arrangement which effectively diverted steel to the American market. This is one reason why no immediate results came from the Wolff Trade Mission in December 1976 -- how can you rectify a condition which you can not prove?

Nevertheless, the Japanese-European deal was an accepted fact among trade policy officials in the United States bureaucracy, and one upon which certain policy decisions were made. Indeed, there is strong evidence to support the American industry's contention that a "voluntary restraint agreement" or "cartel," as they most often called it between the Europeans and the Japanese did exist. Aside from the facts -- increased imports into the United States, and decreased imports into the European market from Japan -- American officials were aware of the "regular meetings between MITI and the ECSC . . . and that a similar process had not developed between MITI and the United States . . .[1] As one trade official at the Japanese Embassy in Washington, D.C. put it: "We have arrangements with the Europeans . . . no, not arrangements (slight smile) . . . you know . . . cooperation."[2] In their official complaint, the industry referred to

---

[1]Interview, November 2, 1978.

[2]Interview, November 16, 1978.

the "cooperation" between MITI and the ECSC as a "concealed agreement":

> The Agreement is not the result of any specific or particular law or regulation of either ECSC, the European Nations, or Japan. The Agreement was oral and was deliberately to be concealed from the United States.[1]

As pressure from the steel lobby manifested in the 301 case increased in the first months of 1977, the Japanese became noticeably nervous. The question that seemed to trouble them most was whether they would begin to lose control over market shares, i.e., liberal access to the American market. It is interesting that the Japanese government began publishing information, obviously intended for American consumption, about the comparative levels of European and Japanese steel exports into the United States. As an illustration, the *Japan Metal Bulletin* announced that "EC's Steel Exports to U.S. Will Surpass Japanese." The article documented a decline in the Japanese share of the United States steel market during the first half of 1977; and it went on to report that:

> It is apparent that the EC steelmakers have stepped up export drives reducing their selling prices to unbelievable low levels so much so that Japanese steelmakers have lost many deals on the U.S. and South American markets. At present, the EC steel products are sold in the United States at the prices

---

[1] "301 Brief Against the ECSC and Japan's MITI."

> $25 - $30 per ton lower than the Japanese products.[1]

Several reliable sources reported that the Japanese government, at the behest of its major steel producers, seriously considered a voluntary restraint agreement on steel exports to the United States. Understandably, they feared the U.S. might be pressured by domestic constituencies to impose quotas. According to a Wall Street Journal article:

> . . . executives of six major [Japanese] steel companies have discussed the possibility of voluntary export restraints with the Japanese Ministry of International Trade and Investment . . .
>
> The Japanese industry is understood to favor some form of voluntary export restraints, rather than possible imposition of import quotas, such as those already in effect for specialty steel.[2]

The Japanese preference for a voluntary restraint agreement is obvious: while such agreements may carry a great deal of pressure, public, and even private, in the end they are voluntary, and not nearly so tough as outright quotas, which the American government had already displayed a willingness to implement. Understandably, the United States steelmakers were far less enthusiastic about the voluntary approach: a voluntary restraint agreement on steel exports from Japan had been in effect from 1968 to

---

[1]Japan Metal Bulletin, August 25, 1977, "Iron and Steel," p. 1.

[2]Wall Street Journal, February 28, 1977, "Japanese Steelmakers Prod Government for Voluntary Accord on Exports to the U.S."

late 1973, and from the industry's viewpoint they weren't very satisfactory.[1] In the present round of the steel issue, the industry had come to more dire conclusions about prospects for resolving the issue with short term, and in any event, largely unenforceable, solutions like the voluntary restraint agreement. The New York Times accurately described why the industry opposed "voluntary agreements":

> . . . general agreement in the United States that the voluntary quota system did not work the first time partly because it was so difficult to police, and partly because there were loopholes. Steel can always be transshipped from neutral countries, for example, and high profit products can be shipped in quantity as long as quotas are imposed in aggregate terms.[2]

Thus, there was a considerable amount of suspicion regarding the effectiveness of such an approach from the American point of view. The industry had concluded in a major study on the "Economics of International Steel Trade," that:

> Other nations will continue to be under considerable pressure to export large parts of their steel production -- at prices below their average production costs if necessary.[3]

---

[1]For a good discussion of the Voluntary Restraint Agreements of 1968 and 1972, see, William T. Hogan, S.J. The 1970s: Critical Years for Steel (Lexington, Mass.: Lexington Books, 1972); especially Chapter 3.

[2]New York Times, October 17, 1977, "Economic Analysis: How Acute Are Steel's Woes."

[3]Economics of International Steel Trade: Policy Implications for the U.S., prepared for the American Iron and Steel Institute, Putnam, Hayes, and Bartlett, Inc. (Newton, Mass., May 1977). p. 27.

Therefore, the report went on to say, "The major threat to the competitive position of the U.S. steel industry in 1977 and beyond lies in the pricing practices of foreign producers."[1] These conclusions led the industry to take an even less favorable position towards the voluntary restraint agreements as the policy resolution for the steel issue. It was felt that the issue was larger, and deeper.

Ironically, because the 301 complaint pointed to the structural nature of a world steel crisis, the Administration had decided it could not act. Having been referred to the STR's office as provided in the Trade Act of 1974, the industry was told by a high level official that "[STR] couldn't support the analysis that had been reached . . ."[2] While the 301 complaint forced the Administration to recognize the effects of the world steel crisis on the

---

[1]Ibid.

[2]Interview, November 9, 1978. Note: By industry's own admission, there was no direct evidence, only circumstantial, of a bilateral agreement between the ECSC and Japan's MITI. Still, the industry's 301 complaint was rather persuasive: "Japanese exports to Europe," it argued, "began to surge early in 1975 following the termination of the quantitative restrictions ended in 1974. Coincident with the opening of the European market to freer trade, Japanese exports to the United States fell from more than 600,000 tons per month early in the year to less than 325,000 tons in August . . . . Third, commencing in August 1975, exports from Japan to Europe plummeted pursuant to MITI's agreement with the ECSC. Fourth, one month after the short-term agreement was to be enforced in August, exports from Japan to the United States began to climb, reaching highs of approximately 900,000 net tons or more in December 1975 and March 1978." 301 Brief on file with author.

American market, there was at that point no visible domestic political crisis.

For the Europeans, however, the economic crisis had already spilled into domestic politics, creating for them a threat to the governments' mandate to negotiate trade liberalization in the GATT. Thus, for American policymakers, the costs of pursuing the 301 complaint as the industry had framed it, especially given the dearth of direct evidence, were far greater than any advantages. It was feared that pursuing the 301 complaint would, in making matters worse for the Europeans, thereby jeopardize the MTN. The Administration was not willing to take the risk.

Still, by pursuing quotas in the 301 complaint -- a vehicle for pressure which the industry continued to use throughout 1978 -- the industry had accomplished two important objectives: first, they framed the issue in terms of a world structural crisis, and claimed that the American industry was the victim of a series of broad, illiberal trade practices of its trading partners; and second, they cleverly carved for themselves a position which established a hard-line bargaining stand vis-a-vis the Administration and foreign competitors. Combined with the precedent set by the decisions on the specialty steel case which shall be examined below, American steelmakers and their allies in labor had built a formidable case -- one that the Administration couldn't turn down once the domestic political situation exploded.

The Specialty Steel Complaint

On January 16, 1975 a petition by nineteen American specialty steel producers and the United Steelworkers of America was filed under the "escape clause" provisions of the 1974 Trade Act. They were seeking relief from what they argued was "a flood of steel imports which threatened the future of the American specialty steel industry and the security of 65,000 steelworkers' jobs."[1] As stipulated in the Trade Act of 1974, the petition was officially filed with the Treasury Department for a determination of less than fair value -- whether the goods were being sold at less than what it cost to make, or at less than it was being sold in the home market. It was then sent to the International Trade Commission (ITC) for determination of whether the imports had caused injury to the domestic producers. Public hearings were held at the ITC in October 1975, and on January 16, 1976, the ITC determined that imports were a "substantial cause of serious injury" to the domestic specialty steel industry.[2] Accordingly, the ITC recommended to the President that import

---

[1]United States International Trade Commission "Stainless Steel and Alloy Tool Steel" Report to the President on Investigation No. TA-201-5 Under Section 201 of the Trade Act of 1974 (Washington, D.C.: USITC Publication 756, 1976).

[2]Ibid.

limitations be imposed for five years "to give the industry sufficient time to recover."[1] Upon ITC determination of injury to the domestic industry, the President, according to the Trade Act of 1974, is required, with certain exceptions, to provide some form of import relief -- such as duty increases, tariff-rate quotas, quantitative restrictions, or orderly marketing arrangements. The President can choose not to provide any kind of import relief, however, if he determines that it is not in the national economic interest. It is also possible under the Act that even if the President chooses not to provide the relief recommended by the ITC, the Congress can override his decision by passing a resolution of both Houses of Congress which requires the President to implement the relief recommended by the ITC.[2] In this case the President negotiated an Orderly Marketing Agreement with Japan limiting specialty steel imports for three years.

Less cooperative than the Japanese, however, the Europeans refused to negotiate such an agreement. Thus, quantitative restraints (quotas) were placed on imports from the European Community, and all other countries, for the same three year period that was covered by the Orderly Marketing Agreement with the Japanese. As quotas commenced

---

[1]"United States International Trade Commission Report on Specialty Steels."

[2]*1974 Trade Act*, P.L. 93-618.

on June 14, 1976, a New York Times editorial, "The Steel Steal," was tough on President Ford's decision, though it correctly underscored the importance of strong political constituency in influencing it.

> The economic ideologues of the Ford Administration lose no opportunity to sing the praises of the market system and to limit government for social reasons. But somehow all these strictures are easily forgotten when competition proves painful for some part of the constituency . . . . There was no mention of the glories of the free market mechanism in President Ford's decision to restrict imports of specialty steels . . . .[1]

There was still another item which cause controversy among those who worried about the direction in which U.S. foreign trade policy seemed to be headed. Included in the President's message to his Special Trade Representative, Frederick Dent, was an item "instructing" the STR's office to seek sectoral negotiations in steel. A Washington Post editorial, which appeared shortly after the President ammounced his decision, referred to it rather sarcastically as "a second instruction to negotiate solutions at the Geneva trade talks, to cyclical distortions in the whole steel trade."[2]

The Specialty Steel Case is important for two reasons: first, it was the first 201 petition filed under the 1974 Trade Act since it had become law, which passed the ITC screening process, and went on to win a favorable

---

[1]New York Times, March 21, 1976, p. 16, Section IV.

[2]Washington Post, April 10, 1976, p. A-10.

decision from the President. This indicated to many outside the United States how the U.S. would interpret import relief provisions of the Trade Act; it supported the worst fears of the Europeans that "appeals [would be] made easier by the 1974 Trade Act which loosened the qualifications for import relief."[1] And, since the decision led, not only to the imposition of quotas, but to an orderly marketing arrangement as well, many point to it as an indication of the beginning of "the cartelization of the world steel industry."[2]

The second reason this case was so important for a study of the steel issue, is that the specialty steel case was adopted by the steel industry as their own. Many who opposed the President's decision on specialty steel argued that it would have wider repercussions on the United States' efforts to liberalize trade by setting the groundwork for wider market sharing arrangements in "big steel." It lent credibility to the allegation that the industry was really "angling for worldwide market rigging and price fixing,"[3] while it helped to build the steel lobby's case for government intervention to protect the American industry from the unfair trading practices

---

[1]European Community, "The Steel Blues," p. 18.

[2]For example, The Washington Post, April 10, 1976, p. A-12.

[3]Walter Adams, quoted in The Washington Post, June 4, 1978, editorial page.

of its partners.

Admittedly, some of the uproar over the President's "second instruction" to his Special Trade Representative, came from the other agencies usually involved in trade policy which were bitter about having been excluded from this intrabureaucratic development. Apparently, the President had acted on a request from the Special Trade Representative who wanted a special mandate for his office to seek sectoral negotiations in steel.[1] According to an official in the STR's office, "The other agencies involved in trade policy did not know about this . . . it was snuck past them, and they weren't too happy about it."[2] In the final analysis, this interchange made it easier for the STR's office to use the threat of sector negotiations to exact concessions from the Europeans and Japanese in steel. It made their position on sectoral negotiations in the GATT -- a demand of the American industry -- that much more credible. But it also gave the industry more leverage with which to pressure the Administration.

In a very practical sense, the specialty steel case helped to lay the groundwork for the development

---

[1]Even though the Trade Act had recommended negotiations by sectors, and the Senate Finance Committee Report language referred specifically to steel, many policy officials felt that they needed direct confirmation from the President since there was so much political opposition in the GATT to sectoral negotiations.

[2]Interview, November 9, 1978.

of the U.S. foreign trade policy for steel. Through the details of this case the bureaucracy began their education process of the complexities of the steel issue. Of course, there were those who had prior exposure, both to the immediate crisis, and to the steel issue generally. But, for the bureaucracy at large, this was their first real exposure to the details as well as the nuances of the steel issue.

Understandably, it made impressions on the United States' trading partners as well: the imposition of U.S. quotas, or the pressuring of the Europeans and Japanese into orderly marketing agreements, left scars that were to affect the trade negotiations over the next two years. It also emphasized to the other major trading partners taking part in the Geneva negotiations the seriousness with which the Americans would approach the steel issue.

However much the specialty steel case touched on all aspects of trade policy, the focus for the U.S. bureaucracy was on how imports caused the steel lobby to bring pressure on the government for relief. There was, after all, the 1976 election; and President Ford has no popular mandate -- a condition of his governance of which he was constantly reminded. Indeed, the specialty steel case had produced a "curious sight" where the chairman of the American Iron and Steel Institute for 1975-76, Frederick G. Jaicks, and the head of the United Steelworkers of America, I.W. Abel, made common cause in their plea to

President Ford. A powerful coalition like that is not to be discarded, especially in an election year.[1] Thus, in the instance of the specialty steel case, the domestic politics side of the foreign trade policy equation was emphasized -- a rather effective coalition which caused the Ford Administration to impose some strict measures on the U.S. trading partners.

Indeed, the toughness of the U.S. position was underscored when the Carter Administration,[2] upon reviewing the case in 1977, decided to keep the quotas on specialty steels for the duration of the three year period established by President Ford.

As was their right, and probably their responsibility as well, the Carter Administration's first official act in the field of trade policy was to review the specialty steel case. It was significant that the new Administration's initiation into the trade area was in steel -- "it served as a way to begin the education process for the administration

---

[1]For an interesting comment on this, see Barron's, March 8, 1976, "Insult to Injury"; most major newspapers which followed the trade issue throughout the sixties -- The New York Times, The Wall Street Journal, The Journal of Commerce, and The Washington Post -- regularly commented on the unity of steel labor and industry as they turned to government for relief from foreign competition. This development is particularly noteworthy since over the years industry and labor slugged it out across the collective bargaining table, and it was not uncommon for extended strikes as the one in 1959.

[2]See below under the section on the Congress.

in the problems of steel"[1] -- and that their position upheld the Ford Administration's decision -- a decision which was viewed in some circles as a violation of liberal trade policies. But, as we shall see in the next section, liberal trade can only be upheld so long as there is the domestic consensus supporting it. As the domestic political crisis unfolded in the autumn of 1977, support for a foreign trade policy for steel to protect American workers and industry's profits gathered powerful momentum.

---

[1]Interview, November 6, 1978.

IV. Political Crisis -- The Youngstown Effect

Leading to Youngstown

So, the foreign trade policy bureaucracy had, by mid-1977, brought the Carter Administration "up to gear on the steel issue."[1] For them, the specialty steel case provided a convenient hook on which the education process of the broader, more volatile, and politically sensitive, steel issue could proceed. Clearly, the steel lobby "helped" in this process. In addition to the specialty steel case, there was the 301 complaint which had been around since October 1976, and the Advisory Committee framework of the MTN through which the industry continued to lobby for sectoral negotiations[2] and several different variations on what the Administration understood to be an "MFA-type" approach for steel; but, there was also the Gilmore steel case -- the first steel antidumping suit filed by a little-known steel company on the West Coast; and in May there appeared the first of a series of rather impressive American Iron and Steel Institute Documents.[3]

---

[1]Interview, November 6, 1978.

[2]See my section in Chapter 2 on the Advisory Committee framework.

[3]The American Iron and Steel Institute had commissioned an accounting firm from Newton, Massachusetts,

Since there was both a new Administration, and a new Congress, in January 1977, one might have anticipated the six to nine month hiatus until late spring 1977 in which not much would happen. This was especially true on the domestic front. Internationally, the United States government did progress, however slowly, toward institutionalizing the discussion framework for steel in the OECD. While the high level political appointments of the new Carter Administration were not set until four or five months into 1977, thereby making it virtually impossible to make policy-level decisions until after that time, the foreign trade bureaucracy continued to talk to their counterparts in the European Community and Japan. As an illustration, the first meeting of the OECD Ad Hoc Steel Committee, held in July 1977, was attended largely by mid-level bureaucrats. Bureaucratically, the OECD Ad Hoc Steel Committee was an outgrowth of the Wolff Trade Mission a half a year before. It was then that the United States government began to talk to the Japanese and European governments about their "common" problems in the steel sector. Intellectually, however, the OECD steel committee was an outgrowth of the U.S. domestic steel lobby

---

Putnam, Hayes, and Bartlett, Inc. to do several studies on the U.S. steel industry. Several of these have already been referred to. Among the Washington Community, private as well as government, involved in the steel issue, these studies served as important guides to economic details as well as policy recommendations.

pressures on the Administration for sectoral negotiations in the GATT. Since it had already been established that sectoral negotiations in the GATT were unacceptable to the Japanese and the Europeans, as we saw in Chapter 2, the U.S. government promoted them in the OECD. And, it will be remembered, this was also consistent with the European request for meetings in the OECD to discuss the world steel trade.

But it is important to note that the United States had begun formal discussions of the global steel issue with its major trading partners before the issue reached "crisis proportions" domestically.[1] An equally important part of that process was to acquaint U.S. policymakers with the global nature of the steel issue -- a great advantage for them once the issue finally exploded into a domestic political crisis. With all that seemed to be happening in the international arena, largely because the issue had been raised by the Europeans and kept there by the Americans in the context of the MTN, the U.S. policy process seemed only to float along until September 1977, when in the words of one Senate staffer: "All hell broke loose."

By September 1977, it had become clear that (1) Steel had been framed as a foreign trade issue, and that any attempt to emphasize other policy arenas would have little

---

[1]Interview, November 6, 1978.

or no backing; and (2) that simply addressing the import issue straight on was both unacceptable, because it would threaten the trade negotiations in Geneva, and in any event, would not be enough. In the immediate term this is exactly what happened, though an important distinction which we shall elaborate in Chapter 5, was made between a "quantitative" approach, and a "pricing" approach.

In September 1977 a series of politically charged domestic events forced the issue to the surface. Steel moved from an issue which had generated a process without any clearly defined decision outcome, to one which, of a sudden, would command a very specific policy resolution. It is true that the Administration had, by September 1977, formalized the OECD discussions, which, in one sense, constituted U.S. policy; but since it still had a largely undefined form, and in any event never pretended to offer benefits in the short term, could not strictly have been considered policy at that time. In a statement by the United States-Japan Trade Council, a lobbying arm of the Japanese MITI located in Washington, D.C., it was evident that Japan, too, believed there was no specific U.S. policy. It reported:

> While the United States government has not adopted any new policy to deal with the position of the American [steel] industry, it has requested discussions in the OECD . . . there is widespread interest and concern about the state of international trade in steel and its future, but there is no significant conflict between the two industries [in the U.S. and Japan] or their

> governments. The problem will continue to be explored at many levels.[1]

It was also true that the Administration had begun to sense, well before September 1977, that a politically sensitive domestic crisis was developing: accordingly, the Administration, largely through officials in Treasury and at the STR's office began to encourage the domestic industry to file antidumping suits as a way of seeking remedy of the import situation. By framing the issue in this way, the Administration got themselves into what turned out to be a rather uncomfortable position -- one which followed them into the development of the specific policy.

Thus, the process had been moving along for at least a year, but, a well-defined policy response came only after the issue had become sufficiently politically tense that (a) the steel lobby began to focus clearly on the domestic impact of the rising imports, (b) the legislation branch became seriously involved, and (c) as a result of what followed from these two, the Administration perceived there was a domestic political crisis which had to be resolved.

---

[1]"No Confrontation on Steel," U.S.-Japan Trade Council Report, No. 30. (Washington, D.C., 1977), p. 1.

The Steel Industry Acts: Plant Closings and Layoffs

The particular events which led to the politicization of the steel issue domestically began in June 1977, when Bethlehem Corporation announced, "[it had] reluctantly decided to permanently close . . . its Lackawanna Plant effective July 31 . . . [and said that] approximately 350 employees will be affected."[1] Significantly the announcement emphasized that employees would be "affected," suggesting that there might be an alternative to direct layoffs. Note also that the announcement did not mention imports as the cause, but referred to "lack of sufficient improvement in demand."[2] By September, however, it had become clear that the industry was playing "hardball" -- forcing a political crisis to which government would have to respond: Bethlehem had laid off, or eliminated, over ten percent of its 90,000 employees, and in a statement by the company's chairman, Lewis W. Foy, attributed "its troubles to . . . the increasing import of foreign steel . . ."[3] Edgar Speer, chairman of United States Steel Corporation, the nation's leading producer, also

---

[1]Bethlehem Steel Corporation Press Release, Bethlehem, Pennsylvania, June 3, 1977.

[2]Labor has consistently expressed concern over how the industry would treat the "marginal plant" issue. For them, there was an important distinction between permanent job loss and temporary layoffs.

[3]Reported in The New York Times, October 1, 1977, pp. 25, 31, "Bethlehem Steel Eliminating 2,500 from Office

focused attention on imports as the prime source of the industry's troubled condition: "The industry's main problem is dumping by foreign producers . . ."[1] and to further emphasize the point he rebuffed President Carter's assessment that one of the industry's problems was its failure to modernize old facilities: "Carter has been very poorly advised on this point."[2]

There was a good deal of industry "jawboning" against the Carter Administration during the first three-fourths of 1977. Predictably, words begot words: discussions in the OECD stepped up -- the Administration hoped to satisfy the industry's demand for sectoral negotiations -- and the Administration appeared to listen more closely at the advisory sector committee meetings. But, the monthly figures of steel imports into the United States were recorded at higher and higher levels as the year wore on. As imports continued to rise, demand stayed depressed, and capacity utilization rates recorded at all-time low levels, the industry decided to lay off workers and close plants so that their profits might be

---

Staff." At that time, there was still attention focused on non-import factors. The industry argued, "Washington's tendency to hold down the price of American steel, the rising cost of labor and materials, and spending needs to meet environmental standards."

[1]The Washington Post, October 1, 1977, "Strauss Indicates Reversal on U.S. Steel Imports Policy."

[2]Ibid.

salvaged.[1] The following chart lists job-losses in 1977. Note that the vast majority of job losses were concentrated in the Northeast-Midwest section of the country. This heavy concentration contributed to the political tensions; it is especially difficult to absorb job losses in this section of the country where there are generally higher rates of unemployment and older dying industries then in the healthier and more vibrant sections of the country.

There is little doubt that once these decisions to lay off workers and close plants had been reached in the board rooms of the major steel companies, the exact timing was carefully planned in order to provide the maximum political benefits. Indeed, it is not unreasonable to speculate that the timing of these layoffs were planned to coincide with a time when they could score the maximum political advantages -- the new Administration was fully operating by then so that the effects would not be lost on a confused bureaucracy which couldn't appreciate the importance of such actions, and the MTN seemed to be approaching a very critical stage.

But, there also seems to have been an economic argument for taking these measures when they did. In the first place, there was a provision in the pension fund agreements for a number of the larger companies which would have cost close to a half billion dollars had the layoffs

---

[1]See below for elaboration of this point. Note, however, that other factors, like the Johnstown Flood contributed to plant closings.

STEEL PLANT CLOSINGS AND JOB LOSSES, 1977

Firm	Location	Job Losses
	STEEL MILL PRODUCTS (SIC 331)	
Youngstown Sheet & Tube	Youngstown, Ohio	4,100
Taylor, Winnfield	Warren, Ohio	300
Jones & Laughlin	Niles, Ohio	170
U.S. Steel	McDonald, Ohio	160
Bethlehem Steel	Johnstown, Pennsylvania	2,900
Bethlehem Steel	Bethlehem, Pennsylvania	115
Alan Wood	Conschohoken, Pennsylvania	3,000
Washburn Wire	S. Philadelphia, Pennsylvania	500
Phoenix Steel	Phoenixville, Pennsylvania	660
Jones & Laughlin	S. Pittsburgh, Pennsylvania	500
Bethlehem Steel	S. San Francisco, California	320
Bethlehem Steel	Richmond, California	180
Kaiser Steel	Fontana, California	300
S.W. Steel Rolling Mills	Los Angeles, California	150
Bethlehem Steel	Lackawanna, New York	3,850
Jones & Laughlin	Warren, Michigan	550
Tennessee Forging	Newport, Arkansas	160
Tennessee Forging	Harrison, Tennessee	300
U.S. Steel	Fairfield, Alabama	180
U.S. Steel	Baytown, Texas	400
C.F.& I.	Pueblo, Colorado	150
		18,945

Source: Various steel companies and United Steelworkers of America

taken place after December 31, 1977. Second, it made sense to lay off the great bulk of workers in 1977; once the companies recognized that economic conditions were forcing some considerable amount of layoffs, it made economic sense to take the entire writeoff in 1977, thereby setting the foundation for an even better year in 1978.

If words begot words, it made sense that action would beget action. When two plants were closed in Ohio -- one being the famous Youngstown Sheet and Tube Plant,[1] and layoffs were announced at facilities in Illinois, New York, other parts of Ohio, and Pennsylvania, all in a matter of a three week period in late September and early October 1977, steel immediately became a priority issue for the Administration. The importance of these plant closings and layoffs -- producing the "Youngstown Effect" -- was in their social and political costs to government. High unemployment combined with high levels of inflation was already creating a political untenable situation for President Carter's domestic policy. The Administration could not afford to have it look that it was doing nothing about the unemployment in the steel industry. It was this more than anything which forced

---

[1]The name "Youngstown" is closely associated with steel. President Truman's attempt at seizing the steel mills of all the major companies involved in a labor dispute with USW in 1952 was challenged in the Supreme Court case, Youngstown, Sheet and Tube Co. vs. Sawyer. See, for

the Administration to make specific policy decisions. At once, there was no doubt that the situation at home was more urgent than the one abroad: either one, if not handled with appropriate sensitivity, could lead to the unravelling of the MTN.

As Jack Sheehan, legislative direction for the United Steelworkers of America put it, Youngstown meant that ". . . the Administration needed a highly visible, public, steel policy"[1] to offset the social and political costs that were accruing from industry's decisions. Sheehan's view was confirmed by a high level official at Treasury who was instrumental both in developing the Trigger Price System, and in the U.S. participation in the OECD steel discussions. He characterized the domestic political situation in September 1977 as "precarious," and said that in their minds "the layoffs and plant closings were tagged to trade-related problems and had to be treated accordingly."[2] The industry's claim gained more credibility when Bethlehem announced its first loss in 18 years, and United States Steel reported that its earnings were down by 52 percent for the first half of 1977.

---

example, Maeva Marcus, Truman and the Steel Seizure Case: The Limits of Presidential Power (New York: Columbia University Press, 1977).

[1]Interview, December 4, 1978.

[2]Interview, November 6, 1978.

The Steel Lobby Presses the Administration

Even before September 1977, there were a number of policies proposed by the steel lobby. But not all were consistent with one another. For example, the industry pointed to the possible use of "quotas, tariffs, or countervailing duties . . . [to] halt certain unfair trading practices."[1] At the same time, however, they hedged on the overall benefits of tariffs or quotas, since they believed that "applying these remedies . . . across the board . . . may not be the best long-term answer."[2] Understandably, part of the explanation for these apparent contradictions was in the confusion over the long-term and short-term dilemma. No one knew what the appropriate answers were, nor how exactly to fit short-term and long-term solutions together. In any case, it was clear throughout that no policy would be adopted if the Administration believed it would jeopardize the MTN. And this, in its turn, depended on the reaction of its trading partners.

But neither industry nor labor were clear on whether quotas were the correct approach. Previous experience had demonstrated that "they [quotas] are easily evaded by foreign countries and can even be harmful during periods

---

[1]"Report to the President on Prices and Costs in the United States Steel Industry," Council on Wage and Price Stability, October 1977, p. 17.

[2]Ibid.

of economic decline."[1] The industry also expressed the fear that enforcement of quotas "would invite the government to participate even more than it does today in the management of our business."[2] Understandably, the industry has always preferred solutions which preserve both the free market system, and their autonomy -- keeping the government as far away from their board rooms as possible.[3]

An equally important explanation for the lobby's apparent equivocation on the question of "direct imposition of quotas," however, was a debate between industry and labor over the appropriate emphasis on policy. Although it is true that industry and labor presented a publicly united front, and in fact had formed a coalition, which would have seemed incomprehensible in the pre-1963 period, there was something of a family squabble that may yet become divisive.[4] In the course of examining the various approaches proposed by industry and labor,

---

[1]David M. Roderick, President of U.S. Steel, "U.S. Steel Position Paper," issued at the U.S. Steel Regional Stockholders Meeting," Washington, D.C., November 18, 1977.

[2]Ibid.

[3]Not so surprisingly, industry and labor diverge on their view about government involvement. This divergence is similar to the relationships in Europe, though not as polarized. See my Chapter 3, on European Steel.

[4]As an example, consider this trialogue among Mr. Collins of the AISI, Jack Sheehan of the USW, and Congressman Long, Chairman of the Foreign Operations Subcommittee of the Committee on Appropriations.

"Mr. Sheehan . . . I do know that our own steel industries are most reluctant to want to receive the

therefore, we shall gain insights into the sociology of the steel lobby as well.

In oversimplified terms, the difference in form stemmed from a difference in emphasis from one on profits versus one on job preservation. For example, labor had

---

same kind of offer of assistance from our own Federal government . . . .

"Mr. Long . . . I suppose the feeling . . . is that this would lead to regulation.

"Mr. Sheehan . . . some Communities are dependent on the continued existence of the steel mill, and when they close down, like in Youngstown and they may want to build in other places in the country, it is a tragedy to the workers in those areas, and if what is needed is some kind of federal loan guarantee program, I don't think it should be criticized, let alone rejected.

"Mr. Long . . . Isn't it difficult to know when to stop on something like this? As soon as you provide a loan guarantee for one firm in one area, aren't you giving that firm unfair competitive advantage over some other part of the domestic steel industry, and don't they have to get the same loan guarantee, so you can't pick up one firm like Youngstown Sheet and Tube and give that a loan guarantee and expect it to stop there.

"Mr. Collins . . . Looking overall at the question of subsidies for foreign steel industries, I think it is fair to point out that the steel industries in the worst shape today are those which have received massive direct subsidies from their governments. Examples are the Italian steel industry, which is fifty percent owned, and the British Steel Corporation, which is a State corporation. There is some correlation between subsidized steel industries and their lack of ability to compete in world steel. Does the inability to compete trigger the subsidy or, indeed, does the subsidy accentuate the inability to compete?

Our steel industry views it from that perspective, and suggests that the way to do business is to accurately reflect the comparative advantage of the particular industry in prices over the long term, which means full cost pricing over the cycle including steel from Europe and Japan entering our market, and then let everybody compete in the world capital market for expansion funds on the basis of his true advantage, not an artificial one."

expressed a preference for "an orderly marketing agreement [which] established quantitative or quota arrangements to stabilize and prevent further damage to employment and disruption to domestic markets."[1]

Of course, both industry and labor agreed that government should act to limit import penetration. But, labor wanted other aspects of the issue addressed; "commitments by the industry," for example, "to modernize at their existing locations."[2] These were added to those fully supported by the industry; "a long range international safeguard mechanism to provide automatic responses in the future that will prevent harmful disruptions."[3]

Predictably, the steelworkers were more interested in job security than profit statements. Accordingly, in their October 6, 1977, Policy Statement, the steelworkers set forth as their primary concern:

> [T]he jobs of our members, the impact of job losses on their communities and states, the

---

I think it is fair to say that labor would place greater emphasis on what Jack Sheehan has called the "social value," or job losses which come from "marginal plants." United States House of Representatives, 95th Congress, 2d Session, Foreign Assistance and Related Agencies Appropriations for 1979, Hearings before a subcommittee of the Committee on Appropriations, Part 4, "United States Subsidy of Foreign Steel Producers"; especially see pp. 117-26.

[1]"Unemployment in the Steel Industry," Washington, D.C., December 2, 1977.

[2]Ibid. pp. 18, 19.

[3]Ibid.

> present state of the national economy, and the relationship of the Basic Steel Industry to our national security.[1]

What the steelworkers feared as much as anything was that "temporary layoffs" would turn into "permanent job losses"; the "steelworker's nightmare" was that industry would accept a short-term solution -- which could be quotas without contingencies about maintaining employment levels -- to boost its profits just enough such that particular companies could begin to invest in other, more viable, and generally healthier nonsteel divisions. Thus, labor emphasized a long-term commitment to the steel industry qua steel, while the industry seemed more content with a shorter-term solution. For example, industry would have been more ready to accept a policy of quotas at a level which would ensure profits, and accept a loss in their share of the U.S. market in the longer term.

It is not at all surprising that steel executives think that way. But, it is also understandable that labor would be concerned with long-term employment prospects in the steel industry itself.

Thus, labor wanted the commitment that industry would invest, not only in steel divisions of their companies, but in established steel communities where their membership lived. Or, as one labor leader put it, "Keep the money in Youngstown." Indeed, their fears were

---

[1] Ibid.

not unfounded. Take as an illustration the remarks of the vice president and general manager of U.S. Steel's Eastern Division: "You can't put a lot of money into an old factory which is based in a bad geographical location."[1]

The policy implications for labor's central concern had also shifted during the ten year period from 1967, when the United States negotiated its first voluntary restraint agreement with Japan. "The emphasis," in 1977, according to Jack Sheehan, legislative director for the United Steelworkers of America, "[has been] on the marginal plant problems . . . which leads to termination and permanent job losses . . . it is a basic problem of industrial adjustment."[2] In their conference in December 1977, labor listed "low demand," "High imports," and "marginal plants" as the three major problems in American steel industry. This is substantially different from their emphasis in 1967 on generally healthy conditions in the steel industry.

By 1977, labor had realized that their interests lie in maintaining existing steel plants as much as a healthy industry itself. This was clearly illustrated in the debate quoted above in footnote four, page , on U.S. loans to foreign steel plants, between Mr. Sheehan of the

---

[1]"U.S. Steel to Lose Youngstown Mills," _New York Times_, January 4, 1978, pp. 51, 54.

[2]Interview, December 14, 1978.

USW and Mr. Jim Collins, an economist for the American Iron and Steel Institute. Mr. Sheehan supported government loans to the steel industry in the United States if such a strategy could maintain existing facilities. Collins, representing industry, opposed this strategy. This is the only time during this author's two years of following the steel issue that tempers flared between the two factions of the steel lobby coalition.

Labor's peculiar position -- dependence on a healthy steel industry in those parts of the country where employment was highest, even more than industry, resulted in a somewhat more cautious and sometimes more desperate position than industry's with regard to the policy options; they continually protected the status quo of American industry against rising imports, as well as future decisions of steel management with regard to investment, rationalization, and modernization decisions. They worried as much about how industry would treat the marginal plant condition, as they did about imports.

In truth, the debate within the steel lobby over emphasis was not crucial for the development of policy in 1978, though it does highlight an important development in the sociology of steel management-labor relations. Its particular manifestation during the 1976-78 steel crisis lasted until the White House meeting on October 13, 1977. Until that time, the industry had promoted quotas first. There were alternative strategies such as the "orderly marketing agreement" -- a program which they said:

> . . . individual country quotas should be established based upon a representative prior period for each country, with the total for all countries not to exceed ten percent of apparent consumption.[1]

As indicated earlier, they also proposed sectoral negotiations in the GATT, the "MFA-like approach," and the 301 case which would have supported "more stringent quotas" on those countries refusing to enter into a steel orderly marketing agreement.[2] The OMA-quota approach was not looked upon very favorably by the Administration. Less than two weeks after the industry proposed it, Ambassador Strauss said, "You can't put everybody in a room and divide up the world market [by] doling out shares. You can take cough medicine that way, but you can't cure steel's problems."[3] And, Commissioner Davignon of the European Community had echoed roughly the same objection: "I do not believe that you can solve problems by restricting markets . . . that will only lead to commercial wards."[4] To both, quotas raised the ugly spectre of neo-mercantalist blocs -- a result everyone wished to avoid.

---

[1]"Steel Trade Recommendations," September 26, 1977, on file with author.

[2]Ibid.

[3]"Policy Search: Carter is Scrambling to Develop a Program to Aid the Steel Industry," Washington Post, October 19, 1977.

[4]U.S.-EEC-Japan Steel Summit Urged," Washington Post, October 12, 1977.

Hence, on October 13, 1977, the Administration and the industry agreed to a quid pro quo: the Carter Administration promised to begin prosecuting antidumping cases more aggressively and the steelmakers aid they would drop their push for import quotas.[1] It is significant that just one day prior to the meeting, Lloyd McBride, president of the United Steelworkers, and leading industry officers, reported that more layoffs and further mill shutdowns were imminent "unless the government acts swiftly."[2] This time they had called for voluntary quotas from Japan and the EEC, to be negotiated through a voluntary restraint agreement. But, such an approach also had little support from the Administration. Rather sarcastically, Ambassador Strauss said of voluntary quotas: "They're hard to monitor and impossible to enforce. It would sound like you got a home run, but what you'd have hit was a Texas leaguer."[3] In fact, this has been the industry's experience, but the industry as well as labor, sought to force President Carter to act. Therefore, they used every available option.

---

[1]"Something of an Understanding on Steel," Washington Post, October 19, 1977.

[2]"More Layoffs Feared Unless U.S. Acts Swiftly," Washington Post, October 12, 1977.

[3]"Carter is Scrambling to Develop a Program to Aid the Steel Industry," Wall Street Journal, October 12, 1977, p. 1.

President Carter's Promise -- The Antidumping Non-Solution

Even while these closings and layoffs were announced, two other factors which contributed to the domestic political crisis began to unfold. The first was an agreement between the Carter Administration and the steel lobby that the issue should be pursued as a violation of the U.S. antidumping code, and the second was Congressional involvement.

The Presidential agreement was made in all the drama of a White House meeting on October 13 -- not a month after the industry began to announce its layoffs -- to which the President had invited executives from the industry, steel labor leaders, Members of Congress from steel districts, and consumer representatives. President Carter committed himself and his Administration to the "vigorous enforcement of the nation's trade laws."[1] In all the splendor of a gathering in the Roosevelt Room of the White House, the President's commitment to enforce the nation's trade laws was also seen as a symbol of a more general commitment to the steel industry. Admittedly, the President hedged his bets somewhat: "We cannot afford to erect trade barriers around our nation,"[2] and characterized import curbs as a "simplistic answer." But, it

---

[1] New York Times, "Steel Leaders at the White House Get Pledge of Aid in Import Crisis," October 14, 1977, p. 1.

[2] Ibid.

is significant that he supported the view that "free trade has got to be fair trade," a slogan which had become synonomous with a tough trade policy against dumping and foreign governments' subsidization of exported products.

The clear focus of the meeting was to set forth the enforcement of the antidumping laws as the answer to the "import problem," and to convey to the public that the Carter Administration was both sympathetic and responsive to the conditions which led to what appeared to be "massive unemployment" in the steel industry. The steel lobby took the President at his word and began filing the antidumping cases. As one serious observer of global steel trade put it:

> The domestic industry took up the antidumping approach with enthusiasm. By the first week in November, sixteen complaints had been filed covering steel imports of $1.6 billion from nine countries, and it was announced that more were to follow.[1]

Of the cases filed during that period, the two most critical were filed by U.S. Steel against Japan for dumping of sheet, plate, pipe and tubing, and structural steel, and by National Steel against twenty-nine producers in six European countries.[2] Both companies had been preparing their petitions for some months prior to September, but

---

[1]Mathew J. Marks, "Remedies to Unfair Trade: American Action Against Steel Imports," The World Economy, vol. I, no. 2, January 1978 (London: Elsevier); p. 229.

[2]"Dumping Complaint Filed by National," Steel Bulletin, November/December, 1977.

had been reluctant to officially file the complaints because they believed that the political climate was not favorable; until the political climate had changed -- beginning in late September -- the industry assumed that their petitions would be more or less ignored as had been Treasury's practice for "time immemorial."[1] In the wake of the plant closings and layoffs, combined with the Administration's public commitment to the antidumping route, it seemed that the political climate had become more favorable. Indeed, the industry's public position was to shift the burden of responsibility onto the Administration as it was now up to the Administration to do what the President had said they would. Upon filing his company's antidumping petition, George Stinson, chairman of National Steel, said:

> We are taking this action . . . in direct response to press reports that President Carter has pledged . . . a more aggressive enforcement of laws to protect the domestic industry from dumping.[2]

He of course referred specifically to the White House Conference where he reiterated what the President had told them:

> . . . that the "laws against foreign dumping in the American market had not been vigorously enforced," adding: "I have not been aware of this derogation of duty until just this week. We're going to do something about it.[3]

---

[1]Interview, January 23, 1979.

[2]"Dumping Complaint Filed by National."

[3]Ibid.

Thus, the industry gave the antidumping laws a try, and in the majority filed what legal and trade experts considered quality petitions which many thought would be hard for the Administration to reject.

Still, the steel lobby's confidence in pursuing the antidumping alternative was said by some to have been naive. After all, the argument went, no Administration had ever shown any great desire to enforce the antidumping provisions of the Trade Act to the advantage of domestic industry. As Dominic King, Assistant General Counsel for U.S. Steel for twelve years put it:

> The present members of the Treasury Department inherit the transgressions of previous administrations . . . it didn't matter whether it was Democratic or Republican.[1]

Treasury had been accused of favoring importers, and therefore foreign producers, over domestic producers in their desire to promote free trade, and uphold the liberal trading order.

Notwithstanding the industry's frustration with general derogation of enforcement of the trade laws, there was really very little alternative the steel lobby had at the time. Besides, they were reassured by Administration officials that there would be more vigorous enforcement

---

[1]U.S. Congress, House of Representatives, Subcommittee on Trade of the House Ways and Means Committee, Oversight Hearings on the Antidumping Act of 1921, 95th Congress, 1st Session (Washington, D.C.: Government Printing Office, November 1977). p. 74.

of the Antidumping Act. There were at least two reasons to believe them.

First, it was clear that the pressure was great, and in any event the Administration had publicly committed itself.

Second, there was the Gilmore Steel Case that already had tentatively decided (October 3, 1977) in favor of Gilmore -- a small steel company in Oregon. Gilmore had alleged that five Japanese steel companies had "dumped" Carbon Steel Plate[1] and accused them of selling nearly $200 million worth of steel in the American market at "less than fair value." The preliminary determination in favor of Gilmore -- the Treasury had assessed dumping duties of thirty-two percent against the five Japanese producers[2] -- combined with the understanding that "virtually no further imports of Japanese carbon steel plate [had] entered the United States, between the assessment of duties,

---

[1]The five Japanese companies were: Nippon Steel, Nippon Konkan, Sumitomo, Kawasaki Steel, and Kobe Steel, all major producers.

[2]The final determination was announced January 9, 1978, downgraded the "duty assessment" from the original recommendations. Assessments were: Nippon Steel 9.1 percent, Nippon Konkan - 7.3 percent, Sumitomo - 18.5 percent, Kawasaki Steel - 5.4 percent, and Kobe Steel - 13.9 percent, reported in <u>The New York Times</u>, October 10, 1978, "U.S. Penalty Cut in Steel Dumping by the Japanese."

and the time when the industry was asked to accept the antidumping alternative,"[1] added more credibility to the President's alternative than had been warranted in the past.

The Administration's experience in the Gilmore case gave it a sound foundation to argue rather effectively that they were seeking improvements in the enforcement of the antidumping laws which would benefit domestic industries. For example, Gilmore allowed Robert Mundheim, General Counsel for the Department of Treasury to argue persuasively:

> We have built upon our experience in Gilmore to revise the cost of production questionnaires being distributed to the Japanese producers in the U.S. Steel case . . . in relating Gilmore, I am not suggested that it be read as a complete answer to the question of effectiveness; but it is one measure.[2]

Indeed, the Gilmore case did break important conceptual ground in the administration of the antidumping laws. For, as the Gilmore case was being prepared, the Japanese refused to supply necessary data to Treasury, making it impossible to determine "cost of production," and, thus, difficult to determine whether the product was "being sold at less than fair value." So, Treasury constructed Japanese costs on the basis of "known information" -- a concept which would be applied in the

---

[1]Subcommittee on Trade Oversight of the Antidumping Act of 1921, November 1977, p. 11.

[2]Ibid., pp. 7, 9.

Administration's development of the trigger price system. The efforts to determine "fair value" were read by the steel lobby as indications that the Administration might well be more sympathetic to their antidumping petitions than had been the case in previous Administrations.

As indicated in Chapter 2,[1] however, the Administration quickly realized that the antidumping route for the whole of the U.S. steel industry was a non-solution, Gilmore or no Gilmore. In the words of an economics officer at the Department of State, "It would have been like enforcing a zero percent quota -- practically no foreign steel could be exported to this market."[2] The same Foreign Service officer, who also represented State at the interagency steel task force meetings, admitted that they believed it would have "staggering implications . . . excluding over 75 percent of European and Japanese steel . . . and would have an undesirable and destabilizing effect" on our trading partners.[3] Thus, State's position, framed in rather melodramatic terms -- "that the whole structure of European civilization would cave in" -- won easy support from Treasury, which also believed that strict enforcement of the antidumping laws in this case would put unbearable strains on the liberal trading order. When the

---

[1]See my Chapter 2.

[2]Interview, November 2, 1978.

[3]Interview, November 2, 1978.

STR's office acknowledged same, the position against strict enforcement of the antidumping laws prevailed.[1]

So the Administration altered its position accordingly -- a position characterized by one industry leader in rather bitter terms: "The Administration has apparently turned away from the courses they had urged on us . . . they said they would enforce them . . . . I'm somewhat surprised . . .[2] But most accepted the Administration's switch and simply used the petitions, as well as the antidumping concept generally to apply even stronger political leverage for other concessions.

Congress -- A Powerful Guardian for the Steel Lobby

The second domestic factor contributing to the domestic politicization of the steel issue was Congressional involvement. Other than the special provisions for steel in the Trade Act of 1974, the Congress hadn't gotten involved in the steel issue since 1971, when Chairman Wilbur Mills of the House Ways and Means Committee promoted an extension of the 1968 voluntary

---

[1]Interview, November 9, 1978. "Automobiles" and "steel" indicate that antidumping laws cannot adequately deal with "massive dumping."

[2]Quoting Richard P. Simmons, President of Allegheny Ludlum Steel, in the *New York Times*, November 15, 1977, "The Issue of Steel Imports: A Deepening Controversy."

agreement between the United States and Japan.[1]

The proximate cause of sudden Congressional interest in the steel issue can be traced to a well-orchestrated several-pronged lobbying effort by the steel lobby. Predictably, the effort was directed especially at Representatives and Senators from "steel states," notably, Ohio, Pennsylvania, West Virginia, New York, and Illinois. As an illustration, Charles Vanik, chairman of the House Ways and Means Subcommittee on International Trade, and a Representative from Ohio, was an obvious target for Congressional lobbying. As if to confirm the relationship between "the lobbying effort," which emphasized loss of jobs, and subsequent Congressional action, Vanik cautioned the Administration that, "The only way the Congressional pressure will ease is to get the men back to work."[2]

Indeed, Congressional pressure on the Administration grew in direct proportion to the amount of pressure the steel lobby put on them, either by knocking on their doors and asking for help, or by closing down more plants. The common thread which justified the linkage between job losses, steel lobby pressure on the Congress, and Congressional pressure on the Administration, was the well-documented fact that imports were steadily rising.

---

[1]William Hogan, The 1970s: The Critical Years for Steel, Chapter 3.

[2]Reported in the New York Times, "Administration Plans to Cut Import Flood Backed by U.S. Steel," November 12, 1977.

Unless organized, however, Congressional energies, even over a specific issue such as steel, can be diffused and therefore lose a good deal of its effectiveness. By effectiveness, one refers to the degree to which the Congress can illicit adequate responses from the Administration. For, in the steel issue, as with most foreign policy crisis situations,[1] most Congressmen intuitively realized that their power to actually effect policy is limited unless they enter into a relationship with the Administration.

There are two points here: first, it is true that the Congress had the ability and authority to make laws -- a very powerful tool indeed. As a practical matter, however, the Congressional lawmaking process is normally cumbersome and unwieldy, not very conducive to responding quickly. Even if this flaw could be overcome, however, the President still has the final word, and it is therefore appropriate to think of the two as more or less equal partners in the law-making process. As one freshman Congressman upon arriving in Washington put it: "I've been lobbied more by the Administration on more things, than by any other interest groups."[2] The reverse is true as well: Congressional offices tend to talk more to the

---

[1]We use the term "crisis" loosely.

[2]Discussion with Joel Aberbach, at Brookings Institution, revealed this.

Administration, on more subjects, than to all other interest groups combined.

Second, it is the Administration, and not the Congress, which has the power to seek "administrative remedies." In the case of steel where the level of pressure was very high, a short-term relief approach seemed to fit more appropriately than the longer term law-making process. Certain aspects of the law-making process were used by Congress to put pressure on the Administration, i.e., hearings, bills, floor speeches, etc.

In this second case, the Congressional-Executive relationship is not quite one of equals -- Congress really plays the role of a lobbying group, using its institutional powers, but usually not acting as an institution. The Congress becomes the advocate for constituent interests with regard to the Administration in a similar way that lobbyists represent their clients' interests to the Congress.

This kind of relationship developed in no small part because Congress wanted it that way.[1] It is much easier, and probably politically wiser, for Congress to avoid taking ultimate responsibility for trade matters. The politics of trade, as Messrs, Bauer, Pool and Dexter[2]

---

[1]This relationship has been enduring in this direction since the 1930s, see, my chapter 1, p.

[2]Bauer, Pool, and Dexter, American Business and Public Policy.

point out, is most often a losing proposition. It is highly unlikely that a Representative -- Senator or Member of the House -- will not find both sides of a trade issue represented in his district. It is in his interest, therefore, to promote a system where he can play both sides of the issue -- "to protect himself," as I.M. Destler put it.[1] Such "positioning," as it were, is only possible if the ultimate responsibility for policy is fluffed off -- to the Administration. It will be noted, for example, that in all its "noisemaking" over the steel issue, the Congress hasn't once acted as a body, taking legislative responsibility for the issue. As we shall see, even the Senate and House Steel Caucuses may be seen as buffers -- an ad hoc committee created outside of the legislative process qua legislature, however much it may have been a very real manifestation of Congressional interest and concern for a very sensitive issue. This is not to suggest that individual Congressman, and groups of Congressmen, didn't play real and significant roles in the development of the policy for steel. Rather, we are suggesting that Congress as a body chose not to enter the fray -- passing a steel quota bill, or amending the trade laws themselves -- and instead pushed the Administration

---

[1] I.M. Destler, "Protection for Congress? The Politics of Trade Policy," prepared as background for the June 26, 1978 meeting of the Joint Discussion Group on Executive-Congressional Relations, the Council on Foreign Relations and the Carnegie Endowment for International Peace.

toward developing administrative solutions[1] to manage the effects of other governments' policies on the U.S. market.

So beginning in September 1977, when the issue exploded politically, the Congress pursued the course which pressured the Administration to take certain remedial administrative actions. Probably the best illustration of this occurred during the House antidumping hearings held in November. Chairman Vanik, and other members of the committee, were emphasizing the point to an Administration witness from Treasury's legal office, that the Treasury should apply the antidumping laws more vigorously. The chairman asked why Treasury was not "self-initiating" dumping proceedings, as was their right under the trade laws in cases where dumping was obvious. Upon receiving a "non-answer," Vanik, in somewhat dramatic fashion for the normally boring Congressional hearings, scribbled off a request to Treasury, and signed it with four other colleagues who happened to be at the hearing. The hand-written petition, on Agriculture Committee notepaper, read:

> We the undersigned members of the trade sub-committee hereby petition the Treasury Department to investigate the dumping in the U.S. of British Steel which is injuring or likely to injure, the domestic steel industry.

---

[1]Part of the reason for this was also to wait for MTN-implementing legislation.

> The other essential information appears on page #12306 and 7 of the Congressional Record of 11/3/77.[1]

As indicated above, Congressman Vanik, and his colleagues, were clearly more interested in pressuring the Administration, than in amending the trade laws.

By emphasizing Administrative remedies, the Congress was able to ensure that the burden of responsibility went to the President, a burden which, in any case, was already there, but could have shifted had the Congress acted differently. It was, of course, easier for the Congress to follow that line, and it was ultimately justifiable since the Executive is better equipped to resolve foreign policy issues -- trade, security, or others -- than the Legislature. And in the case of steel, the steel lobby had already gone to the Administration, and expected it to respond to the impending conditions anyway. But, the Congress did play a critical role.

Serious Congressional consideration of the steel issue began on September 20, 1977, when the House Subcommittee on International Trade held hearings "to obtain information on world steel trade -- current trends and structural problems."[2] Chairman Vanik set the tone for

---

[1]Subcommittee on Trade Oversight Hearings on the Antidumping Act of 1921, November 1977. Original on file with author. Other Congressmen who signed the petition were: Frenzel, Steiger, Jones, and Rostenkowski, all members of the House Trade Subcommittee who attended the hearings.

[2]United States House of Representatives, World Steel Trade: Current Trends and Structural Problems, p. 1.

the hearings in his opening statement by emphasizing the "social" effects of the steel situation. He said that the hearings were held for the purpose of:

> . . . developing information on a growing crisis in the American scene affecting the American steel industry. [He said that] the newspapers carry accounts of cuts in production plans, reduced employment, and plant closings, and the termination of plans for replacement of steel production facilities in the U.S.
>
> These decisions will have a traumatic effect throughout this country and a disastrous effect in the specific areas in which these plants and facilities are located.[1]

Thus began the process of focusing Congressional attention on the issue, and of signalling to the Administration that the Congress was serious about it. Typically, the House, rather than the Senate, held hearings; Representatives, more than Senators, hold hearings on any number of detailed subjects which the Senate may consider in broader, more general terms. In part, this reflects a different relationship between the Representative, or Senator, and the electorate: the Representative is always running for office and is more disposed to play to what might be called "the whims of his electorate."

In addition, the difference in the committee structure between the House and Senate -- where the House tends to have more subcommittees with "real" responsibilities -- makes it more likely that the House will

---

[1]Ibid, p. 2.

address a greater number of issues since its subcommittees hold mark-ups, and vote on legislation. This is particularly true of the difference between the Senate Finance Subcommittee on International Trade, which defers to the full committee on substantive matters, and the House Ways and Means Subcommittee on Trade which performs "real functions" such as mark-ups and committee votes.[1]

In the case of steel, the peculiar fact that Congressman Vanik was chairman of the relevant committee also played an important part in the different attitudes between the trade subcommittee on the House side, and its counterpart in the Senate. While Chairman Vanik's political fortunes were tied to steel since he came from the steel state of Ohio, and had at least one major company's plant in his district, Senator Ribicoff, chairman of the Senate Subcommittee on International Trade, had no troubled steel constituents in his State of Connecticut to shake his undying support for "free trade." Senator Long, chairman of the full Senate Finance Committee also had no "special interest" in steel. Therefore, as we shall see below, the Senate Steel Caucus provided the framework for Senate discussions and actions on the steel issue.

---

[1]While there is no institutional rule which determines that the Senate Finance Committee be structured as centrally as it has been over the past decade, its present chairman, Russell Long (D-La.) has successfully run it that way.

The House and Senate Steel Caucuses

Since the Senate wasn't afforded the institutional convenience of a Vanik as chairman of the trade subcommittee, however, Senators perhaps placed a greater emphasis on their "Steel Caucus," than did the House. So, it was understandable that the first "senatorial" act regarding the steel issue came in the form of a "Deal Colleague" letter from the two Ohio Senators, John Glenn and Howard Metzenbaum, both Democrats from the state which experienced the largest number of plant closings.

On September 23, 1977, the Glenn-Metzenbaum letter arrived in the other ninety-eight offices; it began, "As we are certain you are aware, substantial foreign steel imports . . . are having serious effects on the domestic steel industry . . ."[1] The letter went on to list the events in Ohio, which, it said, "indicate what may lie ahead for the national steel picture."[2] In predictable Congressional fashion, the letter then highlighted the worst of these events, appealing to their colleagues intuitive understanding about the relationship between job losses and their own political futures:

---

[1]In personal files of author. Please see Appendix for comments on notes referring to personal files.

[2]In personal files of author.

> Youngstown Sheet and Tube announced an immediate layoff of 5,000-6,000 people in Ohio; Armco Steel in Middletown, Ohio is terminating six hundred employees, and Wheeling-Pittsburgh is threatening severe cutbacks along the Ohio River communities . . .[1]

The rule of thumb is that Senate offices will pay close attention to an issue when a couple hundred, or more, jobs are at stake; there were a number of steel states which had already been alerted by their respective constituencies that similar levels of job losses were imminent for them. And still other Senators emphathized because they had experienced similar conditions in other sectors. Thus, Glenn and Metzenbaum ended their letter by inviting Senators to a meeting "to participate in the formation of a bi-partisan caucus of Senators interested in the American steel industry."[2]

Two days later another "Dear Colleague" letter arrived on each Senator's desk, this time from Senators Heinz of Pennsylvania and Randolph of West Virginia. The purpose of this one was the same as the Glenn-Metzenbaum letter, with one difference: it was meant primarily to appeal to the steel constituencies in Pennsylvania and West Virginia instead of Ohio. And, one day latter on September 27, still a third letter came around, this time from the four -- Glenn, Metzenbaum, Heinz, and Randolph. It reemphasized the "tragic and disastrous developments

---

[1]In personal files of author.

[2]In personal files of author.

in the steel industry,"[1] and announced that one, coordinated meeting would be held.

So on September 28, 1977, the Senate steel caucus was formed thereby creating the institutional framework through which organized senatorial efforts on the steel issue would be channeled. Nineteen Senators, plus staff from over thirty other offices, attended.[2] The Administration sent up the President's Special Trade Representative, Ambassador Robert Strauss, which gave two important signals: first, that the President was serious, for it was common knowledge around Washington that Strauss had become one of Carter's top advisors;[3] and second, that the Administration viewed the issue as a foreign trade one, even though the steel lobby, and the Congress, showed some interest in non-trade areas such as the high cost of environmental regulations.

The Administration was wise in responding to the Senate's first formal coordinated effort with an appropriate level of concern. But, the Senate was also clever:

---

[1]In personal files of author.

[2]More Senators might have attended, but the Metzenbaum-Abourezk filibuster on the Natural Gas Bill, kept a number of Senators on the floor of the Senate who might have attended the Steel Caucus meeting.

[3]_The Washington Post Magazine_, March 19, 1978 "Bob Strauss Reenters Laughing"; also see "America's Chief Horsetrader," _Wall Street Journal_, February 13, 1978, editorial page.

skillfully, the Senate Steel Caucus had made Senator Jennings Randolph its chairman. Randolph was an elder statesman, and thereby accorded proper senatorial courtesy. But more importantly, he was a senior member of the Senate, and chairman of the public works committee, one of the powerful few to whom any Administration would look for support on a whole range of issues. Since Randolph didn't have the obviously high level of constituent interest of a Heinz, Metzenbaum, or Glenn, making him chairman avoided potential resentment among those who could have argued equal right for chairmanship if it were based solely on constituent interest, in addition to lending a greater degree of strength and respectability to the caucus in its relationship with the Administration.

Even though the House channeled much of its energies through Vanik's subcommittee, a House steel caucus was formed on September 22 and took several important initiatives. By September 28, it had already met three times: an organizational meeting on September 22 attended by seventy Members (which increased to 170 over the next few weeks), and two more over the next week, from which specific policy recommendations came.

Predictably, the chairman of the House Steel Caucus was Charles J. Carney, Representative from the 19th District in Ohio, which included Youngstown. In a letter to the President on September 27, the House Steel Caucus stated that the purpose of its first meeting was to "discuss the Administration's policy with respect to steel imports."[1] It is significant that the House caucus didn't even mention non-trade issues. In addition, the President was informed of two resolutions:

> That the United States Delegation to the Meeting of the Ad Hoc Group on Steel advise the Members of that Organization of the urgent need for multilateral action on the world steel problem and urge the member States to join in a Washington meeting on this issue before mid-October.[2]

And, the second one resolved:

> That the President direct his Special Trade Representative for Trade Negotiations immediately to undertake international efforts to seek restraints on exports of steel to the United States under section 107 of the Trade Act of 1974.[3]

From the Senate steel caucus meeting came similar commitments -- to resolve the steel issue, and an endorsement of a resolution which was subsequently introduced into the full Senate by Senator Heinz. Heinz's resolution said that the "American steel industry is facing an unprecedented crisis . . . suffered layoffs of more than 12,000 workers."[4] And it underscored "the dumping of imports subsidized by foreign governments into this country" as a "major contributing factor."[5] It blamed

---

[1]In personal files of author.

[2]In personal files of author.

[3]In personal files of author.

[4]In personal files of author.

[5]In personal files of author.

the immediate crisis on the "failure of Treasury to be sufficiently aggressive in pursuing dumping complaints by the American industry,"[1] and also accused "the office of the Special Trade Representative of the failure to resolve a complaint alleging a violation of section 301 of the Trade Act of 1974 by the European Coal and Steel Community and the Japanese Ministry of International Trade and Industry."[2] It therefore resolved that:

> The Senate reaffirms its support for existing laws restricting unfair or subsidized competition from imports, particularly the Antidumping Act of 1921 and the Trade Act of 1974, and urge the President to direct federal agencies, particularly the Treasury and the Office of the Special Trade Representative to enforce vigorously and aggressively existing laws to prevent cases of dumping, trade discrimination, and other forms of unfair competition that have an adverse impact on the American steel industry.[3]

The similarities in how the House and Senate framed the steel issue is easily explained: both were briefed by the same steel lobby, and both were playing to the same audience, for the same audience, i.e., to the president for the steel lobby. A thick, rather thorough packet entitled "Points for Consideration by the Steel Caucus" was put together by the American Iron and Steel Institute for distribution to Congressmen through the companies located in their respective states, or regions.

---

[1]In personal files of author.

[2]In personal files of author.

[3]In personal files of author.

As an illustration, one cover letter from National Steel to its New York delegation emphasized "National Steel employs 500 people in your State where jobs may be jeopardized if something can't be done . . ."[1] The steel "caucus information packet" began by listing the "remedies needed by the domestic steel industry to [solve] its multifaceted problems."[2] Clearly, the industry's intention was to frame the issue in terms of a crisis, and argue that an immediate solution should be applied. Accordingly, Congressmen were told that "this summary is designed to give a quick blueprint of what is needed NOW!"[3] And in a section called "Steel Trade Recommendations," the message was that the American industry had been victimized by its trading partners:

> The steel industry needs immediate relief from rapidly increasing steel imports exported to the United States market a predatory prices by foreign producers, seeking to alleviate unemployment and the deteriorating financial position of their own industries.[4]

Imports and international trade were not the only topics -- environment, taxation, and miscellaneous also appeared -- but trade concerns were listed first, and were

---

[1]Letter from National Steel to Senator Daniel P. Moynihan (D.-N.Y.) in personal files of author. (Similar letters with attachments went to all members of the Senate and House Steel Caucuses.)

[2]Ibid.

[3]Ibid.

[4]In personal files of author.

most lengthy. Its message was roughly the same as the Steel Caucus resolutions; "The caucus should demand of the President import relief which he can unilaterally or by agreement with the foreigners effect."[1] The industry then set forth what essentially constituted a strategy:

> Simultaneously with such demand, legislation imposing some form of quantitative limitation on steel imports should be introduced, pressed -- and if the President fails to act within a matter of two or three weeks -- enacted by Congress.[2]

It is not uncommon for interest groups or lobbies to issue position papers, talk to Congressmen, and recommend exact legislative language. It is uncommon, however, for them to be so successful. The Public Relations Counsel for the American Institute for Imported Steel -- the American steel industry's domestic adversary -- summed it up in a plea to a Congressional staffer:

> There hasn't been a lobby in the history of the Congress as powerful as the steel lobby . . . we [steel importers] leap at any chance to talk to anyone from a Congressional delegation. We're in hot water . . . and we're trying very hard to win friends in Congress.[3]

An important indication of the steel lobby's strength was its ability to translate their own pressures on the Administration into legislative proposals. In

---

[1]In personal files of author.

[2]In personal files of author.

[3]Interview, November 26, 1978.

addition to those proposals generated by the House and Senate Steel Caucuses, there were a number of bills introduced by individual Congressmen; over twenty bills had been introduced into both Houses.[1] Though all lay idle in committees, there was at least the threat that Congress could begin to act on any one of them at any time. Each posed a different kind of problem for the Administration, but all were linked in some way to the MTN. There were a number of bills designed to place quotas on steel imports at levels determined by the President or Cabinet Secretaries. Some frontally assaulted presidential authority by writing specific amounts of quota levels into the law; still others sought to tighten the antidumping procedures which would have applied to all industries, including steel; and then there was a "Buy American" bill which would have extended the Federal government procurement rules to state and local government procurement activities. Each of these would have affected the negotiating powers of the Carter Administration in Geneva.

The Administration looked upon two other categories of bills as more serious threats: first, there were those

---

[1]The fact that none of the bills became law, indeed few were even considered in Committee, supports this author's contention that the Congress has chosen not to act in trade matters as a body. Rather, it leaves policy decisions to the Executive. But, because of constituent pressure, it must go through the motions of "developing policy alternatives" for United States international trade.

which would have increased the tariffs on certain iron and steel products and which would have provided for increased rates when imports moved above a stated quota level. Since tariff concessions, especially at this stage in the negotiations, represented a central feature of the MTN exercise and were seen by the other major participants in the MTN as an act of "good faith" with regard to the overall MTN objectives, such a law would have damaged the negotiating process in Geneva.

Finally, there was a bill introduced by the chairman of the House Steel Caucus, Representative Carney, which was linked directly to the key controversy over steel at the MTN -- sectoral negotiations. The purpose of Carney's bill was to push for separate steel sector negotiations at the MTN; the bill would have "prohibit[ed] bargaining on any steel tariff until a steel sector trade agreement is reached which establish[ed] international safeguards against steel market disruptions."[1] Representative Carney's bill sought to link the United States reductions on duties or tariffs on steel mill products at the MTN to international guidelines, monitoring procedures, and safeguard provisions for steel, each of which were to be achieved through separate sectoral negotiations. Since the Europeans and Japanese had already made it clear

---

[1]Representative Carney's bill number was H.R.10039. It never became law. Interestingly, Representative Carney (D.-Ohio) was defeated in the 1978 election.

that they would not negotiate a separate sector for steel in the MTN,[1] the Carney bill caused Administration officials particular consternation. What made the Carney bill so troublesome to the Administration was that it echoed the position which the industry already had made clear in their initial Advisory Sector Report in 1975: "The industry seeks to have a multilateral safeguard agreement for steel concluded as a first and principal objective within the steel sector negotiations."[2]

They had not only not given up, but had channeled their demands into legislative form. Of course, this was true of all the legislation which had been introduced. Yet, very little was actually done to push any of the bills through committee for floor consideration. Congress was a willing partner in the coalition which made it virtually impossible for the Administration to continue to "do nothing," but, as in the Burke-Hartke bill of the 93rd Congress, Congress was still unwilling to make policy itself.

In the next section we shall look at still another method the Congress used to pressure the Administration to satisfy constituent demands.

---

[1]For an elaboration on this point, see my section on "sectoral negotiations" in Chapter 2.

[2]"Industry Communication to Administration Through to the Industrial Sector Advisory Committee, October 1975.

Pressure on the President for the Specialty Steel Decision

In addition to the House and Senate Steel Caucuses, the hearings held by Chairman Vanik and the bills introduced into Congress, there was the review of the specialty steel case which provided an important vehicle for the steel lobby to build momentum for their position in the Congress. Even while institutional support in Congress was building, the Congress had already begun to press the President on the specialty steel issue. As with the Administration, the steel lobby used President Carter's review of the specialty steel case as a way to educate the Congress in the broader steel issue. Though there was interest in the specialty steel issue itself -- in some respects it was considered part of the "big steel" issue -- the underlying motive of the steel industry in promoting it was to generate support for the "big steel" or "carbon steel" issue. For example, the American Iron and Steel Institute didn't play as critical a role as it did in other aspects of the steel issue; a private Washington law firm, and the companies themselves, played a much larger role in soliciting support for the specialty steel case.[1] However, "Big Steel" benefited enormously from the overlap in the time of the two.

---

[1]This is explained partly by the fact that specialty steel companies tend to be independent corporations from "Big Carbon Steel" companies like U.S. Steel, National, and Republic.

As described above, the specialty-steel industry simply wanted to keep the quotas for the period that they had been granted in 1976 under the Ford Administration. Compared to the complexity of the larger steel issue, it was a rather simple matter: the idea was to impress President Carter with the merits of "doing nothing," -- keep the quotas in place -- an objective which it was believed could be reached by organizing enough Congressmen to tell him so. The facts supporting this position were there: the President's own International Trade Commission, in a 1977 study initiated by him, confirmed that the industry deserved the protection it had received under the original judgment in 1976. And, the President's policy advisors were recommending the same.

The industry wanted Congress to reenforce this position. At first, it was not clear which approach would best suit the occasion -- legislation, letters to the President and other relevant policymakers in the Administration, or speeches. One option -- to introduce a resolution or a bill which would affirm the Senate's support -- was discarded on the basis that it was too cumbersome and impractical an approach.

Representatives for the industry had gone to Senator Moynihan since a number of plants were located in New York, and one of the more politically active of the industry's leaders was from his state. Discussions between lobbyists, industry leaders, and Senator Moynihan, led to the decision that a "Steel Colloquy" on the floor of the U.S. Senate, among as many Senators as could be organized, would serve the occasion.

In the event, Moynihan was joined on the floor by se[illegible]teen Senators, and over twenty others who submitted statements for the Record. "Particular attention," as Senator Moynihan put it, [was] addressed to the question of specialty steel,"[1] but it was an occasion on which the Senate could bellow across town to the White House, and across the ocean to our major trading partners, about the larger problems in steel. The steel lobby promoted this, as was evident from a news release which appeared immediately following the Colloquy. It quoted Moynihan as saying:

> Maintaining the quotas which the President has under review would be a clear signal to the rest of the world that the United States will enforce its international trade laws when the competition from abroad is proved to be unfair . . . the nation could no longer afford to sit idly by and countenance the collapse of basic industries like steel.[2]

All participating Senators echoed Moynihan's sentiments. It is not uncommon to find so many Senators on the floor to discuss such a controversial and important issue as steel. But it is almost inconceivable to find

---

[1] Congressional Record, October 19, 1977, Senate Proceedings and Debates of the 95th Congress, 1st Session, pp. S.17259-S.17265.

[2] News Release of the Specialty Steel Industry of the United States and the United Steelworkers of America, October 19, 1977, "Senators Ask President to Keep Quotas on Specialty Steel Imports to Help Restore Free World Trade and Make It Fair."

them in agreement over the issue. Usually, one finds both sides of an issue, and more, represented on the Senate floor. Even Senator Javits, the ever-strident "free trader" began his statement with a sort of apologia by citing his record in the House and Senate over his twenty-some years, as one which was marked by ". . . support of open trade as being in the highest national interest of the United States and in the highest interest of a peaceful and prosperous world . . ."[1] but admitted that in this case he supported retention of the quotas. According to Javits, "a phasing-in period . . . must be given . . . for industries to adjust to a sudden situation which imperils them."[2] He had implicitly adopted the "fair trade" theme. The message that Moynihan, Javits, and the others, sent to the White House, and to Europe and Japan, was surely read as a most powerful one; the Senate's intentions were clear both with regard to the specific matter of specialty steel, and for "big steel." As Senator Moynihan put it upon opening the Colloquy: "Mr. President, we are commencing this morning on an event that is unique in the history of the United States Senate."[3]

It was evident that Congressional consensus on the steel issue had formed around support for the industry's

---

[1]Senate Steel Colloquy, October 19, 1977, pp.

[2]Ibid.

[3]Ibid.

position. Both individual and cum "institutional" support had been generated -- a condition which was again apparent in another set of important hearings held on the "antidumping" issue by the Vanik subcommittee in November 1977. All of these events were part of the process by which Congress pressured the Administration to reach a policy decision on the immediate political crisis engendered by the domestic steel industry. It was probably the single largest, and by some standards, most effective effort. For in the end it would be the Congressmen to whom the President would have to turn for approval of the Multilateral Trade Agreement he hoped to complete in the coming months.

V. Summary

So, by November 1977, the steel issue had moved onto center stage in U.S. politics. As we have indicated throughout this chapter, there were really two separate, but interrelated issues. On the one hand there was the structural crisis in world steel brought on primarily by surplus capacity among the industrial nations, and exacerbated by recessionary conditions of the mid to late seventies. On the other hand, there was the immediate problem of increased import penetration which was rather successfully established by the steel lobby as the prime cause for increased unemployment and depressed profits.

In fact, the latter was really a part of the former, and was the part which forced U.S. policymakers to examine seriously and expeditiously the entire problem. In effect U.S. policymakers were able to finesse the longer term problem under the guise of seeking an international political economic solution. But once the issue exploded domestically the subtle difference between the two was lost. Not only were policymakers forced to step up the international economic negotiations on steel, but they were also forced to develop an immediate answer to the import problem. Thus, in addition to the commitment to enforce the antidumping laws made at the October White House meeting, President Carter also said, "[We intend] to negotiate with other countries that export steel to us a resolution to these problems,"[1] in an obvious reference to the development of the OECD International Steel Committee. As we shall see in the next two chapters, the problems -- short term and long term -- were still kept separate in terms of policy development. But, in the minds of all participants -- U.S. domestic interests, the Administration, and the foreign interests -- there was a direct relationship.

---

[1]"Steel Leaders at the White House Get Pledge of Aid in Import Crisis," New York Times, October 14, 1977, p. 1.

CHAPTER 5

THE TRIGGER PRICE SYSTEM

Introduction

Among Congressmen, the press, and in the public, the domestic political crisis in steel overshadowed the longer term, global-economic problems. Except for an occasional remark by the STR's office, and rather oblique references by some of the other trade policy officials in the government about the OECD discussions all efforts by government and by the steel lobby were directed at seeking immediate relief from the "import problem." Labor, for example, recounted its position as one which "focused upon the need for immediate relief . . . of the steel import problems."[1]

Industry also emphasized the steel import problem as their "uppermost concern." Industry officials were rather direct in their characterization of the problems as having been "created by the attitudes and actions of [U.S.] government over the past twenty years to encourage imports and ignore unfair trade practices."[2] In part, it should be noted, this allegation against government

---

[1]"Unemployment in the Steel Industry," Basic Steel Conference (Washington Hilton, Wash. D.C., December 2, 1977) p. 27.

[2]"U.S. Steel Position Paper," delivered by David

practices was also a defense of their own position. Quoting a study by the Council on Wage and Price Stability (COWPS), the president of U.S. Steel, David M. Roderick, set out to refute what had become the commonly held notion that the United States domestic steel industry had become inefficient and noncompetitive in comparison to the industries in countries like Japan and West Germany. According to Roderick, the study found that "our productivity -- in terms of man hours per ton of steel produced -- is equal to the best of foreign industries and considerably better than most."[1] In particular, he continued, "we are cost-competitive with foreign producers in serving our domestic market."[2] And Roderick concluded by citing the assessment by the COWPS Study which supported industry's basic proposition: that the basis for foreign competition in the American market was massive subsidization by government. The COWPS Study stated: "The only way large volumes of foreign steel can be marketed in this country is by pricing it below their costs of production and shipping. And that is a violation

---

M. Roderick, president of U.S. Steel, at Regional Stockholders meeting, Washington, D.C., November 18, 1977.

[1]Ibid., quoting "Report to the President on Prices and Costs in the United States Steel Industry," Council on Wage and Price Stability, October 5, 1977, p. 17.

[2]Ibid.

of this land."[1] Thus, the Council on Wage and Price Stability had recognized that the increase in import penetration came largely from subsidized foreign competition. The Study continued:

> Worldwide demand for steel is expected to fall short of supply over the next few years, creating pressures in many countries to increase exports to maintain operating rates and employment. The United States, a net importer with low tariff barriers, will be sharply affected by these competitive pressures from imports.[2]

Thus, the COWPS Study provided American industry and labor leaders with an even firmer basis to argue that the government had been negligent in their duty to enforce the trade laws. As Roderick put it:

> We realize that enforcing the trade laws is a matter of political will, requiring attitudes on the part of government that favor a strong and viable steel industry in this country. Such attitudes have not been evident for a long time.[3]

As we have indicated earlier, the political will seemed finally to be present. Even as the Administration realized that the antidumping solution was a nonsolution for foreign policy reasons,[4] it also recognized that

---

[1]"Report to the President on Prices and Costs of the United States Steel Industry," Council on Wage and Price Stability, October 5, 1977, p. 17.

[2]Ibid.

[3]Statement by David M. Roderick, November 18, 1977.

[4]This point is elaborated in Chapter 2, Section III, but also later in this chapter. For reasons of foreign policy, the Administration could not strictly enforce the antidumping laws, since such action would have substantially damaged European steel and might have led to the unravelling of the MTN.

a solution was necessary for domestic policy reasons. And it soon became evident that legislative activity -- the most poignant manifestation of the pressure which caused the Administration to act -- served two important purposes: first, and most important, it dramatized to the Administration the magnitude of the steel lobby's influence, and focused it in the Congress -- the single most powerful interlocutor of the President. Congressional mobilization over the steel issue from September 1977 was seen by the Carter Administration as a preview of potential Congressional stonewalling on the MTN agreement if influential lobbies like steel were not satisfied. Second, the various bills provided important clues as to the specific issues the steel lobby wanted the Administration to address.

Whether any of the bills, especially those calling for quotas or sectoral negotiations in the GATT, would have actually passed both Houses of Congress, is unclear. If they did, and the President vetoed them, which he surely would have, it is even less certain that Congress would have overridden the veto. What was perfectly clear, however, was that the costs were simply too high for the Administration to call the Congress' bluff. It was equally unclear what the results of the antidumping petitions filed by industry would have been, had they been pursued. But the chances that Treasury would have found dumping were high. Again, the risks were simply too great for the Administration to take what would have amounted to a cavalier "wait and see" attitude. As the political crisis became even more tense through October 1977, something had to be done to begin to relieve it. Shortly after the White House meeting on October 13, 1977, and the President's commitment to "fair trade" through enforcement of the antidumping laws, the press began to report that a steel plan was on its way.

The Solomon Task Force

In October 1977, when the Solomon Task Force was created, STR, Treasury, Commerce, State, and Labor had been meeting for over a year on an ad hoc, interagency basis. They had been meeting since January 1976 when the steel steering committee had been created; it was a spinoff of the Trade Policy Staff Committee which was already actively working on industrial sector MTN-related matters. For the first few months the effective co-leaders of the steel steering group were Dick Heimlich, Assistant Ambassador to the STR for Industrial Products, and William Barraclough, Assistant Secretary of State.[1] This was understandable since the *raison d'etre* of the steel steering group was to address problems raised by the steel issue at the MTN and in the international sphere generally. The steel issue was still largely a foreign policy matter with special emphasis on its relationship to international

---

[1]Interview, November 27, 1978.

political economic affairs. Because of the obvious controlling issues -- the trade negotiations in Geneva, the condition of the world steel industry, and the status of United States trade laws -- STR and State were joined by Treasury as central participants in the steel committee's business.

As the domestic political crisis began to unfold throughout the latter part of 1976 and 1977 it appeared that the steel steering group would play a larger role than just overseeing the MTN process. But, by September 1977, the Carter Administration recognized that an even more specialized task force was needed to address the immediate and specific domestic political crisis. While the steel steering group was quite familiar with the steel issue since it had been dealing with the longer term international negotiations,[1] it was not itself equipped to respond to the quick moving pace of the domestic situation. Of course, there was the additional political mileage to be gained from creating a new committee to deal with the problems in the steel sector. The President could announce publicly his concern and interest in the issue, and point to specific action. Thus, the President asked Secretary Solomon to develop a steel plan which would respond

---

[1]As we shall elaborate in the next chapter on the International Steel Committee, the steel steering group had been working in the OECD on steel problems for over a year before the Solomon Task Force was finally created in September 1977.

appropriately.[1] In effect, the President had given the steel steering group a "special mandate" and appointed Under Secretary of the Treasury Anthony Solomon as its head. "We are addressing the steel industry with a multi-departmental approach," the President said in a press conference on September 29, 1977. At the same press briefing the President went on to describe the Task Force:

> This is under the control of an Assistant Secretary in the Treasury Department, Mr. Solomon, who's an expert on the steel industry. He's working with Robert Strauss, our Special Trade Representative, and with Charles Schultze, my Council of Economic Advisors Chairman, and with the Secretaries of Commerce and Labor.[2]

While the Solomon Task Force was a product of the steel steering group, it had been folded out of that particular bureaucratic box. In fact, there were representatives from agencies in the federal bureaucracy which hadn't been part of the steel steering group itself; it consisted of representatives from Treasury, STR, State, Labor, Commerce, the Council on Wage and Price Stability, the Council on Economic Advisors, and the Federal Trade Commission. That was on paper. In fact, the actual decisions were made in the very large part by Secretary Solomon with some considerable help from Assistant Ambassador Heimlich.

---

[1]Interview, November 6, 1978.

[2]"President Carter's Press Conference," New York Times, September 30, 1977, p. 8.

As a top aide to Secretary Solomon put it: "The task force was winnowed down once we were at the point of actually making decisions. After all, you couldn't convene an eight member task force to make decisions."[1] But the aide was quick to add:

> This was not done in isolation. We took input from all the agencies involved. And, all through the process we gave briefings to Cabinet-level officials to indicate where we were going and what we were proposing to do.[2]

There were three major reasons why the prime responsibility fell to Treasury. First, it had already been clear in the White House, at the Secretary level, and at the Assistant Secretary level of policymaking that whatever specific policy did evolve, it would be a variation on the antidumping theme. Since Treasury has jurisdiction over the administration and enforcement of the antidumping laws, it was natural that the lead go to Treasury.

Treasury's key role in actually writing the steel plan was reenforced by two other factors. The "bureaucratic-politics model" seemed to apply in reverse; no one really wanted the issue, but someone had to take it. STR, State, and Treasury agreed that Treasury should take it since Treasury had jurisdiction over the dumping laws.[3] Besides, STR had already taken the lead in the international

---

[1]Interview, November 6, 1978.

[2]Interview, November 6, 1978.

[3]Interview, November 6, 1978.

discussions, and was the unspoken leader in the overall trade negotiations anyway.

A final, but very important reason the responsibility went to Treasury was Under Secretary Solomon. Most of the officials who had been representing their respective agencies both at the interagency meetings in Washington, and at the international ad hoc meetings at the OECD in Paris, realized that there was a fortunate coincidence in the person of Anthony Solomon, Under Secretary of Treasury for Monetary Affairs. Solomon had been largely responsible for negotiating the voluntary restraint agreement for steel in 1968, then as an Assistant Secretary of State; he knew the issue firsthand, was familiar with industry and labor leaders, and was well respected by his counterparts at STR and State. He was sophisticated both in the politics of international trade and in the economics of the issue.

Therefore, by mid-October 1977, the Solomon Task Force was already feverishly hammering out the details of a trade policy for steel. Even more than addressing the long-term economic problems of the world steel issue, the Solomon Task Force was responsible for producing a plan which would diffuse the domestic-political crisis in steel. President Carter had asked Under Secretary Solomon to produce a plan which would ease the domestic political tensions in steel. Probably because everyone in the federal bureaucracy associated with the issue realized that a quick response was critical, and the President had already "chosen his man,"[1] there was little if any struggle to undercut or outmaneuver Solomon in his efforts. For his part, Secretary Solomon made a genuine effort to take account of all possible policy options. As one Solomon aide put it:

> We looked at quotas, tariffs, tariff-rate quotas . . . there was virtually nothing excluded before we actually made the decision to go with a Trigger Price System.[2]

In both the development of the plan, and the plan itself, Solomon had to convince the steel industry that the Administration was serious about helping it. But, at the same time it was already clear to members of the Task Force that "strict enforcement of the antidumping laws was untenable."[3] As he later implied, the Task Force decided to respond to the import problem by seeking an administrative solution which would ensure fair trade without strictly enforcing the antidumping laws.[4] In exchange for a steel policy, largely based on a self-initiating antidumping mechanism, the industry would withdraw its

---

[1]Interview, March 22, 1979.

[2]Interview, March 22, 1979.

[3]Interview, November 14, 1978.

[4]Secretary Solomon speaking at Senate Steel Caucus meeting, February 6, 1979.

antidumping petitions and do what they could to call off Congressional pressures for quotas.[1] It worked.

The TPM: The Answer to the President's Commitment

The Solomon Report was submitted to the President for final review by the last week in November and was publicly announced on December 6, 1977. Trial balloons had been already floated. For instance, while the plan was still in the development stages, Secretary Blumenthal said, "It will try to protect the industry from unfair competition from abroad, help it meet its cash flow problems and spur new investment."[2] As it happened, the final report consisted of five parts, with clear emphasis on the trade problem: relief from unfair trade practices, modernization, rationalizing environmental policies and procedures, community and labor assistance, and a hodgepodge of general measures such as loosening Justice Department controls over antitrust matters.[3]

In fact, the Trigger Price Mechanism -- the central element in what was to be a system designed to provide

---

[1]Labor continued to press for quotas, but without the backing of industry they were in a rather weak position. As events overtook them, they too dropped their efforts at pressuring the Administration for quotas.

[2]"White House Weighs Steel Tariff Plan," _Washington Post_, November 18, 1977.

[3]See my conclusion to Part II, where I elaborate on the failure to seriously address aspects of the Solomon Plan other than the TPM.

domestic producers with relief from unfair trade practices -- turned out to be the only part of the proposal that was seriously pursued. This was understandable since large numbers of imports had already been tagged as the proximate cause of the industry's problems. And it was in that context that the domestic-political crisis had been framed. Accordingly, the immediate solution was to limit such practices through a trigger price system based on price levels. As one Treasury official put it: "The Trigger Price Mechanism emerged as Treasury's approach . . . under the Antidumping Act which would rapidly and effectively deal with unfair priced imports."[1]

In the "Report to the President: A Comprehensive Program for Steel," Solomon introduced the trigger price system with a description of the global steel problem as it affected U.S. producers:

> The global slump in steel demand and the substantial excess capacity in the world steel industry have led to aggressive exporting by foreign steel makers, in particular, those in Japan and the European Community (EC) countries. The U.S. market, because of its size, its relatively higher rate of economic recovery, and its openness to all suppliers, is a primary market for sales of foreign steel producers.[2]

---

[1]William A. Anawaty, "The United States Legal Response to Steel Dumping," speech delivered on September 30, 1978 at the University of Western Ontario, London, Canada.

[2]"Report to the President: A Comprehensive Program for the Steel Industry," Anthony Solomon, Chairman, Task Force, November 8, 1977, p. 9.

It went on to critique the present system by which the U.S. enforces, or fails to enforce, its antidumping laws. Understandably, it was phrased in a way clearly intended for industry's consumption:

> The steel industry has suggested that the traditional response is too cumbersome to provide relief quickly from sudden surges of imports that may cause injury to an American industry.[1]

But, in an implicit reference to the Gilmore case, Solomon's plan was also sensitive to the adverse effects the U.S. dumping laws could have on its trading partners: "High margins of dumping . . . have resulted in a virtual halt in orders for that product from the foreign supplier."[2] Solomon wanted to provide the Secretary of Treasury with a handy way to initiate antidumping investigations without a prior industry complaint.[3] While the Task Force sought an effective remedy against unfair trade practices it did not want to make the antidumping laws a tool for improperly shutting off foreign trade and inviting retaliation.[4]

---

[1]The Solomon Report, p. 13.

[2]Ibid.

[3]The Solomon Report did point out that "self-initiation" is provided under the Antidumping Act of 1921, and set forth in the Trade Act of 1974. But, it admitted that it has not been used in recent years.

[4]Secretary Solomon reflected the general concern among many in the Administration that import restrictions would invite retaliation, which they feared could lead to a condition not unlike the period immediately preceding the Great Depression. For a general discussion of the relationship between "beggar they neighbor" trade policies, and the

The Trigger Price System (TPS), according to the Solomon Report, was intended as a more expedient way of enforcing the antidumping laws. According to William A. Anawaty, the Director of the TPM enforcement division:

> The TPM is a method of implementing traditional antidumping remedies in expedited fashion . . . . It is a benchmark for quickly focusing Treasury resources on antidumping investigations of steel mill products when the situation warrants. The trigger prices are an objective standard against which Treasury can measure entries [at the port of entry into the United States] and spot those which are likely to indicate sales at less than fair value [the definition for dumping] . . . it centers on Treasury's authority to self-initiate under the [antidumping] statute.[1]

Accordingly, the Solomon recommendation to the President was that Treasury:

> . . . set up a system of trigger prices, based on the full cost of production, including appropriate capital charges of steel mill production, by the most efficient producers (currently the Japanese steel industry), which would be used as a basis for monitoring imports of steel into the United States and for initiating accelerated antidumping investigation with respect to imports priced below the trigger prices.[2]

Thus, a "price" solution was less politically disruptive of U.S. relationship with its trading partners than a quantitative restraint solution such as that tried in 1968-72. And, the proposal also won support from the U.S.

Great Depression, see, for example, Charles P. Kindelberger, World in Depression (Berkeley: The University of California Press, 1973).

[1]William A. Anawaty, speech delivered at Western Ontario University.

[2]Solomon Task Force, p. 13.

major trading partners. Spokesmen from the Japanese steel industry have commended the TPM for introducing a measure of discipline into the pricing of steel in the U.S. marketplace.[1]

Indeed, the TPM provided an elegant solution for the Administration to a seemingly unresolvable dilemma between domestic and international pressures.

Before the Trigger Price System developed, the Administration had three policy options: (a) to do nothing; (b) to impose quotas; (c) or to enforce "fair trade" -- what had effectively become a code term for strict enforcement of the antidumping laws. None of those options was acceptable. Understandably, it was equally unacceptable for the Administration to admit that they were unacceptable. How, for example, could the Administration publicly refuse to pursue a policy of "fair trade" or refuse to enforce the trade laws as they appeared on the books? Thus, the TPM sought, rather skillfully, to allow the Administration to pursue a policy of fair trade based on politically workable principles, i.e., to balance its domestic and foreign policy needs. So Solomon reported to the President: "It is reasonable to assume that the Trigger Price Mechanism will lead to rapid amelioration

---

[1]"Nippon's Saito Praises, Criticizes Trigger Pricing," American Metals Market, August 25, 1978, p. 1.

of the problems the U.S. industry has endured from unfairly priced imports.[1] Never did the Solomon Report, or the Carter Administration in subsequent pronouncements, even hint that the TPM, or the antidumping laws, should become a carte blanche against imports. To the contrary, the emphasis was on "organized free trade" by ensuring that products were fairly priced so that "the industry [c]ould recapture a substantial share of the U.S. market that it has lost to . . . unfairly priced imports."[2]

Solomon was ever so careful not to recommend to the President a system that would "upset the applecart in Geneva" -- still a priority goal for Administration trade policy. Rather, the TPM sought to penalize "unfair practices" which they hoped would actually rebound to the benefit of the negotiating process in Geneva. For it would lead to "the elimination of the need for domestic steel companies to file new antidumping complaints and encourage them to consider the prospect of withdrawal of the petitions now under investigation."[3] Indeed, this is exactly what happened. As an illustration, one company which had filed petitions against French and British steelmakers for the dumping of carbon steel rod, accompanied its withdrawal letter to Treasury with this point:

---

[1]Solomon Report, p. 18.

[2]Ibid.

[3]Solomon Report, p. 13.

> We understand . . . that if the continuation of antidumping complaints brought before the TPM became effective it could adversely affect the administration of the TPM. We believe that rigorous and systematic enforcement of the Antidumping Act by Treasury pursuant to the TPM can be a desirable and efficient method of assuring that imported steel products will be sold in the United States at fair value.[1]

Upon withdrawal of such petitions, Treasury affirmed its commitment to:

> continue carefully to monitor wire rods [or whatever product was in question] under the trigger price mechanism and [to] take appropriate action to ensure the effective enforcement of the Antidumping Act with respect to that product.[2]

Treasury also confirmed its responsibility to "expeditiously conclude disposition" on any refiled complaints if the TPM turned out not to work effectively.

But the domestic industry was not going to receive any "unfair advantages" either. Accordingly, the "level of import reduction" was dependent on "the price behavior of the domestic steel companies," and the domestic industry was warned "the more sharply the domestic firms raise their prices, the smaller will be their recapture of the market."[3] Thus, the Trigger Price Mechanism was a way to keep unfairly priced imports to a minimum, but it had built into it an incentive to ensure a reasonable lid on domestic

---

[1]"Georgetown Withdrawal of Antidumping Petitions," Department of Treasury Press Release, July 14, 1978.

[2]Ibid.

[3]Solomon Report, p. 19.

prices as well. If a foreign producer sold at less than the determined level (to be adjusted quarterly), it would be subject to sharply higher duties. Since the price level was keyed to the most efficient foreign producer, and not the U.S. price level, any price increases by the domestic industry would widen the spread between their prices and the reference price, making the selling price of the import that much more attractive relative to their own.[1]

Hence, the trigger pricing system cleverly applied a pricing mechanism to ensure that foreign producers were not selling at below fair costs of production which would outcompete efficient domestic producers. The purpose was not simply "to keep out low cost imports,"[2] or, as Secretary Solomon put it: "We never intended to protect the industry against imports as such, but to protect them against dumping."[3] Nor did Solomon ever intend for the TPM to be permanent: "We don't think of the trigger price system as a permanent feature in the trade landscape."[4] It was a clever economic response to a political crisis

---

[1]The TPM was calcualted on Japanese "cost of production" figures. See the Solomon Report, p. 14-18.

[2]William A. Anawaty, speech delivered at Western Ontario University.

[3]Secretary Solomon speaking at the Senate Steel Caucus meeting, February 6, 1979.

[4]Ibid.

that was caused by a series of economic and political conditions in the United States and abroad. Therefore, Solomon wrote: "When conditions warrant, the system will be terminated and the more traditional procedures restored."[1] There is little doubt that a substantial factor in determining whether conditions would ever warrant termination would be the level of political tensions and that the level of import penetration per se would be a less substantial factor. Thus, Solomon's primary responsibility was to keep the industry at bay by ensuring fair trade. Whether consciously, or subconsciously, policymakers continued to address the steel issue with "a series of ad hoc decisions to deal with short term crises,"[2] as one member of the Task Force candidly characterized their approach.

Not only weren't there any contingencies developed in the event the TPM were to fail, but a minibureaucracy was established to oversee, administer, and enforce the Trigger Price System (TPS). Understandably, one wonders what effect the TPS bureaucracy will have on subsequent decisions about the success or failure of the TPM, and the ease with which the system might be dismantled as the Solomon Report indicated. However, there were good technical and political reasons for creating a separate division in Treasury for implementation and administration

---

[1]Solomon Report, p. 20.

[2]Interview, November 27, 1978.

of the TPS. Thus, the Trigger Price enforcement office was set up as part of Treasury, but it was separated both physically and conceptually from the divisions in Treasury responsible for the administration and enforcement of the traditional antidumping laws.

This separation was established in part because "there was no more room in main Treasury,"[1] but in part to ensure a distinction between the two kinds of antidumping cases. In this way the Administration was able to project an even more serious concern about their ability and willingness to implement the TPS. After all, Treasury had developed a terrible reputation for their apparent unwillingness to enforce the antidumping or countervailing duty laws. Therefore, by establishing a separate office -- technically part of the Special Programs Division of the Department of the Treasury -- the steel lobby was given more reason to believe the Administration would act "responsibly" in spite of Treasury's default on strict enforcement of the traditional antidumping laws.

William A. Anawaty, a young, intelligent Treasury lawyer with little background in trade policy or steel, generally, was appointed Director. He was promptly given his own staff -- several economists, a couple of lawyers, some trade experts, one specialist in steel, a computer expert, and a number of clerical-type office workers. At

---

[1]Interview, November 14, 1978.

the same time that Anawaty's office was set up, Treasury formed another Task Force from which Anawaty's office drew a substantial amount of important information to help in the enforcement process. This (second) Task Force was still under the stewardship of Solomon, although he did not participate much because the policy level decisions had already been made, and the guidelines for the pricing structure had already been set. It was comprised mostly of nongovernment economists, accountants, and technical steel consultants. Their job was to review the categories of steel products covered -- (not all steel was covered, though the Solomon Task Force worked closely with the American Iron and Steel Institute to determine the most sensitive products) -- and study the appropriateness of the trigger prices which had been established.

Key members of the Task Force were: Donald Barnett, a steel economist from the American Iron and Steel Institute, and a former economist for the Canadian government; Robert Crandall, economist at the Brookings Institution, and a member of Solomon's original Task Force, then representing the Council on Wage and Price Stability; Dale Montgomery, an independent steel engineer; partners from the accounting firm of Alexander-Grant; Frank Vucmanik, top aide to Solomon; and a host of other trade policy bureaucrats from Customs, the Special Trade

Representative's office, Commerce and Labor.[1]

Although Anawaty's office didn't begin operating until April 1978, the second Task Force had been feeding them information on the details of the system, and a number of officials, including Anawaty, had been to Japan to collect data for the trigger prices since December 1977 when the Solomon plan finally had been announced.

The Solomon Task Force, the Solomon Report, the Trigger Price Enforcement Division, and the second consultative Task Force signalled to the steel lobby that the President had kept his promise to "do something," even though it clearly wasn't strict enforcement of dumping as he had orginally promised. Still, Secretary Solomon had devised a solution which fulfilled the presidential mandate that had been given him -- a politically workable solution to the dumping problem. The overall effort, symbolized in large part by the establishment of an enforcement agency in Treasury, indicated that the Carter Administration was serious about the steel issue.

Steel Lobby Acceptance

The greatest success of the Solomon Task Force was its ability to diffuse the domestic political crisis which had been seething since late August 1977. Industry's qualified endorsement of the Trigger Price System led to

---

[1]Interview, March 22, 1979.

a remarkably prompt withdrawal of antidumping petitions, and a virtual end to individual Congressmen's pursuit of legislative remedies. The bills were technically still pending, and not all of the antidumping petitions were withdrawn; both were used over the course of the next year as a constant reminder to the Administration that the industry still held rather strong leverage over them. And, as indicated above, even those which were withdrawn were done so on the condition that they would be immediately refiled and given priority consideration if the TPM wasn't working. In reality, however, industry executives hoped that they wouldn't be forced to resort to the traditional antidumping petitions. In a response to Congressional inquiries, speaking for the other industry executives, Lewis Foy summed up their attitudes: "We hope we can work with the TPM System to make it better."[1] So, with the announcement of the TPM, the pressure did ease.

In that sense, Solomon's Task Force fulfilled its presidential mandate: to draw up a plan that would strike a balance between domestic political needs and international acceptability. It also provided the Administration with a way to fulfill what Solomon called "their Congressional mandate for fair trade . . . we set out to stop dumping, which the industry claimed would allow them to compete

---

[1]Lewis Foy speaking at the Senate Steel Caucus, February 6, 1979.

against foreign producers."[1]

Thus, the domestic-political needs were satisfied, more or less. As an example of the "more," consider the statement by the chairman of U.S. Steel, David Roderick, where he essentially endorsed the TPM principle by encouraging a specific reference price level of $360/ton imported. This was an important signal that he had entered into a substantive discussion with Administration officials in trying to make the TPM work. He said that the reference price would be "fair and enable the industry to compete with foreign producers."[2] Over the next months the other presidents and chairmen of the boards of the major steel companies weighed in with various degrees of support for the TPM. For example, Bethlehem Steel issued a statement in late January which extended "appreciation that the Administration and many members of Congress who have recognized the problems which must be dealt with to encourage and maintain a strong competitive steel industry in the United States."[3] Bethlehem said they would "cooperate to the fullest extent possible," but also offered this critical judgment with regard to details: "The Trigger Price Program is in jeopardy due to the erroneous basis

---

[1]Secretary Solomon at the Senate Steel Caucus, February 7, 1979.

[2]"$360 Reference Price for Imported Steel Urged by Roderick," New York Times, December 9, 1977, p. D-1.

[3]"Bethlehem Steel Statement on Trigger Price Mechanism," January 27, 1978, on file with author.

for calculating the Japanese-based trigger prices."[1] Bethlehem, along with other American companies, questioned the accuracy of the Japanese costs -- a central element in developing the actual trigger prices. But, the important point is that however qualified, support was forthcoming.

And the Steelworkers offered their support as well. As with industry, it was support generated more for what the Administration was trying to do, since no one knew if the system would actually work, than an unequivocal endorsement. For example, Lloyd McBride, president of the United Steelworkers of America said of Solomon's Trigger Price Plan:

> We regard the mere existence of the TPM as good since it puts the world on notice that the U.S. government cares about the health of the American steel industry and workers. In that regard, the TPM is beneficial, and it is certainly better than doing nothing.[2]

This view was also contained in a policy statement by labor sent to Congress not one day after the Solomon Report became public:

> We welcome the recommendations of the proposed Solomon Task Force as an important indication that the government has finally accepted the necessity of attaining our goal . . . to put our members back to work immediately and to assure them that they will have long-term protection against the loss of their jobs.[3]

---

[1]Ibid.

[2]Lloyd McBride speaking at a Senate Steel Caucus meeting, March 22, 1979.

[3]"Steelworkers Legislative Appeal," issued December 7, 1977, on file with author.

In particular, labor was optimistic about the new prospects for the antidumping laws:

> We endorse the concept of prompt antidumping relief encompassed in the reference price proposal of the Solomon Task Force. We support the concept of fair market price for imported steel.[1]

Their statement went on to outline what they believed the details of the reference price ought to be if it was going to work. And, there was approval of the concept and the intentions:

> The United States Steelworkers of America supports the President's steel industry plan as a significant first step toward a necessary long range program for developing a stronger steel industry and a stronger economy . . .
>
> The reference price mechanism in the President's program does provide a "fast track" remedy for the dumping problems, and therefore we accept it.[2]

The economic problems were still there -- industry still could not meet its cash flow demands, for example -- but the domestic political crisis had been diffused. U.S. policymakers had developed a system which proposed to reintroduce into the steel trade a number of important elements: a degree of predictability since the exporter would know that sales above trigger prices are likely to be safe from dumping investigations; a speed up of the investigatory process; to provide protection against dumping without insulating the domestic industry from price

---

[1]Ibid.

[2]Ibid.

competition; and to focus on "price" as a determinant of fair trade rather than "quantity."

Not everyone supported the system, however. An article which appeared in the Wall Street Journal in mid-December, pointed to those who were "less" supportive: "Steel Trigger Price Plan has Loopholes." "Foreign Mills May Exploit, Skeptics Say."[1] In fact, in his report to the President, Solomon had included a section called "Potential Problems" in which the Task Force outlined the "problems which may not be fully met by the proposed system." Indeed, there were a number of kinks in the reference pricing system, some anticipated, and others which were not so apparent during the development of the system.

One "unanticipated consequence" was its effect on fabricated steel products. What was sold as raw iron and steel before the TPM, could be sold in the form of fabricated products -- nuts, bolts, and screws, for example -- after the TPM. Even if the TPM helped the iron and steel industry, it was therefore argued, it could hurt other, related industries.[2] Opposition also was heard

---

[1]"Steel Trigger Price Plan Has Loopholes," Wall Street Journal, December 16, 1977.

[2]For example, the "Frabricated Steel Industry" argued that trigger prices would work to the detriment of their industry. See for example, comments to this effect at the U.S. House of Representatives hearings on Nuts, Bolts, and Screws; U.S. Congress, House of Representatives, Hearings on Fabricated Steel Products, 95th Congress, 1st Session, (Washington, D.C.: Government Printing Office, 1977).

from distributors of imported steel. As expressed by one owner of several New England steel distributing firms, it was felt that the TPM would "devastate the American steel distribution business . . . . It will allow foreign mills to open their own distribution centers and will <u>sell</u> rather than buy at the reference price."[1] "American mills," the argument went, "will find their supply customers unable to compete with foreign supply chains and even more steel mills will close."[2] And, in a statement subsequently delivered as testimony before the Senate Small Business subcommittee, the point was underscored:

> The new regulations allow foreign steel mills with fully or partly owned captive steel warehouses (depots and distributors) in the U.S. to receive stock below reference prices, and then to resell steel to accounts at those identical reference prices, adding no charges for transportation, slitting, shearing, burning or other processing, storage or profit.[3]

Finally, there were those who believed that the TPM was inflationary -- some estimated that the reference price system would cost the American consumer one to five billion

---

[1]Interview, Central Steel Supply Company, Inc., Sommerville, Massachusetts, February 14, 1978.

[2]Ibid.

[3]Testimony of Bernard Featherman, Chairman of ASD Government Relations Committee, before the Senate Small Business Committee, February 7, 1978. See, for example,

dollars.[1] But, defenders of the TPM in the Administration argued that "it was no more inflationary than is inherently true of our antidumping laws . . . ."[2]

In spite of these criticisms, the Solomon Report and the Trigger Pricing System provided the Administration with a response to "Youngstown" and helped to diffuse the immediate domestic political crisis. Domestic political conditions during the late summer and fall of 1977 had forced the Administration to develop a "quick solution" to a long-standing structural problem. Secretary Solomon came through. Whether it would actually work was another question.

The TPM: A Concession to Europe

In fact, the question of whether the TPM worked is not so easily answered. For it turned out that not everyone's intentions were the same. The Administration, as we have pointed out over and over again, wanted a plan which met its foreign policy needs as well as its domestic ones.

So, while the Solomon Report was primarily intended as a response to the domestic situation, the Trigger Price System had to be squared with conditions in the international arena as well. "We spent the better part of November and early December [1977] gaining acceptability

---

[1]"Massive FTC Report Calls Steel Reference Prices as Pernicious as Quotas," American Metals Market, January 4, 1978, volume 86, no. 2.

[2]Interview, November 6, 1978.

abroad,"[1] according to a top Solomon aide on the Task Force.

As the time approached for the unveiling of the TPM the Japanese and the Europeans both reacted positively. For the most part, they simply were relieved that the United States had decided not to impose quotas, either through adjustment of the tariff rates, an orderly marketing arrangement, or voluntary restraint agreements. Understandably, the Japanese were fearful that their share of the U.S. market would continue to fall. And, of course, the TPM was a more attractive solution than straightforward prosecution of the antidumping cases which had been filed in September, October and November of 1977.[2]

In particular, the Japanese saw the reference price system as an indication that the Carter Administration had taken charge, a development they viewed as positive; the government was thought, correctly, to be more reliably a free trader than the industry, and the Executive more predictable than the Legislature. In their first public statement on the proposed reference price plan, a senior MITI official was reported to have said, "Though we are not yet aware of any details, Japan would be receptive to government to government talks on a reference price proposal."[3]

---

[1]Interview, November 6, 1978.

[2]"The Dumping Solution," National Journal, Fall 1977.

[3]Japan Economic Survey, volume 1, number 1, November 21, 1977, p. 2.

Along the same quiescent lines, the leading Japanese financial daily, Nihon Keizai Shimbun, quoted another MITI official as saying: "The Japanese government is flexible in its attitude toward solving this issue either on a quantative or price basis."[1] Mostly, MITI was receptive to what they called "the U.S. government's new approach to a steel agreement."[2] In addition to the rhetoric, however, they were cooperative in providing the Treasury Department with the economic data necessary for constructing the reference price.[3]

To the Japanese the Reference Price System represented the least worst solution. In any event, their huge trade surplus by this time had become a source of embarrassment, not to mention the very real political tensions it had caused with the United States. There was a substantial amount of bitterness directed by

---

[1]Ibid.

[2]Ibid.

[3]Industry argued then, and continues to allege, that much of the data is "questionable." For example, in a statement by the American Iron and Steel Institute to the Treasury Department on January 29, 1979, several changes in the methodology of the TPM were suggested. As an example: "Treasury should conduct random audits of both importers and exporters to assure that complete and accurate information is being put in the Customs documents required of such exporters and importers . . . Treasury should augment its TPM enforcement team to allow in-depth audits of exporters, importers, and purchasers of imported steel where two or more of these parties are related in order to minimize the available subterfuges that permit avoidance of the TPM . . ."

both American officials and the American public at Japan. With some justification, the Japanese were blamed for the large balance of trade deficit which was accumulating in the United States. And the Japanese were aware of these attitudes. For example, in a joint statement by Minister Ushiba of Japan, and Ambassador Strauss of the United States, it was agreed "that in the present international economic situation, the accumulation of a large current account surplus was not appropriate. Accordingly, Japan has undertaken steps aimed at achieving a marked dimunution of its current account surplus."[1] In the eyes of U.S. trade policy officials, Japan was largely to blame for what the Wall Street Journal called "the fading of the Tokyo dream -- the world being wafted into an era of wider affluence by the benign winds of ever-freer trade . . . ."[2] -- which even the Joint Communique between the United States and Japan claimed not to be able to halt.[3] The effect was that Japan was likely to react rather positively toward almost any U.S. initiative, especially one which they viewed as the best of the lot. In addition,

---

[1]Joint Statement by Minister Ushiba and Ambassador Strauss called the U.S.-Japan Joint Communique, January 13, 1978, on file with author. Also see, "U.S.-Japanese Trade Communique," The New York Times, January 14, 1978, p. 35.

[2]"Fading of the Tokyo Dream," The Wall Street Journal, January 20, 1978, editorial page.

[3]"U.S.-Japanese Trade Communique," New York Times, January 14, 1978, p. 35.

as we shall see, this attitude made it easier for the Administration to develop a system which prejudiced Europe.

Unlike the Japanese, the Europeans did not feel responsible for the trade problems facing the industrial world, nor were they made to feel that way. If anything, their public image was one of the victim, and their eroding steel situation lent that image a good deal of credibility.[1] By December 1977, the European steel industry had fallen into an even more desperate situation: the Simonet Plan wasn't working, and they too were talking about a Reference Price System , but one which would explicitly limit steel imports into the Community. Davignon, Simonet's successor as the European Commissioner for Industry, made it known that he was holding up action on a European plan for fear that it would "set off a worldwide protectionist spiral."[2] Once the United States decided on a Reference Price System, the way was clear for Davignon

---

[1]It may be argued that individual European government policy decisions to nationalize their steel industries, and thereby support inefficient, old, and noncompetitive facilities through government subsidization, have contributed as much to the structural crisis in the global steel industry as the unprecedented and precipitous Japanese growth. Nonetheless, it was the Japanese, and not the Europeans, who were perceived as the villains.

[2]"A Protectionist Christmas Parcel," The Economist, December 24, 1977, p. 42.

to go ahead with his.[1]

There was a direct relationship between the development of the TPM and the condition of European steel. As indicated earlier,[2] the Europeans had to contend with both edges of the trade sword: there was the import penetration problem, but also the constraints on the amount they could continue to export. They hoped, therefore, that the American reference price plan would help them on both counts. It did. On the one hand, it would serve as the precedent for them to construct their own system of protection[3] -- the Davignon plan -- while on the other, it would control import penetration into the U.S. market through a pricing solution from which they could benefit. In fact, Solomon's reference price plan was based on Japanese cost of production which made it possible for the Europeans to "dump," and not get caught, if they stayed above the reference price. This is exactly what happened, though it should be added that the

---

[1]Ibid.

[2]See my section on European Steel in Chapter 3.

[3]Secretary Solomon vigorously argues, probably correctly, that there is a basic difference between the U.S. TPM, and the Davignon Minimum Price Plan: "Ours is not an import-limiting Plan, nor is it minimum prices"; Secretary Solomon speaking at the Senate Steel Caucus, February 6, 1979.

Europeans were constrained by the TPM to dump at slightly higher levels than before. It was still dumping, however. British steel, for example, was able to continue to subsidize its steel exports to the United States just enough so that their cost stayed above the reference price, but assured them a highly competitive price on the American market. Had the United States devised a plan based on quantity, the Europeans would have been denied the flexibility that the pricing plan offered.

But why did the Administration construct a steel policy for reducing imports from unfair trading practices that only really applied to one trading partner and discriminated in favor of the other by allowing it to dump? And why was this plan accepted? As Senator Schweiker, Republican from Pennsylvania cynically put it, "I can't understand why we built a system which rewards the inefficient producers [the Europeans] and penalizes the efficient producers [the Japanese] . . ."[1]

There are three probable explanations, the first two related to the Administration's obvious interest in the MTN. As part of these explanations it should also become clear why the American steel industry accepted it.

First, the Administration hoped to get important agricultural concessions from the Europeans at the MTN.

---

[1]Senator Schweiker speaking at the Senate Steel Caucus, February 6, 1979.

By devising a pricing system which discriminated in favor of European steel and against Japanese, the Administration figured it could get the Europeans to open up their market to American agricultural products. The Administration assumed, correctly, that a program for the benefit of the European steel industry was one of the few incentives it could offer for Europeans to consider agricultural concessions. Under the Trigger Pricing System, Solomon cleverly ensured that the domestic steel industry would benefit from an effective limit on steel from Japan, and because of the "pricing" approach domestic industry could charge higher prices leading to increased profits. Apparently, the U.S. industry was willing to take the long-term risk of a constricted share of their home market for the short-term benefits of higher profits.

A related explanation for developing that kind of system was that the Administration feared that if it didn't help the Europeans on steel they would retaliate in a host of other product areas, including, and especially, agriculture. As one Administration trade policy expert put it:

> [Ambassador] Strauss was especially concerned about European retaliation . . . if the Reference Price System looked to be unveiled protection against them. After all, the Europeans could retaliate, particularly by further limiting our agricultural exports . . . since there was so little entering Japan anyway, there was little they could threaten us with.[1]

---

[1]Interview, January 5, 1979.

A third explanation stems from the Administration's general concern about stability in Europe. There were those in the Administration who feared that excluding European steel from the American market, either by straightforward enforcement of the antidumping laws, or by any other system which limited to a considerable degree subsidized steel sold at less than fair value -- a characterization of a substantial tonnage of steel exported from Britain, France, Italy, and Belgium -- would lead to increased levels of unemployment that those governments probably could not withstand. It has been suggested that Administration officials who developed the steel plan were very much aware of the threat of Eurocommunism[1] during the period 1976-78. An American steel plan which effectively led to higher levels of unemployment could have left many of the European governments more vulnerable to the strains and tensions already present. Accordingly, the Administration was disposed to develop a steel plan which could simultaneously allow European steel to sell in substantial quantities in the United States, and allow prices only slightly higher than in 1976-77 so long as profits for domestic industry were still encouraged by the mechanics of the plan.

---

[1]Interview, March 22, 1979. Author's personal observations of the concern in Washington during 1977 over the threat of Eurocommunism supports this suggestion.

Thus, there were some very good reasons for a United States steel plan to tilt in favor of Europe. It discriminated against the Japanese, but then that was acceptable policy in 1977 because Americans in and out of government had developed a stark bitterness against the Japanese balance of trade surplus. "[The Japanese] were irresponsible," as one government bureaucrat put it, "and deserved anything they got."[1] Besides, as indicated earlier, the Japanese were delighted not to have to contend with quotas -- a device which they correctly feared could become permanent. The elegance of the Solomon Reference Price System was that it helped the Europeans and also provided the U.S. domestic industry with a chance for increased profits.

As an import-limiting device the TPM failed. But then the TPM was never offered as an import-limiting device, per se. In fact, in 1978, the first year in which the TPM was operating,[2] imports were recorded at an all-time high of 21 million tons, an increase of 9.5 percent over

---

[1]Interview, December 5, 1978.

[2]To be completely accurate, however, Administration officials set the official starting date of the TPM at April 1978. But, it is fairly certain that exceptionally inflated quantities of imports were shipped between the announcement of the Trigger Price System in December 1977, and April 1978, in an effort to ship products at the lower levels before the TPM would go into effect. Industry officials argue that this happens in the period immediately prior to each quarterly adjustment to the TPM, however, and that this inflated quantity should be accepted as a part of the system, rather than as an excuse for high levels of imports.

over 1977.[1] As significant however is that European steel imports as a percentage of the overall imports into the American market increased from about one-fourth to about thirty-five percent. During the same period Japanese imports as a percentage of imports into the American market decreased. The chart on the following page shows the relative shares of the American market captured by Japan and the EEC between 1973 and 1978. Understandably, industry and labor officials have expressed dismay over this development. For example, one industry official commented, "The TPM has given the Europeans a license to dump, and they've taken full advantage of it."[2] In light of their willingness to accept the TPM, and the associated profits, one can only approach such an attitude with extreme cynicism.

Summary

The importance of the TPM is that it represented a willingness on the part of the U.S. government to intervene in the international trade of steel. The fact that the system itself favored one set of producers over another further underscores the point that U.S. foreign trade policy officials are becoming increasingly aware of the need to emphasize the politics side of the equation over

---

[1]"Few Like Steel Trigger Prices," New York Times, January 17, 1979, pp. D-1, 4.

[2]Senate Steel Caucus, February 6, 1979.

Imports to the U.S. by Country of Origin

1973 - 1978

Year	EEC	% of Total Imports	Japan	% of Total Imports
1973	6,509,732	43.0	5,637,402	37.2
1974	6,423,907	40.2	6,158,961	38.6
1975	4,117,575	34.3	5,844,005	48.6
1976	3,187,600	22.3	7,984,131	55.9
1977	6,832,850	35.4	7,820,376	40.5
1978	7,463,394	35.3	6,487,166	30.7

Source: U.S. Department of Commerce

over the economics side in the foreign trade policy calculus for industrial products. In the particular circumstances, U.S. policy officials were remarkably successful in offering a program which quieted domestic political tensions at home without making unnecessary enemies abroad. It is to their credit that they balanced, at least for the short term, what at one time appeared to be irreconcilable positions: on the one hand the steel lobby pressing for strict enforcement of U.S. trade laws, and on the other hand U.S. trading partners arguing that trade laws should be interpreted loosely and based on political discretion. The Administration chose to move against dumping from Japan but allow the Europeans the luxury of easier entrance into the American market. That was a political decision. It was made possible by devising a system which has effectively permitted the industry to raise prices and therefore increase profits.[1] But then there were the longer-term structural problems which the TPM didn't even begin to touch upon. We shall see in the next chapter how another U.S. policy initiative sought to address the long-term problems in the steel sector also by accepting government intervention in international trade to try to secure more stable conditions.

---

[1]"Trigger Prices Misfire?"; NewsWeek, November 20, 1978, p. 105; the industry raised prices by twelve percent in 1978.

CHAPTER 6

INTERNATIONAL STEEL AGREEMENT

Introduction

While the Trigger Price System successfully diffused the domestic-political tensions in the short term, it was by no means the end of the "late seventies round" of the steel issue. In the first place, the TPM did not address the long term, worldwide structural problems in the steel sector. And secondly, by January 1978, the MTN in Geneva had just entered the critical stages of negotiations. Therefore, the steel issue was "to remain on the front burner,"[1] as an aide to Ambassador Strauss put it. In a joint statement by the American Iron and Steel Institute and the United Steelworkers, this point was underscored and marked in bold black letters:

> . . . the advent of the Trigger Price System does not change the original position of the AISI and USW. Sector negotiations in steel are more urgently needed now than they have been in the past.[2]

1Interview, November 2, 1978.

2"Joint Statement by the American Iron and Steel Institute and the United Steelworkers of America," attached to a letter to Chairman of the House Ways and Means Committee, Al Ullman, dated January 20, 1978, signed by Lloyd McBride, president of the USW, and E.B. Speer, Chairman of the AISI (1978-79), p.3. Hereafter cited as "Joint Statement," on file with author.

In fact, industry and labor had called consistently and persistently for sectoral negotiations since early 1973 when the Congress began consideration of what became the Trade Act of 1974. It was their belief then, and one reiterated still, that sectoral negotiations were necessary, regardless of other, interim measures which might be applied. In an original policy statement by the industry, sectoral negotiations were recommended "so that the many special issues which distort trade flows and prevent fair competition internationally, can be surfaced, discussed and, hopefully, resolved."[1] As this condition hadn't changed even after the establishment of the TPM, industry's and labor's position also hadn't changed.

At the bottom of their recommendations to the Administration was the notion that special conditions in the steel industry lead to the situation where international relations in steel must be conducted through a multilateral framework, rather than a unilateral or bilateral one. Thus the Trigger Price System, a unilateral action, was considered by itself inadequate: "U.S. unilateral Trigger Price System, without tariffs as an element in the final price might not alleviate further

---

[1]"American Iron and Steel Institute Trade Policy Overview," submitted to the Office of the Special Trade Representative and the Commerce Department in conjunction with materials on the MTN; on file with author.

market disruptions."[1] But even a TPM, with tariffs as an element in the final price, was not thought to provide optimal conditions:

> We seek, therefore, a recognition of the need for a responsive international mechanism in the GATT to alleviate market disruptions caused by imports which may occur after steel trade barriers, including tariffs, have been reduced.[2]

Neither industry nor labor was wedded to sectoral negotiations in the GATT as such. But they were committed to the principle of establishing some kind of multilateral framework in which problems that arise from unfair practices leading to trade distortions could be resolved. For them sectoral discussions in a multilateral framework was the elemental principle. Otherwise, they cautioned, U.S. trade policy would continue to follow an inappropriate, and possibly, damaging course:

> Failure to obtain sector negotiations is an admission that future steel crises are to be considered as domestic crises, and therefore, amenable only to unilateral or bilateral treatment -- not multilateral.[3]

A separate "Legislative Appeal" issued by the Steelworkers emphasized the same point -- that the Reference Price System was an immediate response to a crisis. But, they strongly urged, "We must move away from the crisis-oriented

---

[1]"Joint Statement," p. 7.

[2]Ibid.

[3]Ibid., pp. 7-8.

approach which we now pursue regarding stéel trade problems. The global undercurrent which causes those problems will continue to persist."[1] The longer term answer, they wrote, is to develop a "separate steel sector agreement . . . so that when the problems arise in the future they can be resolved through international consultation and negotiations."[2] Finally, their joint statement went on to explain how the use of tariffs would minimize the damage in the short term, but in the end wouldn't do either:

> In such a scheme of unilateral national responses, steel tariffs become an essential part of any pricing solution. The steel industry is an import sensitive industry, and therefore its tariffs ought not be subject to GATT negotiations, if there is no steel sector agreement. <u>However, our joint position is that the international steel problems can only be handled adequately through an internationally negotiated multilateral approach.</u> Hence, we do not seek <u>absolute</u> exceptions of steel tariffs, but only <u>conditional</u> exceptions.[3]

This explains industry, labor, and Congressional pressure on the Administration to negotiate special conditions for steel, with regard to tariffs, at the GATT negotiations in Geneva. But since tariffs represented

---

[1]"Steelworkers Legislative Appeal," December 7, 1977. Submitted to Members of the Senate and House Steel Caucuses; on file with author.

[2]Ibid.

[3]"Joint Statement," pp. 7-8.

an important part of the overall MTN negotiating process, both in substance as well as for symbolic value, it also explains why the Administration pushed its trading partners for special steel sector negotiations.[1] Indeed, an official at the Department of State has suggested that the steel lobby's position on tariffs at the MTN was the "immediate catalyst for our [the U.S. negotiating team] insistence on negotiating sectorally." As this State Department official explained it:

> State was opposed vigorously to sectoral negotiations in any form . . . but as the steel lobby pressed harder and harder for us to withdraw the concessions we had given in steel, we knew that the pressure would ease only when we delivered sector negotiations. You must remember that withdrawal of the steel tariff concessions would have opened us to reciprocal withdrawals from the Europeans in other meaningful areas [like agriculture].[2]

At the same time[3] there were equally compelling reasons for the Administration to avoid sector negotiations in the GATT as the steel lobby wanted. It was quite apparent that Japan and the European Community unconditionally opposed sectoral negotiations in the GATT on the assumption that sectoral negotiations in the

---

[1]I elaborate on this point in Chapter 2.

[2]Interview, March 22, 1979.

[3]Mostly because the Europeans and Japanese were unalterably opposed to them. This point is elaborated in Chapter 2, and later in this chapter.

GATT[1] would lead to technical, legal, and generally nondiscretionary rules about export market penetration. Since both the Japanese and Europeans relied heavily on exports, particularly to the American market, while the U.S. steelmakers relied only on production for home consumption, the Japanese and European negotiators feared, probably correctly, that an American position would reflect the demands of its domestic constituencies for protection from their imports. They concluded that they could only lose in such negotiations. Such a loss under the terms of GATT negotiations, they reasoned, could be especially harmful since it would be codified in GATT language, and politically connected to other concessions they also considered valuable. But with the steel lobby in the United States adamant in their demand for sector negotiations, and threatening to force the withdrawal of tariff concessions on steel if sectoral negotiations were not granted, the Administration was forced to develop a compromise position.

The compromise was a multilateral framework outside the GATT to discuss the steel issue. Thus, a cardinal rule of politics: you solve a problem by divorcing it from its context. So steel was taken out

---

[1]See my section below in this chapter on the distinction between sectoral negotiations in the GATT and discussions by sector in the OECD.

of MTN, "de-linking" it, as it were, from the MTN. In effect the Administration was free to pursue their original level of steel tariff concessions so long as a multilateral framework for steel sector negotiations was established.

It should be remembered, however, that there were a number of other issues being negotiated in Geneva in which the steel lobby maintained very considerable interest. For example, the negotiation of the subsidy/countervailing duty code, the antidumping code, and the safeguard code, were each of major concern to steel interests in the United States. But the steel lobby's interest in these negotiations were of a more general nature, associated with the effects they would have on U.S. domestic trade law, especially the countervailing duty, antidumping, and escape clause provisions of the Trade Act of 1974. In each case the negotiations would have effects on how easy or difficult it might be for the steel industry to "be remedied" as a result of complaints against "unfair foreign competition" through subsidization, bilateral or multilateral cartel arrangements distorting trade, or sales at less than fair value. Concepts, definitions and procedures in domestic trade law were all subject to change as a result of the negotiations in Geneva on these nontariff barrier codes. Understandably, the steel lobby would join a host of other "import sensitive" sectors, such as textiles, to lobby the Administration and the Congress on those issues. They expressed a serious interest in all of those negotiations as their resolution would set the stage for U.S. foreign trade policy debates over the next ten years. But they waged their most fervent fight on the sector negotiations battlefront itself -- precisely that to which the European and Japanese were opposed.

Therefore, the steel lobby's main international battle was folded out of the MTN -- it was taken to Paris under the OECD -- even as related battles were fought in the heat of the negotiations at Geneva.

Origins of the OECD Discussions

Beginning in November 1975, when the Europeans first called their meeting in the OECD to discuss what they then termed "the international steel crisis," the major industrial trading partners used the OECD for general discussions about problems in the global steel trade. By the autumn of 1976, however, the initiative for action on steel in the OECD was seized by the United States. As indicated above, it was clear by that time that the U.S. steel lobby's request for sectoral negotiations in the MTN held hostage the U.S. tariff concessions on steel. Because their concessions were so important to the overall MTN package which was being negotiated, the steel lobby "forced us into forcing our European and Japanese trading partners to go beyond discussing steel, and to agree to sectoral negotiations,"[1] according to an economics officer at State responsible for international negotiations in the GATT.

As the United States took control of the OECD discussions in late 1976, they were transformed over the following year and a half from a loosely organized discussion forum with no apparent objective, to a more clearly defined structure with specific goals about how to respond to structural problems associated with surplus capacity and inappropriate national adjustment policies. From all indications this is not at all what the Europeans had intended when they originally asked that the OECD discuss the world steel crisis. But, U.S. officials had become increasingly convinced that sector negotiations in the OECD were the only possible solution to an otherwise irreconcilable dilemma. That is, it was the only way to keep the domestic steel lobby from demanding withdrawal of tariff concessions in Geneva, a situation which surely would have led to the unravelling of other critical aspects of the negotiations. Accordingly, the United States trade policy bureaucracy began to formalize its efforts in the OECD.

---

[1]Interview, March 22, 1979.

U.S. participation in the OECD was channeled through the steel steering committee, an interagency task force on steel responsible to the Trade Policy Staff Committee in the Administration. As indicated in the last chapter, the Solomon Task Force was also created from this steel committee.[1]

But, at that point in 1976 and even into 1977, the domestic political crisis in the United States had not yet erupted. So, the steel steering group concentrated its efforts on the OECD discussions. From late 1976 to July 1977, the steel steering group met with their counterparts from Europe and Japan to discuss "the world steel crisis."[2] During this period, the discussions remained at a relatively slow and uneventful pace.

The U.S. delegation was led by Assistant Secretary of State William Barraclough, and Assistant Special Trade Representative for Industrial Products, Richard Heimlich, and included representatives from the Departments of Treasury, Commerce, and Labor. Noticeably, the domestic

---

[1]The Solomon Task Force was both wider and narrower than the steel steering group. It included some members of the steel steering group, plus some "non-trade" economists to work on the details of the TPM. For example, Robert Crandall, an economist on leave from the Brookings Institution, to work with the Council on Wage and Price Stability, worked closely with Solomon on developing the mechanics of the TPM system.

[2]Interview, November 6, 1978.

policy representation from the Council on Wage and Price Stability, and the President's Council on Economic Advisors which served on the Solomon Task Force, was missing here. Equally as noticeable, the leadership had a clear bias toward the international dimension of U.S. foreign trade policy.

U.S. Pressure for a Steel Committee

As pressure from the steel lobby for withdrawal of steel tariff concession grew, the U.S. delegation to the OECD stepped up its efforts to move discussions into a more formalized structure. This was not an easy task, as the Europeans and Japanese continued to oppose the concept of sectoral negotiations and still just wanted to "discuss" steel. Thus, there were two cumbersome stages in which U.S. officials pushed the other members of the OECD (all but Iceland participated) to accept the notion that an "Ad Hoc Steel Committee" should be formed. The initial stage of negotiations lasted from January 1977 to about mid-April 1977; and then it took until July 1977 when the OECD Ad Hoc Steel Committee was officially established.

This process was not made any easier for the STR's office, which by this time had clearly taken the lead of the U.S. delegation, since the majority of the U.S. agencies involved -- Labor, Commerce, and State -- continued to regard the effort as "unnecessary," and it was therefore treated rather casually.[1] State made it difficult because they opposed sectoral negotiations and resented being held hostage by the steel lobby; Labor and Commerce treated the "whole affair as a secondary concern."[2] Indeed, from the point of view of Labor's representative, a mid-level bureaucrat "there was a void of sorts, until November 1977 when the United States decided there was a need to go beyond just discussing data."[3] In fact, it wasn't until the end of 1977, according to a high official at Labor, that "policy-types got involved." The same was true for Commerce. Not so coincidentally, that was the period when the domestic political crisis had erupted.

Nonetheless, throughout 1977, it became increasingly clear that the initiative in the OECD was being taken by the United States and that the STR's office was its leader. STR's position was understandable since it was that office in the U.S. government which had the responsibility for a successful MTN. While State clearly supported the effort toward trade liberalization, and wanted a successful Agreement, it was more sensitive to the European and Japanese opposition to sectoral negotiations than to the domestic pressures. STR, on the

---

[1]Interview, November 7, 1978.

[2]Ibid.

[3]Ibid.

other hand, felt both, and realized that strong opposition to the final MTN package by the domestic steel lobby could be just as damaging as strong opposition to sectoral negotiations by the United States' trading partners during the process of negotiating. Therefore, the STR's office was more disposed to press the Europeans and Japanese, and effectively assumed the leadership role in the OECD steel talks even though it was officially shared with State. By the fall of 1977, the United States had begun in a serious way to press the other OECD countries to include in the discussions substantive policy issues, in addition to the data gathering exercise which had comprised their entire agenda since 1976. As one U.S. participant in the ad hoc group said, "We had been meeting without any terms of reference . . . we felt there was now a need to go beyond just discussing data."[1]

Even though the Europeans had called the first meeting in the OECD, in response to their particular conditions in late 1975, neither they nor the Japanese were prepared to upgrade the group to a policy level. Both sustained opposition to sectoral negotiations, in or out of the GATT on the grounds that they would eventually lose substantial market access under such arrangements. But the United States, clearly at the behest of a powerful

---

[1]Ibid.

lobby at home, although formally and even practically under the stewardship of the STR's office, continued to push the OECD toward establishing an international steel committee with a "policy" as well as an "information gathering" mandate. Finally, in November 1977, the OECD Ad Hoc Working Group on Steel agreed to a "declaration of principles."

As a result of American initiative the informal OECD discussions had passed through several stages to the establishment of a "permanent ad hoc working group."[1] Still, it wasn't until October of the following year that the OECD Member States would finally agree to the working principles for an OECD International Steel Committee. But the central question -- Would the OECD steel committee be a "discussion group," or a "policy group?" -- was effectively settled before year-end 1977. Thus, for the United States, the decision to establish a "declaration of principles" signalled a victory in the battle between "policy" and "technical information" in the OECD, and still another chip to be offered to the steel lobby at home.

There were clear reasons why the OECD had finally agreed to the position which the U.S. had championed for close to a year. Most of them had to do with unusual pressure by the U.S. negotiators because of increased

---

[1]This is the term used by Administration officials.

pressure on them. For one thing, the domestic political crisis in the wake of "Youngstown" brought the steel issue "to the top of the list for the Carter Administration." While the Administration responded to the domestic political crisis with the TPM,[1] the explosive situation at home made it that much more urgent that an acceptable agreement be secured internationally. Thus, on November 30, 1977, the OECD Ad Hoc Working Group on Steel reached an understanding on several principles. Since this understanding become the basis for the International Steel Agreement, which officially established the International Steel Committee, we shall list them:

> First, sustained priority attention must be given to the long-term need of restructuring and modernization . . . to promote a rational allocation of productive resources with an aim to achieve fully competitive enterprises . . . . The group agreed that Member Countries . . . should avoid shifting the burden of adjustment from one producing nation to another.
>
> Second, any immediate measures must be consistent with the longer-term need to rationalize the world steel industry as well as with the free and fair flow of international trade. No solution for the fundamental problems of steel industries can be found in reliance on quantitative restrictions.
>
> Third, the Group agreed that special attention should be given to the problem of pricing. In times of slack demand prices are expected to fall and there may be tendencies toward sales at a loss. No nation can be expected to absorb for sustained periods large quantities of imports at unjustifiably low prices to the detriment of

---

[1]See Chapter 5.

> domestic production and employment, but any measures to deal with such imports should take into account customary patterns of trade.[1]

Each point addressed substantive policy issues. In addition, however, the Group reiterated its commitment to collecting "important data":

> The Group also decided to establish a system for gathering information which can make an important contribution on a continuing basis to the participants' understanding of trends within and among countries and to their ability to devise long and short term measures consistent with the principles cited above. The Group expects that this system, in addition to serving as an early warning system to identify incipient problems, will facilitate rational investment decisions in the future through increased transparency in the industry worldwide.[2]

Interestingly, not much was said publicly in the United States about the OECD Steel Committee. There seem to be two probable explanations. One is that it was drowned in the overwhelming publicity about the Trigger Price System. For example, some articles that appeared at the time only mentioned the developments in the OECD in the last paragraphs after having discussed the TPM.[3] A second probable explanation is that the Administration

---

[1]"Declaration of Principles," working draft for the OECD Steel Committee, on file with author.

[2]OECD Press Release, (77) 54, November 30, 1977, Paris.

[3]See, for example, "Imported Steel Pricing Plan To Start February 21", <u>Washington Post</u>, February 11, 1978, pp. C8,12

didn't want to appear to be doing too much for the steel industry. After all, the commonly accepted image of steel has been that of a powerful oligopoly which raises prices, exacerbating the inflationary spiral, and generally hurting the consumer. Besides, too many deals for one sector during a time when the Administration was trying to conduct multilateral trade negotiations would give other sectors ideas about what they weren't getting, but deserved.

So, quietly, but successfully, the Administration pursued a framework for sector negotiations in the OECD. The "Declarations of Principles" was an important breakthrough, but there was still some distance before the OECD Steel Committee would actually be established. Another important breakthrough came in the period following the establishment of the Davignon Steel Plan for the European Community. For, the Davignon Plan was another development which led to increased steel lobby pressure on the U.S. negotiators.

Two aspects of the Davignon Plan were viewed by the U.S. government, and steelmakers alike, as inimical to U.S. interests.[1] The first is obvious: it set up a "base price system" which automatically limited imports

---

[1]This point is also discussed in Chapter 3 in the section on European steel.

into the Community. As indicated earlier,[1] this was different from the Solomon Reference Price Plan in that it limited imports which were actually priced above what European steel sold for intracommunity. In other words, imports were not limited on the grounds that they were unfairly dumped, but on the grounds that they were imports. The Davignon Plan sought to help European steelmakers by allowing them to raise prices by fifteen percent. This was to be accomplished, in part, by keeping out low-cost imports on a minimum price scheme.

The second aspect of the Davignon Plan which prompted the United States to push even harder for a formal steel committee in the OECD were the "bilaterals." The Davignon Plan encouraged the Member States of the European Community to conclude bilateral deals on steel imports. It has been the United States position that "bilateralism" places international transactions beyond the influence of the market, and may therefore constitute obstacles to fair and open international trade.[2] According to a recent Congressional Budget Office Report on United States trade Policy:

---

[1]This point is also discussed in Chapter 5, under the section "A Concession to Europe."

[2]"U.S. Trade Policy and the Tokyo Round of the Multilateral Trade Negotiations," The Congress of the United States, Congressional Budget Office, March 1979, p. 39.

> . . . these arrangements reserve some fraction of a nation's total imports for particular countries. Products from other nations not party to bilateral arrangements can be displaced, even if these products are cheaper than those that the importer has agreed to buy . . . . Bilateralism poses a particular problem for the United States. Because the Federal government has relatively little control over private firms in the United States that carry out the bulk of U.S. international transactions, it cannot enter into bilateral arrangements as easy as can governments that exercise effective control over important industries.[1]

Thus, U.S. policymakers opposed this aspect of the Davignon Plan which encouraged a development that they regarded as contrary to the spirit of the liberal trading order, and against the interests of the United States. Therefore, they sought to overcome the effects of increased "bilateralism" in steel by pushing for an even more firm commitment from the Europeans in the multilateral arrangements envisioned under an OECD Steel Committee.

Still another catalyst working on the U.S. steel negotiators in Paris to increase pressure on the Europeans and Japanese for the establishment of a steel committee is associated with domestic acceptance of the TPM itself. Unlike the Trigger Price System government officials never pretended that there was a direct relationship between the domestic political crisis which exploded after "Youngstown," and the discussions in the OECD. Indeed, it would have been politically naive, and probably somewhat foolish, to rely

---

[1]Ibid, pp. 40, 41.

on foreign policy to solve the domestic crisis. However, it was understood that the acceptance of the TPM was contingent to a certain degree on successful international negotiations for steel. Industry and labor accepted the TPM, though not entirely satisfied by it, in part because of the progress the Administration seemed to be making on the development of an international agreement i.e., recognition of an industry-wide steel sector for international trade negotiations. So as a result of the "Declaration of Principles" the foundation for the Steel Committee and the broad outline for its mandate were in place by the beginning of 1978.

While industry and labor were quite aware by late 1977 that it was highly unlikely they could secure sectoral negotiations in the GATT, they continued to use that demand as a leverage to ensure the best possible deal in the OECD; this strategy became more evident during the winter of 1977-78.

Consensus at Home and Abroad for an OECD International Steel Committee

By June 1978 the Administration's representatives at the OECD ad hoc steel meetings had returned to Washington with a preliminary text of what would become the International Steel Agreement. The June text was submitted, along with other central elements of the GATT trade negotiations, to the President. Politically, sectoral negotiations on steel were still separate from the MTN; but as a technical matter the documents relating to the OECD steel discussions, as well as the final text of the International Steel Agreement, were submitted together to the President and to the Congress with the various codes negotiated at the MTN. This was a domestic matter. Indeed, it had always been for purposes of foreign policy that the steel discussions were folded out of MTN politics per se. And for domestic purposes, it was important to underscore the link between the two. Even at the international level, however, the OECD Steel Committee began to get folded back into the MTN; this only happened once the agreement was essentially in place, thereby assuring, as much as these things can be assured, that steel would not upset the overall agreement in Geneva. Therefore, while the Ministers of the European Community were reviewing the proposed steel agreement, they were also preparing for the "political" agreement on the MTN which was to have been reached by July 15 when the heads of the industrial countries were to have met in Bonn.[1]

At the same time the European Commission was preparing for the July meetings, the steel lobby in the

---

[1]The Bonn meeting was held, but political agreement on the MTN was not reached at that time. At the time of writing, final agreement has still not been accomplished for the whole of the MTN, though considerable progress has been made on a number of the important aspects of the MTN.

United States called on the Congress for the first time to press directly and singularly on the Administration for support of the OECD Steel Committee. The Congress acted through the Senate and House Steel Caucuses which had been established in response to the domestic-political crisis. Key members of both Caucuses had become quite familiar with the steel issue, and were unusually well-briefed on the Trigger Price Mechanism. But they knew little of the OECD Steel Discussions, and even less of the subtleties of its politics. Still they responded to constituent pressure. Indeed, a number of the Congressmen involved with the steel issue began to take some credit even if it might not have been well deserved. For example, Senator Randolph referred to the Congressional responsibility for the President's response in developing the Trigger Price System and the OECD Steel Committee: "Cooperation came after the members of the Steel Caucus went to the White House." Then in a reflective moment by this long time chairman of the Senate Public Works Committee, traditionally the dispensor of pork barrel: "There are times when those downtown need to be jogged by us on the Hill."[1]

The steel lobby understood the importance of Congressional pressure on the Administration. Thus, in

---

[1]Senator Randolph speaking at the Senate Steel Caucus, February 6, 1979.

a letter to each member of the Senate, Lloyd McBride, president of the Steelworkers, and Lewis Foy, chairman of the American Iron and Steel Institute, set forth the position of labor and industry on the impending international steel agreement:

> The ultimate objective must be elimination of predatory and other unfair trading practices . . .
>
> An effective International Steel Agreement amongst governments must at a minimum contain steel-specific rules governing dumping and safeguard measures.[1]

The Senate and House Steel Caucuses responded accordingly. On June 30, 1978, the Senate Steel Caucus sent a letter to Ambassador Strauss expressing concern about "the progress of international negotiations on steel."[2] And the Caucus received a response from Ambassador Strauss on July 26. In part it said:

> After more than one year of discussions and nearly six months of intensive negotiations, we now have a tentative agreement on the text of a draft steel arrangement . . .
>
> The central feature of this arrangement is the establishment of an international steel committee under the auspices of the OECD to develop agreed guidelines for government policy in the steel sector. This committee would serve as a forum for notification of

---

[1]June 19, 1978 letter to the Senate Steel Caucus, from Lloyd McBride of the United Steelworkers of America, and Lewis Foy, acting chairman for the American Iron and Steel Institute, on file with author.

[2]Senate Steel Caucus letter of June 30, 1978; on file with author.

> governmental actions relating to steel trade and for multilateral review of national governmental policies and actions in the steel sector. In addition, the steel committee would monitor steel production, capacity, trade flows, and other indicators in an attempt to spot potential steel trade problems . . . Another key feature of the draft arrangement is that government steel policies should not shift the burden of structural adjustment to other countries.[1]

It was quite clear that Ambassador Strauss had already realized that keeping the steel talks out of the MTN was the only protection he had against an unravelling of the MTN itself. He had by this time been told what had been implicit since the Congressional hearings on the 1974 Trade Act: "If you don't get an [steel] Agreement, you won't have an MTN." Some of the substance industry and labor wanted, indeed demanded through their Congressional voices, couldn't be delivered.[2] More important, however, was the broad framework of a steel Agreement, and the International Steel Committee itself, which offered the same principles that were sought by sectoral negotiations in the GATT. That could be delivered. Therefore, consensus was finally built around steel sector negotiations

---

[1]Letter from Ambassador Strauss to Senate Steel Caucus, July 26, 1978, on file with author.

[2]As indicated in Chapter 4, most of the Congressional pressures on the Administration avoided institutional or legislative channels, but used more informal ones such as letters to Ambassador Strauss. In other words, the Congress didn't act as a body, per se.

in the OECD. For example, as the Europeans and Japanese came around to supporting it, even the State Department dropped its opposition. The domestic steel lobby was also resigned to the fact that they weren't getting sectoral talks in the GATT.

Once the Congress began pressing the Administration, the steel lobby's concern about tariff cuts in the GATT was somewhat alleviated. Consider, for example, Ambassador Strauss's reply to the Senate Steel Caucus letter referred to above:

> With respect to the negotiations on steel tariffs, I can assure you that it is unlikely that our final offer will be even close to 40 percent reduction and that we intend to complete our negotiation of an international steel arrangement before commitments are to be made on steel tariff offers.[1]

Therefore, by late summer 1978, it seemed to be in everyone's interest to support the establishment of an OECD International Steel Committee. Once the politics were in place, there were a number of very good reasons which could be recommended in support of the result.

There was much about the OECD which, for the Europeans and Japanese, made it far more attractive than the GATT. Even getting them to the OECD to talk about "policy" -- production levels, expansion plans, investment plans, pricing, etc. -- was "tedious." As one steel trade

---

[1]Ambassador Strauss' letter of July 26, to Senate Steel Caucus, on file with author.

official at the STR's office described it: "They came," he said, "but they were kicking and screaming all the way."[1]

Virtually every Administration official who took part in the development of an International Steel Agreement, and setting up the International Steel Committee, are now in agreement that there were essentially five reasons that the appropriate home was the OECD, rather than the GATT.[2] At the bottom, of course, was that the OECD was politically acceptable to their major trading partners, and the GATT was not. But let us review the arguments now made:

1. While a clubby, friendly and generally informal atmosphere tends to pervade the OECD, the GATT is clouded by a more staid, formalistic atmosphere which makes it less easy to reach consensus on controversial subjects. In a word: the legalistic structure of the

---

[1]Interview, November 9, 1978.

[2]One suspects that these reasons were constructed to conform to the reality of the situation. That is, because of the position of the Europeans and the Japanese, sectoral negotiations in the GATT were virtually impossible, and so as the Administration realized that they could only pursue sectoral discussions in the OECD, they began to find reasons why this was a better approach anyway. For a good discussion of the role of the OECD, see, Miriam Camps, "First World Relationships: The Role of the OECD," The Atlantic Papers, February 1975, Council papers on International Affairs: 5 (New York: Council on Foreign Relations, 1975).

GATT was seen by the Europeans and Japanese as a reason not to discuss steel there.

2. Particularly because of the controversies in the Tokyo Round of the GATT, and the degree to which industrial sectors like steel were a part of the controversies, any attempt to talk openly and candidly about steel -- something the Americans hoped to do in the International Steel Committee -- would have been difficult, at best. One assumption, probably correct, was that the discussions in the GATT would be used more for "positioning," than for the supposed purpose of solving its problems. Of course, there will always be some amount of political "cat-and-mouse," but it was felt that the delicate nature of the MTN might not withstand such shenanigans.

3. There were those who argued that there was no place in "GATT-lexicon" to talk about such items as pricing structures, production levels, etc.

4. Even if the obstacles in (1), (2) and (3) could have been overcome, however, the OECD had the desirable institutional characteristic of a limited membership. Limited in number: in the GATT it would have been nearly impossible to talk about the kind of topics the United States wanted to discuss with close to one hundred countries participating. But limited in type as well: the Western industrial countries and Japan wanted to talk to one another. It was felt that

bringing the Third World into the discussions, en masse, would so politicize the issue from the start as to render any discussion nearly valueless. One U.S. policymaker put it in rather sobering terms:

> It would have been physically unwieldy, and politically unhealthy, to try to negotiate such sensitive matters in the GATT with ninety-eight other countries, many of whom either do not have a direct and large stake, and/or are your enemy.[1]

5. Finally, unlike the OECD "officio-crats"[2] who are familiar with industry and industrial sectors like steel, GATT technicians tend to be lawyers who are trained in the legal details of the GATT, but know little or nothing of industry. This argument gained strength as time went on: in the first place, the OECD ad hoc steel group had been meeting for over a year before the International Steel Agreement was finally approved. Thus they knew even more than when they started. Secondly, the OECD Secretariat for Industrial Policy, which had met seven times between July 1977 and October 1978 when the International Steel Committee was formally established, had developed an impressive network of valuable contacts in the steel industry, accumulated a data base of considerable depth, and knew the issue quite well. Thus,

---

[1]Interview, November 9, 1978.

[2]"Officio-crats" is a term which has been used by a number of Administration officials when referring to professional members of the OECD technical staff.

the OECD's natural advantage had grown even wider by October 1978 when the International Steel Committee began to operate.

These reasons for setting up the International Steel Committee in the OECD apart, the governments were still cautious about conforming to GATT rules. As Ambassador Strauss indicated in his letter to the Senate Steel Caucus:

> . . . further, the signatories of the draft steel agreement will undertake specific commitments regarding intervention in trade during crisis periods, including an obligation to make such actions consistent with GATT provisions, and to notify such actions to the steel committee and the GATT . . .[1]

They were, after all, engaged in an MTN, and at least one important reason they worked so hard to get an Agreement and a Committee was to maximize the chances for a successful MTN Agreement.

Addressing the Structural Crisis

If the Trigger Price Mechanism was aimed primarily at diffusing the domestic-political crisis, the point of the OECD International Steel Agreement was to keep an international crisis in world steel trade from erupting -- a far more ambitious effort, indeed. The Administration operated under the assumption that the breakdown of the MTN talks would lead to an international political crisis

---

[1]Ambassador Strauss' letter to the Senate Steel Caucus, July 26, 1978.

over trade among the OECD countries. They were probably correct. Unlike the TPM, which was never intended as anything but a temporary measure, the International Steel Agreement, through the International Steel Committee, was expected to "meet regularly" to deal with the present and future problems in international steel trade. As Secretary Solomon contrasted it to the TPM: "The International Steel Committee has relevance for the long term solution."[1] Therefore, while it sought to contain the potential political explosion over the steel issue among the OECD countries, and probably would never have been set up had the MTN not forced the participating countries to reach consensus in the short term, it was surely intended to deal with "the steel industry's . . . serious difficulties of both a cyclical and structural nature,"[2] i.e., the economic and political-economic problems which threatened the steel industries in "virtually all major steel-producing nations,"[3] in the long term.

As the mandate listed the "problems," it was therefore indicated that all signatories recognized them as such and had thereby "committed" themselves to

---

[1]Secretary Solomon speaking at the Senate Steel Caucus meeting, February 6, 1979.

[2]OECD International Steel Agreement.

[3]Ibid.

the ambitious effort of seeking solutions: The problems as listed are:

> Persistent excess capacity; an exceptionally low level of demand; unjustifiably low prices on world markets; marked changes in traditional trade patterns; major dislocations of labor, frequently in areas already experiencing high unemployment; depressed financial performance among producers, which holds down investment needed for modernization and rationalization of plants; increasing governmental intervention in steel supply and demand, especially with foreign trade.[1]

Clearly, it was not easy to reach consensus even on what the problems were. Everyone agreed with the first two points; they were understood as facts describing the condition of the world steel market. But the others were certainly more controversial. The Europeans and the Japanese, for example, were most concerned about how the "traditional trade patterns" were changing: were they to lose access to foreign markets they depended on for their exports? They understood that U.S. domestic producers were alarmed at the growing import penetration into their own market. If overall import penetration had increased to twenty percent of apparent consumption in 1977, would the United States set that as the limit, or set a lower level? Foreigners might be able to live with less than twenty percent, but how much less and what proportion of the overall percentage would each get? The TPM had

---

[1]Ibid.

given the Europeans a greater percentage of the import market in 1978 than they had in the prior decade during which time the Japanese had steadily increased their share. Could the Europeans maintain that position, however? And how would the Japanese react? Thus, it was important to those countries which relied on exports to ensure that they were not denied a share of the U.S. market, or any other market, which they had "traditionally" come to depend upon.

Since the United States producers didn't rely on exports, they weren't as concerned about "changes in traditional trade patterns" so long as those changes didn't cut into their own market, and they surely had some control over that. Rather, the American producers' *raison d'etre* for an International Steel Agreement was to address the import problem caused by unfair trading practices. And, the Carter Administration had committed itself to penalizing unfair trade practices which resulted in injurious import penetration to American producers. Thus, the "problem" described as "increasinq governmental intervention" was a recognition by the International Steel Committee of the claim the United States had brought against its trading partners: Unfair trade practices were recognized as those actions of government intervention which distort trade by dumping and/or subsidizing products for sale on foreign markets. As more and more Western

European governments nationalized their steel industries U.S. producers found more and more rationalization for claiming "injury" from governmental intervention which the mandate stated was distorting "steel supply and demand, especially with foreign trade."[1] Accordingly, the American position on this issue prevailed; the International Steel Committee acknowledged the existence of inconsistencies in government intervention and implied a recognition that such government involvement could lead to unfair trading practices.

Typical of decision by consensus, everyone got something. The International Steel Committee was to continue the work of the Ad Hoc Steel Group, and try to smoothe the way for the adjustments that all agreed were necessary in the global steel market.

It if fair to ask, however, how serious the participants will be in trying to achieve the objectives set forth by the International Steel Agreement. In many cases, even a government's seriousness will not make it any easier to withstand the political and social tensions that may result from adjustments in world steel production. What has been said of the relationship between the European Community and its Member States, may apply here as well: "There are nine countries and ten views on any

---

[1]Ibid.

particular issue."[1] One hopes that such cynicism would not apply in the case of the International Steel Committee, though it is also hard to believe that the French or the British will be willing or able to promote as a matter of government policy the high levels of unemployment which surely would follow from rationalization and adjustment of steel production as implied by some of the Steel Committee's Objectives. On the other hand, it has been argued that the existence of an international body such as the OECD Steel Committee will give both the European Community, and individual governments, a "fall guy" on which to blame the tough decisions to cut back production levels. This situation may make it somewhat easier, but it will still be the national governments which will bear the brunt of the political and social tensions.

Still, there were two indications that the participants have established an International Steel Committee that they intend to help promote a situation which "will make the next crisis less severe."[2] That is, that they are serious about addressing the problems in the world steel trade. The first indication is related to the way in which the Committee was set up; the second indication is an effort to include some of the more advanced Third

---

[1]Interview, March 26, 1979.

[2]Interview, November 27, 1978.

World countries in the Committee on the assumption that these countries will be contributing increasingly significant proportions of world steel production. Both were United States initiatives, but have been accepted by the other members of the Committee. Let us look at both of these.

One clear indication of the OECD members' intentions was the decision to negotiate a separate mandate for the Steel Committee. According to OECD procedures there were two alternative courses: the first would have been to leave the steel working group under the control of the Council, which itself consisted of ambassadors from the twenty-four member countries of the OECD. Under this procedure there wouldn't have been a mandate for specific actions. It was decided, therefore, that a separate mandate would be negotiated which would give the working group the authority to do what they wanted without first getting approval from the Council. The Steel Committee got its own mandate, its own Secretariat, a staff of eight permanent professionals, plus four clerical types, a not insubstantial budget, and the authority to "act" on issues relating to steel. And under this arrangement, the Steel Committee's responsibility to the Council was limited to pro forma.

The second indication of the members seriousness with regard to the Committee's success, also an American initiative, was the Committee's invitations to the more advanced of the Third World countries to ask them to participate. While the Europeans put forth some opposition at the beginning, presumably based on the fear that including them could adversely affect the bilaterals they were negotiating under their Davignon Plan, they have now agreed not to block any Third World country which has been asked to join and accepts.[1] Invitations have gone to a handful of Third World countries which, in GATT terminology, have "graduated," or are about to "graduate" from "developing" to "developed." While U.S. officials are reluctant to specify which Third World countries have been asked to participate, one can assume that invitations have gone to those which now have reasonably substantial steel making capacity: for example, Brazil, India, South Korea, and Mexico.[2]

At the time of writing, none of these countries have accepted membership. Their hesitation is understandable, as the perceived political stakes are quite high. Acceptance to the "Rich Man's Club" would probably mean rejection from the Third World, a transformation of great significance in the political affairs of the countries taking the step. Most of the countries reflect

---

[1]Interview, March 26, 1979.

[2]Interview, March 26, 1979; for reasons having to do with normalization of relations with the People's Republic of China, Taiwan can not now be asked to join.

this concern in the internal politics over the decision. According to a U.S. State Department officials, most Foreign Ministries of the prospective Third World participants are against joining, while most Economic Ministries support the move.[1]

The reason we point to these invitations as indicators of the seriousness of the Steel Committee is that the Committee will not be in a position to cope with future crises in world steel trade unless it considers all countries which will likely be important producers of steel.

In its mandate the International Steel Committee did purport to address <u>world</u> steel problems -- "persistent excess capacity; and marked changes in traditional patterns."[2] Even though the Third World countries comprise a small proportion of global production in the 1970s, and engaged in an equally small fraction of the steel trade during that period, they will surely affect these "problems" in the 1980s and beyond. Thus, members of the Steel Committee set forth among its "Objectives," to "avoid encouraging economically unjustified investments while recognizing legitimate development needs."[3] Trade

---

[1]Interview, March 26, 1979.

[2]OECD International Steel Agreement.

[3]Ibid.

officials in the United States, even more than the Europeans and the Japanese, were concerned that the International Steel Committee would be seriously limited in its capabilities if it did not include some of the more advanced of the developing countries.[1] According to one official:

> You will have a whole new set of participants by the time we're faced with the next crisis . . . . And if you don't bring [all of] them into this consultative process under the Steel Committee, then you won't be very effective.[2]

U.S. officials were hopeful that the International Steel Committee would promote a process of multilateral consultation which would serve U.S. interests. Their intentions were to minimize distortions in the international steel trade by trying to coordinate supply and demand. They sought preventive rather than remedial measures. No one in high policy level positions had quixotic visions about what an ISC could accomplish, but they did know that the effects of Third World investment in steel making capacity would grow. And, if they wanted

---

[1]The U.S. steel lobby, particularly the industry, wanted to use the Steel Committee to control future investment, production levels, and prices. They argued, probably correctly, that this could only be accomplished if the advanced developing countries were included in the discussions of the Steel Committee. The Administration trade policy officials reflected this view in their negotiations with the other OECD countries.

[2]Interview, March 26, 1979.

to intervene in the global steel market such that economic conditions like excess capacity could be politically controlled to limit the assault on the U.S. domestic market, they would have to account for countries like South Korea, India, Brazil, and Mexico, as well as the Japanese and the Europeans.

By attempting to address problems in the world steel trade through the formation of an international steel committee, U.S. policymakers have indicated a willingness to accept the principles of organized liberalism. This kind of response which has been developed for steel is likely to be applied in roughly similar terms for a number of other industrial sectors experiencing structural changes and associated adjustment problems. But, it will be necessary that the steel committee, or similar arrangements for other industrial sectors, helps to promote the development of positive adjustment policies in the older industrial regions of Western Europe and the United States, while also organizing the emergence of the developing world. For we should be certain that we learn the lesson of Japan: that rapid and precipitous economic growth can impose uncomfortable burdens on individual governments and produce unhealthy strains on their abilities to govern effectively. We have seen that the liberal trading order, itself supported and in many respects made possible by the liberal policies of the United States, can lead to a set of conditions that ironically threaten the very principles from which that system grew and prospered.

From the case of steel, 1976-78, it has been clear that U.S. policymakers have begun to recognize these fundamental problems, and seem willing to modify and amend liberal trade policies in a manner which helps promote policies of positive adjustment among the industrialized countries experiencing the adverse effects of structural change. At the same time it is also necessary that U.S. policy encourage a more rational and steady approach to the way the system should cope with new entrants. Thus, policies of organized liberalism, as manifested in the formation of the International Steel Committee, ought to be viewed as a way to protect the liberal trading order from defeating itself. For we have learned that liberal economics within national economies, and principles of free trade among national economies, can bring us higher levels of prosperity and welfare. We have also learned, however, that there are limits on the speed at which these benefits can be absorbed. In the United States, Western Europe, and Japan, there are segments of the populations which depend on standards of production and employment in specific sectors. The U.S. government has a responsibility to these expectations in its own society, just as U.S. foreign trade policy has a responsibility to the liberal trading system which has provided the critical foundation in which these expectations have been grounded.

As the structural changes in the world economic system shed doubt on the degree to which these expectations can be reached, U.S. policy must begin to question practices which were previously accepted with a frightening degree of automacity as part of its goals regarding liberal internationalism. Consider, for example, that the Moroccans may wish to build a plant for the production of steel bars for use in a proposed public housing project in Morocco.[1] And consider that the government of Morocco may be perfectly capable of securing the necessary financing for the project. Regardless of how competitive or uncompetitive the steel plant may be, it is still the case that that additional steel plant will contribute to the condition of excess capacity in global steelmaking facilities. The liberal economist will argue that the key here is whether the Moroccans can produce the steel more efficiently than some of the older steelmakers in Western Europe, Japan, or North America. And if they can, then they should build the steel mill, produce the steel bars for the public housing project, and then begin to export the steel

---

[1]Interview, May 7, 1979.

when the consumption in Morocco falls off as a result of the public housing project having been completed. There is the additional problem not addressed by the liberal economists, however: that of the additional political strains in those societies whose workers will have been replaced by the Moroccans.

So the International Steel Committee, or any such arrangement organized to cope with the problems which come from structural changes in the international economy, must apply itself to the hard question of who should produce when. To avoid harsh political and social strains it may be necessary to provide Morocco, for example, with incentives to not build the steel bar plant, by providing them with unusually low priced steel, and other low interest loans or grants for a sector from which Europe, the United States, and Japan may be better able to adjust. Thus, the Moroccans would get their public housing, and the industrialized nations will have gotten a reprieve in which they might complete a restructuring and rationalization policy away from producing steel bars which in the end could be produced more efficiently elsewhere. That of course assumes a good faith effort toward positive adjustment on the part of those who have kept the Moroccans from building their own plant, and a willingness on the part of the Moroccans to develop in another sector. Organized improperly, these trade-offs would never work. But if there isn't an attempt at organization, then the industrial world may find that the structural changes taking place in the international economy are imposing burdens on individual societies and governments which will lead to further instability and tensions that may cause the connecting principles of the liberal trading order to unravel. And in the end if the liberal trading order were to fail to adjust adequately to structural change, a process which may be accomplished through gradual rather than precipitous change, "future" Moroccans will probably not have the chance to look for the financing to build that steel plant.

Summary

The International Steel Committee was officially established on October 21, 1978 and has already met in November 1978 and January and April 1979. Predictably, the Committee has done little more than to collect data but it has made progress on deciding the type of data to be collected. For example, it has made substantial progress in addressing the "data comparability problem" among countries which many claim is one of the central technical causes of overcapacity, i.e., producers in one country not having a firm grasp on what capacity exists elsewhere. Of course, one must emphasize "technical cause" since many of the decisions to build steel capacity and to produce it are politically motivated. Still it is fair to say that the Committee is moving in a direction consistent with how the United States has defined its interests and objectives. For example, Ambassador Alan Wolff, U.S. Assistant Special Trade Representative, was elected chairman of the Committee. Officials in the U.S. government read this as an indication that the rest of the Committee membership is willing to accept the U.S. position that the Committee "should address substantive policy issues in addition to information gathering."[1]

More important than the details of what it will do, however, the International Steel Committee represents a successful effort by the United States trade policy bureaucracy to balance the pressures of domestic constituencies with those of its trading partners in the international arena. In some ways even more than the Trigger Price Mechanism, the International Steel Committee is a prime example of how the United States is responding to conditions in the global economy caused by increased government involvement in international trade. It is the compromise between "fight[ing] or join[ing] the trend towards increasing government involvement abroad,"[2]

---

[1]Interview, March 26, 1979.

[2]C. Fred Bergsten, "International Economic Policy -- Where We Stand," Statement before the Joint Economic Committee of the United States Congress, July 19, 1978.

as C. Fred Bergsten put it. Indeed, the objective of the International Steel Committee is to organize the "policies of government intervention in international trade" in order to stabilize existing arrangements of global production and competition. While it is far different from the economic strategies and foreign trade policies of intervention practiced by its trading partners, it symbolized that U.S. policymakers recognize the need to intervene in international trade to satisfy pressures from domestic constituencies. The willingness to talk about organizing markets, controlling production levels, and setting price guidelines is seen by some as an infringement on the free market system. It is seen by others, however, as the only response to a situation of growing protectionism among industrial nations in international industrial sectors like steel.

CONCLUSION TO PART II

As we have seen, the United States government developed two programs specifically to address steel trade problems. The most important policy distinction between the two is between a long-term and short-term approach. The International Steel Committee focused on the long-term problem created by structural shifts in global steel production and exacerbated by foreign governments' actions which effectively shifted the burden of industrial economic adjustment to other countries. During the 1976-78 period, a disproportionate share of that adjustment was shifted by the Japanese and the Europeans to the United States. Its practical and immediate effect was to increase the amount of imports. Its long-term effect was to further erode the U.S. steel industry's competitive position in the global market.

Since steel is a cyclical industry, where periods of downturn will be particularly exacerbated by excess capacity, one expects the problems of 1976-78 to recur.[1]

---

[1]Interview, January 5, 1979; also see, "Report to the President on Prices and Costs in the United States Steel Industry," Council on Wage and Price Stability, October 1977; "Report to the President: A Comprehensive Program for the Steel Industry," Anthony Solomon, chairman, Task Force, November 8, 1977; "International Steel Agreement, Organization for Economic Cooperation and Development,

Therefore, the ISC has been widely acclaimed throughout American policymaking circles, and supported by industry and labor as well, as "a significant step towards resolution of the longstanding problems in steel trade."[1] In a statement by Lewis Foy for the industry on "Steel Trade Policy," he said, "the industry fully supports the Steel Committee."[2] Fundamentally, it was intended to address the problem of excess capacity. But in that sense, the ISC has the distinct advantage of being subject only to prospective analysis, i.e., it purports to monitor global steel production, investment policies of companies and countries around the globe, and pricing levels, in order that countries will be better equipped to adjust to new conditions. Simply, it seeks to minimize the distortions in international trade which come from structural shifts in world steel production and competition. Its purpose is to protect existing steelmaking facilities[3] from future challenges. It seeks

---

Paris, 1978; "Economics of International Steel Trade: Policy Implications for the United States," an analysis and forecast for the American Iron and Steel Institute, Putnam, Hayes, and Bartlett, Inc. (Newton, Massachusetts, May 1977).

[1]Secretary Solomon speaking before the Senate Steel Caucus, February 6, 1979.

[2]Lewis Foy speaking before the Senate Steel Caucus, February 6, 1979.

[3]International Steel Agreement, Paris, October 1978.

to address the causes, not the sumptoms, i.e., restructuring policies and adjustment strategies rather than quantities of imports.

By contrast, the Trigger Price System was designed to address the immediate import problem caused by unfair trading practices. It had to produce immediately; in that sense its task was more difficult. Thus industry and labor were less sure about their support for the TPM: "We still hope that the TPM can be made to work effectively. If properly administered, we think the TPM should substantially reduce imports from their high levels of the past years."[1]

While both the TPM and the ISC address the trade problems in steel, both were viewed by industry and government alike as tools to reinvigorate the American steel industry. As industry officials put it:

> The industry must achieve higher levels of profit for a sustained period to obtain enough investment capital through internally generated funds to achieve some vitally necessary expansion of capacity. This will also position it to obtain more funds from private capital markets.[2]

Thus, industry's concern about the level of imports stemmed from the degree distortions in international trade through others' economic strategies eroded its ability to generate

---

[1]Lewis Foy, as representative for the steel lobby, speaking before the Senate Steel Caucus, February 7, 1979.

[2]David M. Roderick, speaking before the Senate Steel Caucus on "Capital Formation," February 7, 1979.

capital from within or obtain it from othér sources because of the debilitating effect imports have had on its competitive position.

The TPM alone, even if it did more than diffuse the domestic political crisis, and cut back the amount of imports, was not equipped to address the long-term problem of competition against modern and efficient and/or subsidized steel industries.[1]

In fact, imports into the United States in 1978, rose 9.5 percent over 1977, to an all-time record of 21.1 million tons.[2] This is especially significant since the amount of imports was higher in 1978, after the TPM went into effect, than in 1977.[3] Based on these figures, therefore, one might expect that the amount of steel imported into the United States may have, in the words of Lewis Foy, "moved to a higher plateau."[4] Indeed, the

---

[1]Secretary Solomon, speaking before the Senate Steel Caucus, February 6, 1979.

[2]The steel trade deficit was roughly $6 billion in 1978, or about thirteen percent of the overall U.S. balance of trade deficit, "Steel Industry Statement for Submission to the Department of the Treasury," January 29, 1979 (xerox). (All data which appeared in the Steel Industry statement and is quoted here, has been confirmed by author with the Department of Commerce, Bureau of Economic Analysis.)

[3]Ibid.

[4]See Chart I, Chapter 3, which shows that the level of import penetration has not only increased, but appears also to level off at higher plateaus.

average imports for 1977 and 1978 exceeded twenty million tons, a forty-three percent increase over the 1973-76 period, which had reached a still higher level than previous periods. In other words, the overall trend line shows a steadily increasing level of the amount of imports since 1960. And, if this trend continues one might expect that the domestic industry will be in an even worse position to withstand the pressures of the international trading system in the next period of cyclical downturn.

For, the steel industry benefited in 1978 from two conditions which may fade over the next few years: first, a more buoyant U.S. economy -- apparent steel consumption in 1978 was 116.4 million tons as compared to 108.5 million tons in 1977, 101.1 in 1976, and 89.0 in 1975[1] -- combined with the improved health of the other industrial economies; and second, a reluctance on the part of U.S. trading partners to "dump" since "they knew they couldn't get away with it,"[2] as one Treasury official put it. Thus as the cycle turns for the worse, a condition which virtually all economists expect for steel, the U.S. steel industry may face similar dilemmas

---

[1]See Chart I, Chapter 3.

[2]Interview, March 19, 1979.

as it did in 1977. Since the European and Japanese steel industries continue to operate at low levels of capacity utilization, and Third World countries continue to build steel mills which tend to produce more than their domestic economies can absorb, it appears that the problem of excess capacity will persist as well. But there is still a distinction to be made between the short term and long term problems -- a distinction which may be clarified by an assessment of the industry's performance in 1978.

In spite of the increase in imports in 1978, the industry recorded a better year than 1977, with regard to a number of indicators. For example, in 1978, it reported a profit of about $804 million, considerably more than the loss of $40 million in 1977; cash flow tripled from $974 million to about $3 billion; and capacity utilization went from 78.4 percent to about 86.5 percent.[1] But how does one interpret these numbers, and what implications do they have for an assessment of the TPM? More importantly, even if one is to interpret them positively -- that the industry is now healthy[2] -- and one is to assume that the TPM played a significant part

---

[1]"Steel Industry Statement for Submission to the Department of the Treasury," January 29, 1979.

[2]A high capacity utilization rate in 1978 may be interpretated in two ways. On the one hand it is certainly a healthy sign, since it means that U.S. productive capacity

in promoting the industry's profit picturé, what does it mean for the long term condition of the industry, and for the role of the International Steel Committee?

Lewis Foy, as spokesman for the American steel industry, argued that there were other, more revealing indicators of the health of the industry: "We're still at, or near the bottom of the Citibank list of forty major industries in terms of return on shareholder's equity,"[1] Foy reported to the Senate and House Steel Caucuses. He went on to argue that the $1.4 billion net income for 1978 doesn't represent as important an improvement as some believed. "It represents," he pointed out, "returns of three cents on a sales dollar and about eight percent on equity," traditionally a level which signified trouble. "Similar returns back in

---

is operating near full capacity. This is healthy for the economy as a whole -- demand is up, suggesting a growth in the economy relative to the two or three prior years. On the other hand, however, when the high capacity utilization figure is set next to the fairly large number of plant closings which occurred in 1977 (See Chart VII, Chapter 4), and the continued high level of import penetration in 1978, one suspects that the industry may now supply a smaller share of the American market than it did a decade ago. That is, while the industry is healthy in the short term, it may be a relatively constricted industry, and one which is getting smaller. This is a major fear of the United Steelworkers of America since a smaller share of the market translates into lower employment levels.

[1]"Steel Industry Statement for Submission to the Department of the Treasury," January 29, 1979.

1968," he reminded the Senate Steel Caucus, "created enough concern to convince the Administration to negotiate the VRAs."[1]

In addition, its net cash flow -- about $2.5 billion by industry's estimates -- fell short of the capital expenditures by $.5 billion; and even the $3 billion of capital expenditures, which came partly from borrowing thereby leaving industry's debt at or near peak levels, fell $1 billion short of the Solomon Report's judgment that it "should be investing $4 billion annually just to modernize and update present facilities, without any provisions for expansion of capacity."[2]

The clear implication of Mr. Foy's assessment of the industry's condition was that it competitive position would get worse if its capital base continues to erode:

> Unless we soon start expanding our domestic steel capacity to supply an additional ten million tons of domestic steel consumption, twenty-five to thirty million tons of steel annually are likely to be entering the U.S. market by 1985, at an annual cost of $12 to $15 billion.[3]

Thus another consequence could be an increase in the U.S. trade deficit, further undermining the U.S. position in

---

[1]"Statement on Steel Trade Policy," Lewis Foy, before the Senate Steel Caucus, February 7, 1979.

[2]The Solomon Task Force Report, p. 22.

[3]"Steel Industry Statement for Submission to the Department of the Treasury," January 29, 1979.

the international economy.[1]

There seem then to be a number of contradictory conclusions which one may draw from the above: (a) Imports are up, suggesting an ongoing trade problem and a need for an ISC to contain international capacity and production levels. (b) The TPM is working since the industry improved its profit statement, increased its cash flow position, and raised its level of capacity utilization. (c) Nonetheless, the industry, as William J. Delancey of Republic Steel described it, "has been effectively liquidating since about 1966 -- we've not added one pound of capacity since then." The contradictions may be explained by distinguishing between the short term and long term.

The TPM, for example, seems to have had some positive effect, but in any event doesn't address the structural problem of excess capcity which lends to increasing quantities of imports. The larger question, therefore, is whether the U.S. industry is in fact

---

[1]While this situation could lead to an increased balance of trade deficit, assuming other factors remain as they have during 1976-78, it is not clear that this will lead to an erosion of the American position in the world economy. There is the position, for example, that the United States should continue to transfer to a "service sector economy." In particular, as one economist writing for the Wall Street Journal has argued with this author in private conversations, "We should be designing steel plants, not working in them."

liquidating, and whether it should be if it is? Most economists, government officials, and industry executives agree that the industry is effectively liquidating. Many economists will argue that this is as it should be because it reflects the comparative advantage of other more efficient industries in other countries, and the concomitant comparative disadvantage of the U.S. industry. Advocates for the industry, however, argue that others' comparative advantage is oftentimes achieved through illiberal economic policies and unfair trading advantages promoted by their governments. For example, in their statement to the Treasury Department, the industry stated:

> An an industry, we cannot be indifferent to the liquidation of position in our own market which occurred in 1977 and 1978, essentially through lack of effective national response to unfair trading practices in steel.[1]

They went on to say, indeed threaten, "we must, and will, take action through whatever legitimate political and legal means are available to us to reduce the 1977-78

---

[1]"Steel Industry Statement for submission to the Department of the Treasury," January 29, 1979. Also, it should be noted that even where countries may appear to be gaining the comparative advantage, in steelmaking capacity these same countries may have an even wider advantage in other industries. Even by liberal economic terms, therefore, it might be argued that these countries should not be producing steel, and certainly not for export, but instead should produce in those sectors where they maintain the greatest comparative advantage.

flood of steel imports."[1]

In addition to foreign trade policy the industry has referred to a broader and more comprehensive industrial policy. Interestingly, in its most optimistic projections, the industry views the government's willingness to assist them in the area of trade policy during the 1976-78 period as the beginning of an industrial policy for steel. According to Jim Collins, chief economist and vice president of the American Iron and Steel Institute: "The government has stumbled towards an attempt to formulate an industrial policy . . . to formulate and direct public policy which will enhance [the steel] industry's competitive position globally."[2] Let us look at this: There is some reason for the steel industry to believe that the United States may in fact be "stumbling towards an industrial policy." One indication is the recent formation of a "Tripartite Steel Committee" comprised of government officials, industry executives, and labor leaders.[3] The Committee has been set up under the jurisdiction of the Commerce Department,

---

[1]Senate Steel Caucus, February 7, 1979.

[2]Interview, January 5, 1979.

[3]Predictably, this "Tripartite Steel Committee" has not yet officially acted at the time of writing. In part, it was established for practical reasons of feeding into the OECD International Steel Committee though it seems not to have done that yet. In part this is probably because the MTN is still underway, and the channels already established uder it are still being used. It is also

which may be read as a signal that issues other than foreign trade will be addressed in a rather serious way. One must not forget, however, that the formation of this committee occurred during one of the most critical stages of the Multilateral Trade Negotiations -- January 1979, the final period in the negotiations during which U.S. negotiators needed support from domestic constituencies. However, even if the raison d'etre from the government's standpoint was to ease domestic pressures on the MTN, the fact remains that the Committee exists, and it is more than likely that industry and labor will press quite hard to keep it from fading even after the Tokyo Round of the GATT negotiations is complete. There is also little doubt that they can look to most government bureaucrats serving on the Committee as allies in their efforts.

It is also likely, however, that the Tokyo Round of the GATT, in addressing for the first time Non-Tariff Barriers to Trade as a major part of the negotiations, may have forced U.S. officials, trade and others, to recognize the need for an industrial policy for certain sectors. Therefore, it is possible that, quite apart from the politics, government officials have genuinely

---

interesting that a similar, though less formal, arrangement has been operating for textiles and apparel.

reached the view that a serious effort needs to be made toward developing an industrial policy for steel.

This latter view can be supported by one interpretation of the Solomon Report. As we indicated in Chapter 5, Secretary Solomon's Task Force recommended a number of ways the government could assist the steel industry in addition to the Trigger Price Mechanism. While the non-trade policy recommendations got very little attention, it is worth noting that the Solomon Task Force set as its primary objective to "assist the steel industry in a manner which will stimulate efficiency and enable the industry to compete fairly."[1] It also recommended to the President that he "provide meaningful incentives for plant and equipment modernization through appropriate tax, investment, and financial assistance. Continual modernization is required if the industry is to operate at peak efficiency."[2] For the reasons set forth in the introductory section of Chapter 4, and examine more closely throughout the rest of that chapter, the Administration found itself in a position where the steel issue was framed in the context of foreign trade problems, and policy developed accordingly. There was some minimal effort at the time, which seems to have

---

[1]Solomon Task Force, p. 7.

[2]Ibid.

creeped along only slightly since then, to affect changes in the Environmental Protection regulatory process in order to reduce the industry's expenditures in that area. Another recommendation of the Solomon Task Force which also received little attention was to assist the industry in its "needed investment" to modernize and increase efficiency by "changes in tax laws . . . and reducing the guideline life for depreciation of new steel industry machinery and equipment."[1]

The key question, of course, is what happened to all of these recommendations, and what implications the results have for the development of an industrial policy. According to Administration officials testifying before the Senate Steel Caucus in February 1979, "We're investigating them." In fact, in each case the Solomon Task Force was recommending to the President that some or all of those areas -- tax policy, environmental policy, trade policy -- be "investigated" to determine the appropriateness of government assistance. The problem is that an industrial policy would, be definition, seek to put the health of industrial sectors above other goals and objectives of government. While the President may ask the Environmental Protection Agency to look into "what it can do for the steel industry"[2] there is little chance

---

[1]Ibid., p. 23.

[2]Interview, November 6, 1978.

that anything will come of such a request when even the Solomon Report stated its priorities as follows: "We do not recommend a relaxation of our basic environmental goals. We also recommend against differential or more lenient treatment in the regulation or enforcement for the steel industry."[1]

One concludes, therefore, that at least in the short term, the steel industry, and probably other international industrial sectors in the United States, will continue to look to foreign trade policy for assistance. In the period we have studied, 1976-78, the steel industry was able to squeeze two policies which together do seem to go beyond simple patchwork of normal trade policies like a voluntary restraint agreement, or quotas. But they are still a long way from either an industrial policy, or even a coherent foreign economic strategy of the kind we see in Japan or France, for example.

If the 1976-78 period provided anything about U.S. foreign trade policy it is that the steel lobby, spearheaded by the industry, carries a lot of clout in Washington. According to Lewis Foy, "Government has recognized that a viable steel industry is vital to the health of this country."[2] This is due, in no small part, to the political

---

[1]Solomon Task Force, p. 26.

[2]Senate Steel Caucus, February 7, 1979.

pressures that were brought to bear. Refèrring to these pressures, one economist who has argued that the U.S. steel industry is operating at a comparative disadvantage, marveled at the policy successes it scored in the TPM and the ISC. "Its success," he pointed out, "has to be because of its political effectiveness."[1]

We should also emphasize, however, that neither the TPM nor the ISC required formal consultation with the Congress and so the steel lobby had to forge very delicate relations among itself and the Executive, and the Congress. The TPM and ISC were the result of administrative action by the Executive branch of government. Congress played a larger role in the political process which led to the establishment of the TPM, than it did in the ISC. But even in the case of the TPM Congress did not participate in the formulation of the policy, nor did it participate in the development of the Trigger Price System itself. Its role was purely political, as a pressure group lending greater credibility and influence to the steel lobby in the latter's efforts with the Administration. Congress did not make any decisions as a body, nor did it relate to the Executive "legislatively," except through the use of certain legislative tools such as hearings and floor debates as special

---

[1]Interview, March 2, 1979.

pressures on the Administration. Therefore, the steel lobby is to be given credit for mobilizing the Congress as a lobby, as well as for its efforts with regard to the Administration.

Indeed, the two policies should be seen as an impressive political victory for the steel lobby. Both represent the government's willingness to recognize that foreign industries compete with unfair advantages given them by their own governments' policies, and that U.S. trade policy will use tools of intervention in the market to balance the competitive scale. The principle involved represents a departure of the first order from U.S. industrial trade policy commonly applied since 1945. Ironically, the policy of "intervention" is taken to protect the interventionist trading order from unravelling into inimical protectionist blocs.

The U.S. government has exercised the will to protect domestic constituencies from a condition of liberal internationalism -- a condition ironically constituted from a range of illiberal national policies made in London, Tokyo, Paris, Brussels, and Seoul. For each program, however, U.S. policymakers point to liberal principles on which its policies of protection are based: the TPM adheres to principles of free trade; and the ISC is founded on principles of international consultation and cooperation -- Wilsonian internationalism as it were. The two are promoted as defenders of liberalism. And so they may be. But it remains to be seen whether United States foreign trade policy will continue to intervene in the market even where it can no longer justify its actions as a defense of liberalism.

CHAPTER 7

CONCLUSIONS

I. Organizing Free Trade, Collectivizing Protection and a National Policy

Both at the international and at the U.S. domestic levels, the trend in the conduct of foreign trade seems to be toward protection; a trend which is reflected by, and increasingly embedded in, the institutions at both levels. Accordingly, the trend of United States policy has been to limit access of international products experiencing surplus capacity from easy entrance into its domestic market. While this has been the response of U.S. policymakers to particular sectors, there is also evidence that beyond these responses, an unshakable commitment to the liberal trading order persists. The two positions tend to push U.S. policy toward a delicate compromise. The most convincing evidence of this is found in the rhetoric of those industrial sectors most affected: it is still fundamentally unacceptable to be a "protectionist." Instead, one must frame one's claims in terms of "fair trade" -- a commitment to free trade under fair conditions.[1]

---

[1]See N , pp. in Chapter 2.

As demonstrated by the examination of the steel case during the period 1976-78, the tendency in U.S. policy toward protection is found when influential domestic constituencies pressure government to assist them by intervening in international trade. Nonetheless, one continues to find resistance to such pressures among trade policy officials in the Administration. Such resistance is a result of the Administration's responsibility to foreign governments which seek access for their producers to the U.S. market, as well as to countervailing domestic pressures such as consumer interests. The commitment to the principles of liberal trade is demonstrated by statements such as the one by Assistant Secretary of the Treasury C. Fred Bergsten before the Joint Economic Committee of the Congress:

> The Administration's philosophy centers on two basic factors: (1) the need to maintain and strengthen an open trade and payments system; (2) the requirements of global economic interdependence. The Administration and, I believe, the Congress and the nation as well, place basic reliance on the free market system.[1]

In still another context, Secretary Bergsten reiterated the commitment to liberal trade, but cast it in a slightly different form. At a Labor Department Conference on

---

[1]C. Fred Bergsten, "International Economic Policy -- Where We Stand," statement before the Joint Economic Committee of the U.S. Congress, July 19, 1978.

"International Trade and Its Effects on Employment," he stated that the United States should "fight the policies of our trading partners[1] which unfairly give them a competitive advantage. The implication was that the United States ought to put all its efforts in the free market and free international trading system, rather than "joining" its trading partners in, for example, protecting its market as they do theirs. "Our basic philosophy," he said, "is to resist this trend [toward intervening] in the hope and belief that the market-oriented approach is both far superior, and likely over time, to prevail."[2]

As another illustration of the Administration's commitment to liberal trade, consider Under Secretary of Treasury for Monetary Affairs, Anthony Solomon's rather brazen statement to the Senate Steel Caucus, that he never intended to keep imports out. To be fair, Solomon was suggesting that the TPM sought only to enforce the antidumping laws and ensure fair trade,[3] and not

---

[1]C. Fred Bergsten, "Labor Department Conference on International Trade and Its Effects on Employment, December 15, 1978.

[2]Ibid.

[3]Secretary Solomon speaking at the Senate Steel Caucus meeting, February 6, 1979, in personal notes of author. Labor officials have alleged that they were told that imports as a percentage of apparent domestic consumption would fall to 18 percent as a result of the TPM. Apparently, this is one reason only the steelworkers accepted the TPM program.

necessarily limit imports. Still this was an unusually straightforward comment for that kind of audience.

In still another context, one notices that the most visible and concerted effort toward redressing the U.S. trade deficit has been in the area of "export promotion," rather than limiting imports. The Commerce Department, that agency which typically represents domestic industry in intrabureaucratic policy disputes, has focused its only policy-level effort in the international trade area at promoting exports. Indeed, it is fair to say that the only Administration-wide effort at developing an overall foreign trade policy in 1977-78 was in this area of export promotion through an interagency task force comprised of trade policy representatives from STR, State, Commerce, Labor, and Treasury. In testimony before another session of the Joint Economic Committee of the Congress on "The Need for a New Export Policy," Assistant Secretary of Treasury Bergsten pointed to a National Export Policy as the free traders' answer to the trade deficit:

> The external economic position of the United States is undergoing an important, long-run, structural change. The sharp increase in our dependence on imported oil, and to a lesser extent, other products, means that the share of imports in our GNP has risen sharply. There must therefore be a concomitant rise in the share of exports in our GNP -- where each single

> percentage point now means over twenty billion dollars.[1]

And, emphasizing the need to promote exports, as opposed to limiting imports, he said: "Our growing economic dependence on the rest of the world now dictates that we must become more attuned to exports."[2] In a similar vein, Assistant Secretary of State for Economic and Business Affairs, Julius Katz said, "We look to a policy of increased exports as an important element in improving the current trade account."[3] Interestingly, a fair amount of support for the creation of a Department of International Trade stems from the belief that a Trade Department will provide a convenient way to promote exports and therefore result in a decrease in the trade deficit. Proponents of this view argue that a Department which coordinates import and export functions will give the United States greater leverage in its effort to pressure other governments to provide freer access for American goods and services.[4]

---

[1]C. Fred Bergsten, "The Need for a New Export Policy," statement before the Joint Economic Committee of the U.S. Congress, September 29, 1978.

[2]Ibid.

[3]Julius Katz, "The Need for a New Export Policy," statement before the Joint Economic Committee of the U.S. Congress, September 29, 1978.

[4]Senators Abraham Ribicoff (D.-Conn.), and William V. Roth (R.-Del.), have introduced a bill calling for the

As another indication of persistent support in the Administration for liberal trade, consider the ongoing debate between Treasury, as the enforcing agency for U.S. domestic trade laws, and those domestic interests seeking relief from what they argue are "unfair trading practices causing injury." Typically, Treasury has erred on the side of the foreign producers reflecting its bias against limiting trade, quite often in spite of questionable practices such as excessive subsidization causing distortions in trade flows.

We have now seen how these kinds of attitudes by key Administration trade officials have the effect of checking what might be an otherwise single-minded protectionist policy at the national level. During the course of this study we referred explicitly and implicitly to the Administration's commitment to liberal trade. For the most part, it was characterized in the form of a commitment to the MTN. But domestic pressures set against these kinds of attitudes have led U.S. trade policymakers to devise programs like the Trigger Price Mechanism (TPM) or the International Steel Committee (ISC). They are less protectionist than a quota program, for example,

---

creation of a Department of International Trade and Investment. See, for example, S 1990, U.S. Senate, the 95th Congress. Hearings have been held in Senator Ribicoff's Committee on Governmental Affairs; see S.377, a bill to create a Department of International Trade, U.S. Senate, 96th Congress, 1st Session.

but are also some distance from the liberal trade policies which promote unencumbered "the free movement of goods and services" of which Secretary Bergsten speaks. But the most obvious and farreaching effects of this delicate balance are at the international level.

The first conclusion of this paper, therefore, is that American foreign trade policy continues to promote principles of liberal internationalism manifested in the case of steel and other industrial sectors through an effort to organize national protectionist policies. Policymakers devise strategies to organize national policies of protection, including its own, under the guise of an international framework of cooperation, accommodation, and conciliation.

For steel, the ISC mandate is clear on its responsibility toward promoting cooperation and consultation: "Governments need to work closely together in order to facilitate multilateral cooperation consistent with the need to maintain competition to anticipate, and to the extent possible, prevent problems."[1] Thus the United States has been a leader in creating a multilateral framework which purports to enable steel producers, labor leaders, and their governments to come together to talk about price levels, production, investment

---

[1]International Steel Agreement, Paris, October 1978.

plans, adjustment problems, and market arrangements.[1] But will such an enterprise promote international cooperation and accommodation as its advocates suggest, or will it further institutionalize the policies of national protection which are in many respects its raison d'etre?

Virtually all U.S. government officials, and representatives from the European Community and Japan, whom this author has interviewed, deny they have in any way constructed a framework which is, or will lead to forms of outright protection which run contrary to principles of liberal trade such as a steel cartel. One suspects that Shakespeare's "The lady doth protest . . ." may apply.

The ISC, policy officials argue, is intended to promote international bargaining at the government, industry, and trade union levels, to arrive at mutually acceptable market arrangements and adjustment policies. They insist that the key is for negotiations to take place on a multilateral, and not a bilateral basis. Only in the former, it is argued, can one presume that the most harmful effects of trade distortions may be avoided. Put another way, trade distortions collectively organized may be channeled so that the damage is spread among all participants in its international trade, and

---

[1]Ibid.

therefore minimal to any single country. Under bilateral arrangements, by contrast, restrictions on one country's activities have distorting effects on third markets. Thus in bilateral arrangements, distortions may be limited between the parties involved and both may benefit in the short term. The chances are that the international system itself will be disrupted by these special arrangements and they may therefore have destabilizing effects on international trade as a whole.[1]

U.S. policymakers also sought to accomplish a more stable and acceptable international steel trade through construction of the TPM at the national policy level. While some industry executives and labor leaders in the United States believed, and/or hoped that the TPM would keep unfairly priced imports out (and maybe even fairly priced imports out) it simply raised the price level of unfairly priced imports which were let in. This was done quite deliberately in an effort to organize trade patterns acceptable to domestic producers and foreign governments. The Administration sought to accommodate the pressures from both levels. Combined with the multilateral structure created by the ISC, U.S. policymakers hoped to increase the chances that stable

---

[1]"U.S. Trade Policy and the Tokyo Round of Multilateral Trade Negotiations," The Congress of the United States, Congressional Budget Office, March 10, 1979, especially see, pp. 39-42.

conditions acceptable to all the major producing countries of steel could be secured for a relatively long period.[1]

Typically, status quo powers -- those which are in a strong position and therefore seek to protect it -- will benefit the most from multilateral market sharing arrangements. In the case of steel, American producers find themselves in the unique position where they seek only to protect their own position in their own market, i.e. they seek to limit the level of import penetration so they and not foreign competitors will fill present as well as future demand in the U.S. market. By contrast, the Europeans, Japanese, and some of the Third World countries depend on demand in both their own markets and others' markets. As excess capacity grows, or becomes more troublesome during recessionary periods, they will want to maintain the flexibility to sell in markets other than their own. This explains why the U.S. producers sought sectoral negotiations in the MTN -- arrangements organized under GATT auspices would result in fixed patterns of trade therefore allowing them to protect their

---

[1]As indicated in previous chapters, especially Chapter 4, U.S. foreign trade decisionmakers did not develop the TPM and ISC programs together. But once the U.S. domestic political crisis and the world steel crisis converged in late fall 1977, the development of the two programs became part of one effort by the Administration to cope with the pressures from domestic constituencies and from their trading partners.

position in their own market. It also explains why the Europeans and Japanese opposed them since they would want greater flexibility for penetration into foreign markets.

Therefore, both promotion of multilateral cooperation at the international systems level, and the TPM at the national level, may be seen as ways to organize existing foreign trade policies of other countries and reactions to those policies, so that minimal injury is incurred by any single participant. However, some are less sure about the value of a multilateral framework for negotiating international market sharing arrangements. Skeptics argue that the management of sectors may be well-intentioned, and founded on principles of liberal internationalism, i.e., cooperation and accommodation, but that they are unwittingly moving the industrial world even further away from a liberal trading order. "International organizations concerned with trade matters," according to Susan Strange, may "function increasingly as would be legitimizers of strictly mercantalist behavior," and not as the "administrators or executives of multilaterally agreed regimes."[1]

Most leaders in most industrial states are prone to accommodation and cooperation among one another.

---

[1]Susan Strange, "The Management of Surplus Capacity, Or How Does Theory Stand Up to Protectionism 1970s Style?" (xerox: 1978).

The tradition of prosperity and growth that has built on these principles is embedded in Western culture and ideas. The diplomacy of market sharing, then, may be seen as an effort to bring the realities of national economic strategies of protection which are especially manifest in periods of structural change exacerbated by the instability of recessionary crises, and international tendencies toward cooperation and consultation, together. On the one hand, by participating in the diplomacy of market sharing, indeed leading it in some sectors, the United States may be undercutting the prospects for continued trade liberalization. To use Bergsten's terms, it may be effectively joining in the tendency toward protection, and therefore encouraging it. On the other hand, it may be that U.S. policy directed toward organizing markets in a multilateral framework is the only alternative to a national policy of outright protection. For the pressures for protection have been great in those sectors where it has organized market sharing arrangements. In either case, indicators at the national and international levels point to the multilaterally arranged sectoral bargaining process as the way the United States will conduct its foreign trade policy in the 1980s.

II. The Pressures for Protection: International and National

As we examined the case of steel, 1976-78, it became clear that the United States devised its policies of "organized protection" as a free trader's response to the structural crisis in the international system. Policymakers recognized that they could not ignore the growing pressures from domestic constituencies to balance the competitive scales against other governments' intervention in international trade. They therefore sought to redress the inadequacies of a trade policy based, and operating on, liberal principles in a world where market intervention had become the norm, and increasingly contributed to the structural crisis which its domestic industries faced. Indeed, U.S. policy officials had to account for the effects of the difference between the market-government relationship in the United States, and those in virtually all of its major industrial trading partners. Japan's "industrial policy," the "French Plan," Germany's "Konzertierte Aktion," and the British preference for socialization of its basic industries all result in different social and political organization of the market place which contribute to the structural crisis domestic constituencies in the United States face.

The second conclusion of this paper, therefore, is that United States policymakers are no longer able to withstand the pressures to adopt its trade policy to one which protects domestic constituencies from the adverse effects of other governments' policies.

The case of steel, 1976-78, is an example where U.S. trade policy responded to the pressures of domestic political interests designed to preserve their own markets and jobs.

The steel lobby's efforts to enlist government assistance did not arise suddenly in the late seventies, but has been evolving for nearly fifteen years. And as it grew, industry and labor came together in what was once thought to have been a most unusual alliance. Nonetheless, they have consistently promoted a common, and what has turned out to be, a most persuasive theme. Joseph Maloney, vice president of the United Steelworkers of America in 1967 testified before the Senate Finance Committee using words that could well have been said in 1977 before Congressman Vanik's subcommittee hearings on "World Steel Trade Problems." Maloney expressed concern over the difference between the growth in world steel production, and the comparative decline in American capacity. But, he cautioned, there is a larger concern over the "prospect of continuing overcapacity in world steel producing capacity,"[1] the proximate-cause of the discrepancy between American and world production growth levels, which comes not so much from the relative decline of American proportion of world production, but from the fact that "increase in foreign production . . . [has not] reflected increased demand in their home markets."[2] Rather, he argued, "as world steel making capacity rose, steel producing nations with insufficient demand turned to foreign markets to unload production from excess capacity."[3] It was this situation which Maloney, and others after him, said had caused the strain in world trade, and in particular, "that has resulted in pronounced repercussions upon the American steel industry."[4] They cried "unfair trade practices" against government responses in Europe, Japan, and the Third World, to the condition of surplus capacity. Indeed, they argued that policies to export surplus capacity were promoted at government-supported prices, rather than cutting back on production and accepting higher levels of unemployment or uncomfortable periods of adjustment to other sectors. U.S. labor and industry affected by this development insisted that

---

[1]Joseph P. Maloney, "Statement before the Senate Finance Committee," reported in <u>Steel Labor</u>, October 20, 1967, (Indianapolis, Indiana, Ocrober 1967).

[2]Ibid.

[3]Ibid.

[4]Ibid.

they had not abandoned free trade as a principle,[1] but argued the case in terms of "fairness." as indicated by Maloney's testimony, they built their case around the strategies other governments used to promote their industries. As one American businessman characterized it more recently in the New York Times:

> West Germany and Japan "collaborate" [with industry] by providing to industry low-interest long-term loans and attractive export-credits and insurance granting industry handsome latitude in depreciation schedules and the timing of tax payments . . . foreign government support becomes unfair competition . . . not in the old sense of low wages or poor working conditions, but in the new sense of benevolent governmental attitudes toward return on investment and use of cash.[2]

So when William Verity appeared in November 1978 on behalf of the American Iron and Steel Institute before the Vanik subcommittee, over a decade after Maloney testified, he too emphasized the "unfair trade practices" theme: "Our industry is up to at least its knees in alligators in . . . unfair trade practices, and . . . these trade practices could cripple the economic viability of the industry."[3]

---

[1]See p   Chapter 2.

[2]"Free Trade, Then and Now," New York Times, February 20, 1978, editorial page.

[3]U.S. Congress, House of Representatives, Ways and Means Subcommittee on Trade, World Steel Trade: Current Trends and Structural Problems, 95th Congress, 1st Session (Washington, D.C.: Government Printing Office, 1977) p. 315.

As we found in Chapter 3, the economic policies of most of the OECD countries have been marked by efforts to control their markets. By contrast, the United States has resisted similar economic policies. Indeed, the most basic, and probably the most important difference between the United States and its major trading partners is the willingness on the part of the latter to intervene directly in the market place for political objectives. They do so to promote goals and objectives associated with social well-being and political stability. For the most part the United States supported these policies, until recently, as part of the overall economic and security arrangements of the post-war era.[1] As growth has become more difficult for the United States, and pressures from affected constituencies mount, policymakers in the United States have also begun to devise strategies which try to control markets "to assure gain and avoid pain." But, as John Zysman in a paper on the politics of sociology of global inflation points out, "Controlling markets is not innovative, unnatural, nor an unfortunate disruption of an otherwise

---

[1]See for example, Charles S. Maier, "The Politics of Productivity: Foundations of American International Economic Policy After World War II," in Peter J. Katzenstein, ed., Between Power and Plenty (Madison, Wisconsin: University of Wisconsin Press 1978), pp. 23-89; and Stephen D. Krasner, "United States Commercial and Monetary Policy: Unravelling the Paradox of External Strength and Internal Weakness."

smoothly functioning machine."[1] Rather, he argues, it is part of industrial life -- as much as markets and machines, themselves -- since the market, after all, was a "political innovation," itself.[2] Still, the United States has been reluctant to promote industrial strategies like the ones we find in Japan, France, or even Great Britain. Instead, U.S. policymakers have attempted to use foreign trade policy as a way of deflecting the more severe effects of both the international economic system generally, and its trading partners' industrial economic strategies and foreign economic policies.

In Europe, Japan, and the developing world, governments used economic strategies to promote certain key industries. An important part of the industrial economic strategies used in Europe and Japan has been the willingness to limit access to their own market and to promote exports to other markets. In other words, the unwillingness to leave key industrial sectors to strictly "market forces." As we indicated earlier, for example, part of the explanation for the "Japanese economic miracle" has been their strategy of selecting

---

[1]John Zysman, "Inflation and Industrial Adjustment: The Politics of Supply," prepared for the Brookings Conference on Politics and Sociology of Global Inflation, December 6-8, 1978, p. 5.

[2]Ibid.

key industrial sectors for fast-growth development, oftentimes contrary to what their natural economic advantages might have dictated. As one student of Japanese political economy has observed:

> It [the Japanese government] refused to concede the country's limited natural resources and inadequate capital supply and take advantage of its ample, well-trained labor supply to concentrate on production of toys, textiles, and Christmas tree ornaments.[1]

Japan's primary objective -- fast growth in capital and technology intensive industries to insure long-term benefits in the nation's economic growth -- led to an economic policy in which, as Professor Pempel of Cornell University so aptly put it:

> The state [was given] a considerable degree of control . . . the government served as doorman between domestic and Japanese society and the international arena determining what could enter or leave Japan and on what conditions . . . it filtered the impact [of international factors] through the Japanese state.[2]

For steel, as with a number of other industrial sectors, the governments of Europe, Japan, and the developing world, regularly intervene in their domestic markets. John Zysman has written in his case study of the "State, Market and Industry in France":

---

[1]T.J. Pempel, "Japanese Foreign Economic Policy: The Domestic Basis for International Behavior," in Peter J. Katzenstein ed., Between Power and Plenty, p. 158.

[2]Ibid., p. 157.

> The state stand[s] as an intermediary between a national industry and the international market -- cut off the national economy from the world economy, as it were -- when by its own actions it can assure a stable supply of the product and control the market in which the product is sold.[1]

This is easiest, he continues, for products such as steel and oil where there is a degree of stability because they are "sold to a handful of consumers who are open to influence from the state."[2] Such control tends to seduce governments into a false sense of demand, which encourages the maintenance of higher levels of productive capacity than could otherwise be justified. It is further encouraged by government subsidies which lend what could turn out to be an illusory competitive edge over producers in other countries.

As indicated earlier the condition of oversupply, especially problematic during periods of cyclical downturn, have prompted governments to take further steps to insulate industry from international factors. Governments seek to ensure the survivability and prosperity of their industrial bases in a form to which its society has become accustomed. These tendencies are all the more pronounced in those countries where policy instruments

---

[1]John Zysman, Political Strategies for Industrial Order: State, Market and Industry in France (Berkeley: University of California Press 1977), p. 208.

[2]Ibid.

for market intervention are embedded in the political and institutional arrangements of its society.[1] Japan displayed this tendency at the outset of its post-war economic expansion program. The Europeans, as a Community through the European Coal and Steel Community, but also on a country by country basis, have prompted government intervention too. The Davignon Plan with its minimum price system, and "bilaterals," is a recent example of this strategy. And its effects on foreign markets, like the United States, lead affected groups in the foreign markets to pressure their own governments for protection.

Therefore, the tendency to intervene in the market has been present in the governmental policies of the European countries and Japan. Pressures to do so increase, however, during times of oversupply or cyclical recession. The British, for example, made the decision in 1967 to nationalize the British steel industry. Since then it has cost the British government close to $1 billion annually.[2] They do so for political and social reasons. Part of the problem with the British steel policy, however,

---

[1]Peter J. Katzenstein, ed., Between Power and Plenty; also Chalmers Johnson, Japan's Public Policy Companies (Washington, D.C.: American Enterprise Institute for Public Policy Research 1978).

[2]England, House of Commons, "First Reports from the Select Committee on Nationalized Industries," Session 1977-78, The British Steel Corporation, volume I, II, November 9, 1977 (London: Her Majesty's Stationery Office).

is that steel is an international industry, and the effects of the domestic social policy therefore scatter far beyond Britain. As William Diebold put it, "The international aspect of . . . structural problems intensifies the pressure [on government] to foster exports and shut out imports that already comes from cyclical factors."[1]

As the steel crisis worsened in Europe during 1977-78, the governments of Belgium and France joined the nationalization policies of their neighbors -- Britain, Ireland, Italy, and the Netherlands. Thus each government continued to support higher levels of production than consumption in their home markets warranted. The willingness to intervene in the market was great, because the pressure was great from those in society resisting adjustment. Put another way, many of the European governments have been unwilling to absorb the costs of cuts in production and higher rates of unemployment that would almost surely follow from self-imposed limits during periods of oversupply; they resort to protectionist measures instead.

Thus, from an international perspective, and also from the perspective of affected U.S. domestic industries, the economic situation seems to have been exacerbated

---

[1]William Diebold, "Adapting Economies to Structural Change: The International Aspect," International Affairs, Fall 1978, p. 576.

by state involvement. As Susan Strange has written: "The power of the state [in the 1970s] has been used to exacerbate rather than remedy the problems of capitalism, making adjustment more difficult through competitive subsidies and putting obstacles in the way of continued growth through expanding markets."[1] To the extent that she is correct, it seems that liberal-plural systems are especially strained during periods of capitalism where structural crises and recessionary cycles converge. The political institutions and arrangements of liberal society pressure governments to operate at a national level in a way which "exacerbates" the international dilemmas of capitalism. They "export pressures for adjustment" as it were. In turn, the crises in the international system lead to increased pressure on individual governments to continue to resist adjustment. As growth has become more difficult, and national economies are more fully penetrated by foreign trade and international production, there are fewer and fewer national political economies which can absorb "the problems of capitalism."[2]

---

[1]Susan Strange, "The Management of Surplus Capacity: Or, How Does Theory Stand Up to Protectionism 1970s Style?" p. 44.

[2]For discussion of this point see, Charles S. Maier, "The Politics of Productivity: Foundations of American International Economic Policy After World War II," in Peter J. Katzenstein, ed., <u>Between Power and Plenty</u>; Andrew Shonfield, <u>Modern Capitalism: The Changing Balance of Public</u>

So economic strategies, and foreign economic policies, which provided government subsidies to maintain wages, employment levels, and profits, in what otherwise might have been uncompetitive industries, tended to institutionalize protection, and therefore increase the likelihood that it would become a permanent feature of the international trading system. Against this background U.S. trade policy is increasingly acting to protect the jobs and profits of its own constituencies from exported surplus capacity in industrial sectors. In principle U.S. policymakers continued to espouse a commitment to liberal trade. In practice they adopted illiberal, interventionist programs -- organizing markets, setting price guidelines, controlling investment, and generally intervening in the market.

---

and Private Power (London: Oxford University Press 1965); also see, Stephen Krasner, "State, Power, and the Structure of International Trade," *World Politics*, April 1976.

III. Rethinking Decisionmaking Approaches for U.S. Foreign Trade Policy in the 1980s

The trend toward protection among the industrial nations had led the United States to respond in certain industrial sectors with a foreign policy of intervention in international trade. However, intervening in international trade is substantially different from intervening directly in the market through the use of farreaching industrial policies as most of the other OECD countries.[1] Therefore, one should not overemphasize the use of foreign trade policy as an economic strategy, since the domestic institutional arrangements within the United States remain more or less unchanged.[2] But the changes in its U.S. foreign trade policies do have implications for the relationship between the government and domestic interests, i.e., between the state and society.

---

[1]For a good discussion of industrial policies in Europe and Japan, see, Lawrence G. Franco, "Industrial Policies in Western Europe," The World Economy, volume 2, number 1 (January 1979).

[2]For a good discussion of how the domestic institutional arrangements determine a country's foreign economic policy, see, Peter J. Katzenstein, "Introduction: Domestic and International Forces and Strategies of Foreign Economic Policy," in Peter J. Katzenstein, ed., Between Power and Plenty.

While U.S. policymakers intervene in international trade to protect domestic interests from the adverse effects of others' interventionist policies, they have also begun to change the emphasis of the U.S. trade policy process itself. As a result, the classic decisionmaking models used to explain the U.S. trade policy process, for example those used by Bauer, Pool and Dexter, or Schattschneider, are no longer applicable. By examining how and why the classic decisionmaking model is inappropriate, we will also explain how the relationship between state and society in the U.S. trade policy process is changing.

These classic decisionmaking models were typically used to explain the policymaking process of a trade bill, where the Executive and Legislature shared roughly equal power. At the same time that they attempted to reflect this relationship between Executive and Legislature,[1] they also implied that policy was the product of competing domestic interests working through the two branches, though probably more directly inspired by the pluralistic nature of the Congress. Most important, however, was the image of the policy as a product of domestic societal pressures.

---

[1]Bauer, Pool, and Dexter do explain that the Congress, since Smoot-Hawley Tariff, has given the lion's share of trade policy responsibility to the Executive. But their emphasis is still on the legislative process, pp. 30 to 39.

Industrial sector policymaking has changed the emphasis from one on legislation, where the two branches try to balance domestic constituent input, and where the end result is a product of competing domestic interests, to one on administrative or adjudicatory remedies where the Executive seeks to manage the effects of the range of non-tariff barriers on the economy. But while the Executive tries to manage the effects of non-tariff barriers, it must negotiate with the foreign governments whose economic strategies and foreign economic policies created them in the first place. Thus, there is an international dimension introduced into the equation which goes beyond an American exporter or importer's interest in the Trade Bill Debate, directly to the practices of foreign governments. In addition to the change of emphasis,[1] then, the circumstances of industrial sector policymaking lead to effective participation of foreign governments in the policymaking process since resolution by administrative or adjudicatory procedure includes international negotiation between the U.S. government and foreign governments.

---

[1]Admittedly, there is an interrelationship between the change of emphasis, and the "international negotiation" aspect of the policy process. On the one hand there is a change of emphasis because of the "international negotiation" aspect of the process. But, the change of emphasis tends to enhance the degree to which the "international negotiations" are, in fact, integrated into the process.

Therefore, the change in emphasis has the effect of shifting the center of power to the Executive even more than occurred subsequent to Smoot-Hawley.[1] The result is a process where domestic constituent interests are diluted by the combined effects of (a) the inclusion of international negotiation in the policymaking process; and (b) the shift of power away from the Legislature to the Executive.

As we indicated in the first chapter, this situation led us to consider the use of the national interest concept, where we constructed a framework in which policy comes from a set of objectives and goals developed by central decisionmakers.[2] As we saw throughout the examination of the steel case, 1976-78, the policy came less from a process imagined by classic decisionmaking theory, than from one where the Administration bargained with domestic interests and foreign governments to arrive at a point acceptable to both and which could also meet their own objectives of trade liberalization.[3] In doing so, the Administration devised

---

[1]Ibid.

[2]For a good discussion of this point, see Stephen Krasner, Defending the National Interest (Princeton: Princeton University Press 1978), especially p. 330.

[3]See the first section of this chapter.

two programs which intervened in international trade to assist the steel lobby. Industry and labor had asked for special assistance in dealing with increased import penetration from other governments' policies. They were successful in getting the U.S. government to move in that direction. But the TPM was not "strict enforcement of the antidumping laws," and the ISC was not sectoral negotiations in the GATT, the two goals which the steel lobby sought. Even the powerful steel lobby, therefore, was not in a position to translate its goals into direct results. That it got reasonably close is a significant accomplishment. Certainly, we are not suggesting that compromise is anything new. But resolution of industrial sector cases to manage the range of non-tariff barriers affecting international trade does envision a new kind of compromise between domestic interests and foreign interests (usually represented by governments, or in this case the European Community, and Japan) and the Administration. This is a substantially different process from the making of the Smoot-Hawley Tariff in 1930, the Trade Expansion Act of 1962, or the Trade Reform Act of 1974, all subjects of former studies on the U.S. trade policy process.

The third conclusion of this study, therefore, is that the consideration of industrial sector cases requires a different emphasis both in who participates and in the actual roles assumed by the participants, as well as in the decisionmaking approach used to study them, from that which has been used in the classic studies.

The most important conceptual distinction, already suggested above, is that resolution of industrial sector cases have an "antiplural bias" with respect to the domestic arena.[1] That is, the policy outcomes are different from the result of competing domestic constituencies; since the policymaker considers one sector at a time, as distinct from the trade-offs they engineered and brokered in the making of a trade law, the process itself tilts toward a bargaining relationship between policymakers and sector representatives. The bargaining is fairly well confined to the sector representative -- but includes the Congress as we discovered in the study of the steel case -- and the Administration, as the Administration simultaneously negotiates with foreign interests. Thus in the examination of the steel case, 1976-78, we found that the development of the TPM and the ISC were derived in part from the effects these programs would have on the Europeans or Japanese, and in part from the effects they would have on domestic constituencies; the two programs developed as a result of pressures from

---

[1]"Antiplural bias" refers to the fact that policy is more than a product of competing domestic interests.

both arenas. Considered in this form, therefore, these issues do not lend themselves to resolution suggested by the typical trade bill debate. It is not appropriate, for example, to seek resolutions by trading off political chips among domestic interest groups as in the classic "logrolling" process familiar to trade bill legislation. Instead of the government -- Executive or Legislature, or both -- acting as an intermediary between the domestic "textile" and "steel" lobbies, for example, the Executive plays an intermediary role between domestic steel interests and international steel interests or between domestic textile interests and international textile interests. So, issues require isolated consideration, and include other governments' economic strategies and foreign economic policies in their individual policy processes. Since it is easiest to address these elements -- negotiating by sectors, and including international political and economic conditions -- if the Executive operates with greater authority than might be supposed by strictly plural decisionmaking theory, it is understandable that the Executive will assume more responsibility. Conversely, the decisionmaking approaches which assume both a more or less equal legislative-executive relationship, and a controlling input by domestic constituencies, are no longer appropriate.

For steel, the Administration was by far the dominant participant -- certainly more than the Congress, which played a role of first among equals lobbying the Administration, but also more than the steel lobby itself. At critical points during the policy process, it was the Administration, and not industry, labor, or the Congress which defined the terms of reference. For example, the industry was reluctant to pursue antidumping laws, but did, nonetheless, largely because the Administration had decided it was the proper course. Likewise, when the Administration realized that the antidumping alternative, as it appeared in law, simply wouldn't work because of the chaos it would have created for European steel, the industry withdrew from its position. They got something for their acquiescence, but that too was an Administration scheme. Similarly, the Administration determined that the "301 complaint" wouldn't be pursued, quite apart from pressure that industry or labor applied. The Administration commitment to "free trade," and the blatant assault on other governments' domestic and foreign policies, both of which the 301 complaint challenged, were controlling.

The redistribution of power between the Executive and Legislative branches points to the basic difference between developing a trade policy in a "crisis situation" that acts to respond to structural changes in industrial sectors,[1] and in the classic trade bill. In both cases, the Congress is lobbied by domestic interest groups. In the case of the classic trade bill, however, the Congress is lobbied for favors it can dispense directly -- a provision here, a modification in a clause there, and of course, the final vote on the bill. The Congress is directly responsible for a trade bill, and the "steel," "textile," and "zinc" lobbies know it. Each lobby also understands that it is competing with the other for attention. But in responding to particular conditions of the international system -- the steel import problem, for example -- the Congress is only slightly less impotent than the "steel," "textile," or "zinc" lobbies themselves. The Congress can impose a substantial amount of pressure on the Executive since it has specific institutional and legal channels that interest groups don't have. Therefore, the lobby pressure on Congress in these instances is more for what the Congress does through the Administration, than what it is likely to do directly. This is noticeably different from the way the Congress is supposed to act in classic decisionmaking theory.

It is important, however, that the Congress has deliberately chosen this role. As a body it has not acted on steel trade matters. Neither the bills, actions by

---

[1]That is, the changing international economy.

the steel caucuses, nor individual Congressmen's letters represented a "responsible" act on the part of the Congress qua the Legislative branch of government.[1] The Congress won't get the blame, but it also won't share in the power.[2]

While Congress has abdicated much of its power in trade policy to the Executive -- some by choice, and the rest by circumstances peculiar to the industrial policy issues -- the Congress can still "make laws." True, it has tended to use its "lawmaking" powers as especially effective pressure tactics on the Administration, but if the strategy is tactfully pursued, then the Administration must always fear that a "pressure tactic" could become law.

For example, the Burke-Hartke bill proposed in 1971, called for "across the board tariffs on any products which comprised over a specified percentage of domestic

---

[1]As indicated earlier, the Congress has played a significant role in the policy process. But, we distinguish here between strictly legislative acts taken by the Congress as a body, and more or less ad hoc acts taken by one or a group of Congressmen. It is the difference between institutionally based acts, and informal ones.

[2]It is fairly well accepted that a Congressman simply can't "win" in trade policy. No matter how he tries to balance constituent interests, there will be some who want protection, and others who want free trade. Thus, Congress gives the ultimate responsibility to the Executive and then tries his best to claim credit for both kinds of policies.

consumption." The bill never became law, though it pressured the Administration, and our trading partners, to negotiate voluntary restraint agreements on steel and similar arrangements for textiles. Similarly, the steel quota bills, the Carney bill which called for sector negotiations in the GATT, and those bills which sought to constrain the Administration's flexibility in negotiating tariff cuts on steel, all introduced during the 95th Congress, pressured the Administration to provide the steel industry with relief from imports. The same has been true for a host of other industrial products. In textiles, for example, Senator Hollings' textile and apparel bill, also in the 95th Congress, added to the pressures from industry and labor already on President Carter and Ambassador Strauss and "helped the domestic textile and apparel industry." The Hollings bill surely must be given a good deal of the credit for whatever special concessions the textile and apparel industry receive during the Multilateral Trade Negotiations and beyond.[1]

---

[1]At the time of writing, it appears that the textile and apparel lobby has been given a special deal encompassing foreign and domestic policy concerns. The "Textile Agreement" was announced at the White House on Tuesday, March 20, 1979, and it does appear that the textile and apparel lobby will now support the MTN Agreement; also see, pp. , Chapter 1.

In each of these cases, the power of Congress was noticeably circumscribed. Still, if it were so disposed, Congress could have done more than pressure the Administration for their desired response. It could have turned any of those bills into law. Thus it would have directly dispensed favors, and would have thereby wielded a larger amount of power than it seems to in its role as "supreme lobbyist."

But the nature of the issues we have described as crises in industrial sectors tends to box Congress into the role of "spoiler" if it chooses to make laws as a response to constituent pressure. For the alternative to a protectionist bill is an internationally negotiated solution, which may or may not lead to specific government programs, but is acceptable to domestic constituencies, foreign governments, and Administration decisionmakers. Since the Congress is not in a position, institutionally or practically, to negotiate international settlements, the ultimate responsibility for policy decisions rests with the Administration. In the end, therefore, it leads to a more centralized decisionmaking process for trade, i.e., centralized in the federal bureaucracy thereby constraining the influence of non-federal participants.

More importantly than the specific empirical conclusions which might be drawn about the relative influence of the Congress, however, are the conclusions relating to the degree of influence domestic constituents have in the policymaking process. The shift of power and influence from the Congress to the Executive has a concomitant impact on the operation of the plural system and therefore on the degree of access constituents have to the governmental process: since the policy formulation resides primarily with the Executive branch, which acts according to a set of goals and objectives only partly derived from domestic interest group pressures, it is therefore likely that the outcome will be less responsive to interest group pressures than traditionally has been the case.

There are two separate, though interrelated, parts of the process which tend to decrease domestic interest group leverage, and therefore undercut the forces of domestic pluralism:

First, there are a limited number of channels through which domestic constituencies can press their claims in a process where the resources of power and influence reside with the Executive. Hence, a classic principle of pluralism -- multiple channels through which domestic constituencies can make their views known in a fairly potent way, and are afforded the luxury of playing policymakers in the Executive and Congress against one another -- is substantially circumscribed in the policy process for industrial sector cases.

Second, while it may be argued that access to government is objectively no more limited than it has always been, access to those channels of government which actually make the decisions is significantly limited. As we saw in the examination of the formulation of steel policy during 1976-78, limited access to the Executive stems from several aspects of the policymaking process itself.

For steel, and the burgeoning number of industrial sector cases, interagency task forces are formed which tend to increase the distance between domestic interests and the decision outcome. That is, the Executive branch is more insulated from constituent pressures than the Congress. In part this is true because the interagency task force undercuts to some degree the effects of pressure tactics which are normally afforded constituents through "friendly" agencies as suggested by the bureaucratic-politics model. The interagency task force, in this case represented by the steel steering group and then the Solomon Task Force, removed the locus of decisionmaking authority from any one agency and gave it to a group of individuals responsible to "the national interest."[1] Obviously, it would be naive to assume that the representatives from

---

[1]See this section in Chapter 5 on the TPM. See Chapter 5 on the TPM.

Treasury or Commerce suddenly shed their interests in their "home" agency. Clearly, they don't. But, taking them out of their respective agencies, and putting all policymakers together, does tend to minimize the imprint of any one agency on the policy outcome. It would be equally naive to assume that policymakers act solely in response to a concept of the "national interest" and discount constituent pressures. However, this process does minimize policymaker's allegiance to both his "home agency" and domestic pressures.

While the steel steering group and the Solomon Task Force were responsible for resolution of the issue primarily from a domestic politics point of view, they perceived an equal responsibility to economic and political factors in the international arena. To be fair, there were special circumstances which applied in this case which encouraged them to consider the factors in the international arena perhaps more strongly than they might have during another period or in another sector. For example, the steel steering group was exposed to the world steel crisis prior to September 1977, when the domestic political crisis exploded. Thus they went into the "post-Youngstown" period from which the TPM actually developed with a set of goals and objectives associated with their prior experience. In addition, of course, there was the MTN which also influenced the outcome.

There are institutional characteristics of such task forces, however, which seem to transcend the particular circumstances of steel, 1976-78. As indicated above, part of the policy process for industrial sector cases is negotiating internationally to manage the effects of the non-tariff measures of other governments. During this process, the Executive branch task forces develop, and to a large degree institutionalize, contacts with their counterparts in the other countries. Thus, consideration of interests quite apart from domestic constituencies is increased.

Indeed, there is reason to believe that the tendency to associate with foreign governments on a sector by sector basis will grow. Under the MTN proposed reform of the GATT framework there will be an international dispute settlement mechanism for a number of the non-tariff barrier codes which will have been negotiated. This dispute settlement will provide both formal and institutional arrangements where governments may negotiate cases in the GATT framework for affected domestic constituencies. In other words, GATT reform will encourage negotiation among governments by sectors not dissimilar from what was organized on an ad hoc basis for steel in 1976-78. In addition, U.S. domestic implementing legislation proposes to amend the U.S. Trade Act of 1974 accordingly. That is, it proposes special provisions where U.S. domestic constituencies may file complaints with the Special Trade Representative to negotiate on their behalf in the GATT.[1]

In addition to the international negotiating aspects of industrial sector cases, however, there is still another aspect of the policy process which tends to limit the access of domestic constituencies to the decisions.

In the case of steel, for example, once it was decided that the Administration would be primarily responsible for the issue -- a decision not consciously taken, but one which resulted from the circumstances discussed above -- policy is then responsible to a particular legalistic framework. The result, as characterized by I.M. Destler, is that "political-economic problems are turned into technical legal ones."[2] Clearly, the interpretation of the laws subject to political influences, but the Administration argues, somewhat justifiably, less freedom of movement than is afforded Congress in the traditional legislative interest-group politics model. This is a feature of administrative

---

[1]Interview, March 28, 1979.

[2]I.M. Destler, "Protection for Congress? The Politics of Trade Policy," paper prepared as background for June 26, 1978 meeting of the Joint Discussion Group on Executive-Congressional Relations, Council on Foreign Relations and the Carnegie Endowment for International Peace.

and adjudicatory proceedings on international trade policy which the Administration tends to use when convenient. For example, the development of the steel issue leading to the TPM, a solution not entirely satisfactory to the steel lobby, was explained by Administration officials in terms of their responsibility to "technical-legal" considerations. While there remains, as Destler points out, "a political safety valve" for either the President or the Congress to override agency decisions in the complaint proceedings of an antidumping or countervailing duty case, the Congress has never exercised its option. The President has exercised his option,[1] but in the great percentage of cases where he has acted, it was to reverse a decision which interest groups tended to regard as relatively favorable. It would seem, therefore, that there is another aspect where the domestic interest groups do exercise less influence in the policymaking process for industrial sector cases. This is a result of the introduction of foreign governments as participants into the U.S. policy process, and a paralleled transfer of power from the Legislature to the Executive. The nature of industrial sector cases points to a solidification of this process, and the power

---

[1]Interview, the International Trade Commission, November 8, 1978.

relations inherent in it, as the direction of U.S. foreign trade policy for the next decade.

IV. Summary

As we have seen, the United States developed two policies for steel in 1976-78. Upon examining the Trigger Price Mechanism, and the International Steel Committee, and the processes leading to each, it became clear that U.S. foreign trade policymakers recognized a need to intervene in the international trading order. While intervention itself may not be a new phenomenon, for even the U.S. has been accustomed in the post-World War II era to regular intervention in the agriculture sector, there is much about intervention in the industrial sector that is new. We saw, for example, that many of the characteristics of the foreign trade policy process have changed as policymakers have tried to conform policy to the objective conditions in the international and domestic political economies.

U.S. officials have found that trade policy in the industrial sector is increasingly about how to manage the effects of foreign governments' non-tariff measures on the domestic political economy. Or, how to cope with the pressure for economic and political adjustment and adaptation which are caused in some considerable measure by the economic strategies and foreign economic policies of other governments. Therefore, pressures for policy from affected constituencies like steel can only be resolved if the international factors contributing to their condition are made an integral part of the policy development process.

As they try to manage the political-economic pressures in the domestic political arena, U.S. policy officials are also adapting to the need for a different kind of management of the international trading order. For example, the change in emphasis in the GATT negotiations from one on tariff-cutting, to one on the organization of non-tariff measures, and the institutionalization of the change with the international dispute settlement mechanism, has paralleled the change in emphasis in the U.S. trade policy process itself. These changes have already had a rather significant effect both on the U.S. policy process, and on the international trading order as well. The policy of "organized free trade," or "collective protection," managed through national policies such as the TPM and initiatives toward multilateral arrangements such as the ISC, represent important departures both in how the United States will conduct its foreign trade policy in the 1980s, as well as the shape the international trading system will take over the next decade.

APPENDIX

The following is a list of documents cited in footnotes as "on file with author."

1. American Iron and Steel Institute Submission to the Department of Commerce and the Office of the Special Trade Representative on their position on the "Status of the Multilateral Trade Negotiations." Documents include submissions beginning in March 11, 1975 and continuing through to February 14, 1979, "Preliminary Report on the Status of the MTN Issues." All of these documents are filed as part of the Industry Sector Advisory Committee (ISAC) Process.

2. "301 Complaint" filed in the Office of the Special Trade Representative for Trade Negotiations, by the American Iron and Steel Institute, under section 301 of the Trade Act of 1974, to the chairman of the Section 301 Committee of the Office of the Special Trade Representative, October 6, 1976.

3. "Chronology of EEC Actions Affecting International Trade," containing European Community Documents from the Official European Journal, September 29, 1975 to April 1, 1978.

4. Senate Steel Caucus materials from personal files of United States Senate Steel Caucus beginning September 26, 1977 to March 8, 1979.

5. Text of the OECD International Steel Committee Mandate.

6. A Report to the President: A Comprehensive Program for the Steel Industry, Anthony M. Solomon, chairman, Task Force.

7. As a Senate aide during the period 1977-1979, the author has attended Senate Steel Caucus meetings with industry and labor officials. Meetings on September 29, 1977, August 1, 1978, August 29, 1978, September 13, 1978, February 6, 1979, February 7, 1979, have been especially helpful in determining both labor's and industry's position on the steel issue during the period under study. In addition, the author has been privileged to confidential correspondence between Congressmen and Administration officials which offered important insights.

8. Names of government officials, and some industry and labor leaders have been withheld upon request. Since the Multilateral Trade Negotiations are not yet complete, in particular that aspect of the process where the Congress and the Administration negotiate implementing language for U.S. trade law, confidentiality has been requested by many government officials and industry and labor leaders who were interviewed. Dates of interviews are cited in footnotes, and all information is on file with the author.

SELECTED BIBLIOGRAPHY

Adams, Walter, and Dirlam, Joel B. "Import Competition and the Trade Act of 1974: A Case Study of Section 201 and Its Interpretation by the International Trade Commission." Indiana Law Journal, volume 52, number 3 (Spring 1977).

Adams, Walter, ed. The Structure of American Industry. New York: MacMillan, 1977.

Allison, Graham, and Halperin, Morton. Bureaucratic Politics: A Paradigm and Some Policy Implications. Reprint 246. Washington, D.C.: Brookings Institution, 1972.

American Iron and Steel Institute Study. "Economics of International Steel Trade: Policy Implications for the United States." Prepared by Putnam, Hayes, and Bartlett. Newton, Massachusetts: May, 1977.

________. "The Implications of Foreign Steel Pricing Practices in the U.S. Market." Prepared by Putnam, Hayes, and Bartlett, Inc. Newton, Massachusetts: August, 1978.

Baldwin, Robert E. Non-tariff Distortions of International Trade. Washington, D.C.: Brookings Institution, 1970.

Bauer, Raymond A., de Sola Pool, Ithel, and Exter, Lewis A. American Business and Public Policy: The Politics of Foreign Trade. Chicago: Adeline, Atherton, 1972.

Bell, Corrine. "Interpretive History of the Escape Clause Under the Trade Act of 1974." The Journal of International Law and Economics, volume 12, number 3.

Belassa, Bela. Trade Liberalization Among Industrialized Countries: Objectives and Alternatives. New York: McGraw Hill, 1967.

Bergsten, C. Fred. The Future of the International Economic Order: An Agenda for Research. Washington, D.C.: Brookings Institution, 1974.

________. Completing the GATT: Towards New International Rules to Govern Export Controls. Washington, D.C.: British North American Committee, 1974.

_______. Toward a New International Economic Order: Selected Papers, 1972-74. Washington, D.C.: Brookings Institution, 1975.

Blackhurst, Richard, Marian, Nicolas, and Tunlir, Jan. "Trade Liberalization, Protectionism and Interdependence." Number 5. Geneva: November 1977.

Brittan, Samuel. "The Economic Contradictions of Democracy." British Journal of Political Science. (April 1975).

Calleo, David P., and Rowland, Benjamin M. America and the World Political Economy: Atlantic Dreams and National Realities. Bloomington, Indiana: Indiana University Press, 1973.

Camps, Miriam. The Management of Interdependence, A Preliminary Views. New York: Council on Foreign Relations, 1974.

_______. "First World Relationships: The Role of the OECD." The Atlantic Papers. February 1975, Council Papers on International Affairs: 5. New York: Council on Foreign Relations, 1975.

Carr, Edward H. The Twenty Years' Crisis, 1919-1939: An Introduction to the Study of International Relations. Second edition. New York: St. Martin's Press, 1962.

Caves, Richard E., and Uekusa, Masu. Industrial Organization in Japan. Washington, D.C.: Brookings Institution, 1976.

Cline, William et. al. Trade Negotiations at the Tokyo Round: A Quantitative Assessment. Washington, D.C.: The Brookings Institution, 1977.

Cohen, Jerome B., ed. Pacific Partnership: U.S./Japanese Trade: Prospects and Recommendations for the Seventies. Lexington, Massachusetts: Lexington Books, 1972.

Cohen, Stephen D. The Making of United States International Economic Policy. New York: Praeger, 1977.

Cooper, Richard N., ed. A Reordered World: Emerging International Economic Problems. Washington, D.C.: Patomic Association, 1973.

________. "Economic Interdependence and Foreign Policy in the Seventies." World Politics. January 1972.

________. Economics of Interdependence: Economic Policy in the Atlantic Community. New York: McGraw Hill 1968.

Dahl, Robert. Who Governs? New Haven: Yale University Press, 1961.

Destler, I.M.; Capps, Prescilla; Sato, Hideo; and Fukin, Haruhiro. Managing An Alliance: The Politics of U.S./Japanese Relations. Washington, D.C.: Brookings Institution, 1976.

Destler, I.M. "Protection for Congress: The Politics of Trade Policy." Paper was prepared also as background for June 26, 1978 meeting of the Joint Discussion Group on Executive-Congressional Relations, Council on Foreign Relations and the Carnegie Endowment for International Peace.

Diebold, William. "Adapting Economies to Structural Change: The International Aspect." Fall 1978.

________. The United States and the Industrial World: American Foreign Economic Policy in the Seventies. New York: Praeger, 1970.

Fisher, Bart. "Dumping: Confronting the Paradox of Internal Weakness and External Demand." xerox, 1978.

Gardner, Richard. Sterling Dollar Diplomacy: The Origins and Prospects of our International Economic Order. New York: McGraw Hill, new expanded version, 1969.

Greenstone, David J. Labor in American Politics. Chicago: University of Chicago Press, 1967.

Hallerman, Leon. Japan's Dependence on the World Economy: An Approach Toward Economic Liberalization. Princeton, New Jersey: Princeton University Press, 1967.

Hamilton, Alexander. "Report on the Subject of Manufacturers." In A.H. Cole ed. Industrial Commercial Correspondence. New York: Kelley Press, 1968.

Hanreider, Wolfram F. The United States and Western Europe. Cambridge, Winthrop Publishers, 1974.

Hansen, Roger D. "The Crisis of Interdependence: Where Do We Go From Here?" In Roger Hansen, et. al. eds. The U.S. and World Development: An Agenda for Action, 1976. New York: Praeger, 1976.

Helleiner, G.K. "Transnational Enterprises and the New Political Economy of U.S. Trade Policy." pp. 102-117. Oxford Economic Papers, volume 29. number 1, March 1977 Oxford: Clarendon Press 1977.

Hexner, Ervin. The International Steel Cartel. Chapel Hill: The University of North Carolina Press, 1943.

Hilsman, Roger. The Politics of Policymaking in Defense and Foreign Affairs. New York: Harper and Row 1971.

Hirschman, Albert O. National Power and the Structure of Foreign Trade. Berkeley, California: University of California Press, 1945.

Hoffman, Stanley. "Obstinate or Obsolete? The Fate of the Nation-State and the Case of Western Europe." Daedelus. Summer 1966.

Hogan, William T., S.J. Economic History of the Iron and Steel Industry in the United States. 5 volumes. Lexington, Massachusetts: Lexington Books, 1971.

________. "The 1970s: The Critical Years for Steel." Massachusetts: Lexington Books, 1972.

________. "Future Plans in the Third World." Iron and Steel Engineer. November 19, 1977.

Hosomi, Takashi. "Japan's Changing Role." The World Economy, volume 1, number 2 (January 1978) London: Elselvier, for the Trade Policy Research Center.

Huntington, S.P. "The Democratic Distemper." The Public Interest. (October 1976)

________. "Transnational Organization in World Politics." World Politics. (April 1973).

Hurnsberger, Warren S. Japan and the United States in World Trade. New York: Harper and Row, 1964.

Johnson, Chalmers. Japan's Public Policy Companies. Washington, D.C.: American Enterprise Institute for Public Policy Research, 1978.

Kaiser, Karl. "Transnational Politics: Toward A Theory of Multinational Politics." International Organization. (Fall 1971).

Katzenstein, Peter J. "Introduction: Domestic and International Forces and Strategies of Foreign Economic Policy." International Organizations. (Fall 1977).

Katzenstein, Peter J., ed. International Organization Journal. (Fall 1977).

________, ed. Between Power and Plenty: Foreign Economic Policies of Advanced Industrial States. Madison, Wisconsin: University of Wisconsin Press, 1978.

Kawahito, Kiyoshi. Japanese Steel Industry. New York: Praeger, 1972.

Keohane, Robert O.; and Nye, Joseph S. Power and Interdependence. Little Brown Company: Boston, 1977.

________. "Transgovernmental Relations and International Organization." World Politics. (October 1974).

Keohane, Robert O., and Nye, Joseph S., eds. Transnational Relations and World Politics, Cambridge: Harvard University Press, 1973.

________. "The International Politics of Inflation." Paper presented at The Brookings Institution Conference on the Politics of Global Inflation." Washington, D.C.: December 6-8, 1978.

Kindleberger, Charles P. The World in Depression 1929-39. Berkeley: University of California Press, 1973.

Knorr, Klaus E. Power and Wealth: The Political Economy of International Power. New York Basic Books, 1973.

Kohl, Wilfred, ed. Economic Foreign Policies of Industrial States. Johns Hopkins University, Lexington Books, 1977.

Kolko, Joyce and Gabriel. The Limits of Power: The World and the U.S. Foreign Policy. New York: Harper and Row, 1972.

Kock, Karin. International Trade Policy in the GATT 1947-1967. Stockholm: Almquist and Wicksell, 1969.

Krasner, Stephen. "State and Power and the Structure of International Trade." World Politics. (1976).

________. Defending the National Interest: Raw Materials Investment and U.S. Foreign Policy. Princeton: Princeton University Press, 1978.

Kreile, Michael. "West Germany: The Dynamics of Expansion." Between Power and Plenty. Katzenstein, Peter J., ed. Madison, Wisconsin: University of Wisconsin Press, 1978.

Levy, Hermann. Industrial Germany: A Study of Its Organizations and Their Control By the State. New York: McMillan 1966.

List, Frederich. The National System of Political Economy. New York: Kelley, 1966.

Lister, Louis. Europe's Coal and Steel Community: An Experiment in Economic Union. New York: Twentieth Century Fund, 1960.

Lowi, Theodore J. "American Business, Public Policy, Case Studies and Theory." World Politics. (July 1964).

Maier, Charles. "The Politics of Productivity: Foundations of American International Economic Policy After World War II." International Organizations. Fall 1977.

Malmgram, Harald. "Coming Trade Wars." Foreign Policy. (Winter 1970-71).

Marcus, Maeva. Truman and the Steel Seizure Case. Columbia University: New York, 1977.

Marks, Mathew J. "Remedies to Unfair Trade: American Action Against Steel Imports." The World Economy. volume 1, number 2 (January 1978). London: Elsevier.

McArthur, John H., and Scott, Bruce R. Industrial Planning in France. Boston: Harvard University, 1969.

McDermid, John F.; and Foster, F. David. "The United States International Trade Commission's 30-Day Inquiry Under the Antidumping Act: Section 291(c)(2)." Mercer Law Review. volume 27, number 3. (Spring 1976).

Morse, Edward L. Modernization and the Transformation of International Relations. The Free Press. New York 1976.

Myrdal, Gunnar. Beyond the Welfare State. New Haven: Yale University Press, 1960.

Olsen, Mancur, Jr. The Logic of Collective Action: Public Goods and the Theory of Groups. Cambridge, Massachusetts: Harvard University Press, 1971.

Ozaki, Robert S. The Control of Imports and Foreign Capital in Japan. New York: Praeger, 1972.

Palmer, John. "The International Steel Cartel." United States Department of Commerce Reports. Washington, D.C.: Government Printing Office, 1927.

Pastor, Robert A. "Legislative-Executive Relations and U.S. Foreign Trade Policy: The Case of the Trade Act of 1974." Prepared for delivery at the 1976 Annual Meeting of the American Political Science Association. Chicago: September 2-5, 1976.

Patrick, Hugh; and Rosovsky, Henry, eds. Asia's New Giant: How the Japanese Economy Works. Washington, D.C.: The Brookings Institution, 1976.

Pempel, T.J. "Japanese Foreign Economic Policy: The Domestic Basis for International Behavior." Between Power and Plenty. Katzenstein, Peter J. ed. Madison, Wisconsin: The University of Wisconsin Press, 1978.

Peterson, Peter G. The United States in the Changing World Economy. Washington, D.C.: Government Printing Office, 1971.

Roberts, John G. Mitsui: Three Centuries of Japanese Business. New York: Weatherhill, 1973.

Rosenau, James N., ed. Domestic Sources of Foreign Policy. The Free Press, New York, 1967.

Russel, Robert W. "Political Distortions in Trade Negotiations Among Industrialized Countries." Scarpalanda, Anthony E., ed. Prospects for Eliminating Non-Tariff Distortions of International Trade. Leider, Netherlands: A.E. Sijthoff 1973.

Schattschneider, E.E. Politics, Pressure and the Tariff. Englewood Cliffs, New Jersey: Prentice Hall 1935.

Shonfield, Andrew. International Economic Relations of the Western World 1959-1971, volume I, Politics and Trade. London: Oxford University Press 1976.

________. Modern Capitalism: The Changing Balance of Public and Private Power. London: University of Oxford Press, 1969.

Schroeder, Gertrude. The Growth of the Major Steel Companies: 1900-1950. Baltimore: Johns Hopkins Press, 1953.

Schumpeter. Capitalism, Socialism, and Democracy. New York: Harper and Brothers, 1942.

Spero, Joan. The Politics of International Economic Relations. New York: St. Martin's Press, 1977.

Stocking, George W., and Watkins, Myron W. Cartels in Action: Case Studies in International Business Diplomacy. New York: Twentieth Century Fund, 1946.

Storing, Herbert J. Essays on the Scientific Study of Politics. New York: Holt, Reinhart and Winston, 1962.

Strange, Susan. "The Management of Surplus Capacity: Or, How Does Theory Stand Up to Protectionism 1970s Style?" xerox: 1978.

________. "Transnational Relations." International Affairs. volume 52. (July 1976.

Treaty Establishing the European Coal and Steel Community. Paris, April 18, 1951. Dublin: Stationery Office, 1951.

Tower, Walter S. "The New Steel Cartel." Foreign Affairs. (January 1927).

"Unemployment in the Steel Industry." Basic Steel Conference. Washington, D.C.: Washington Hilton Hotel. December 2, 1977.

Whitman, Marina. "The U.S. and the International Economy." Foreign Affairs. Volume 57. Number 3. (January 1979).

Wilcox, Clair. A Charter for World Trade. New York: MacMaillan, 1949.

Wolff, Alan. "The U.S. Mandate for Trade Negotiations." Virginia Journal of International Law. Volume 16, number 3 (Spring 1976).

Zysman, John. "Inflation and Industrial Adjustment: The Politics of Supply." Presented at the Brookings Institution Conference on the Politics and Sociology of Global Inflation. December 6-8, 1978. xerox.

________. *Political Strategies for Industrial Order: State Market and Industry in France*: Berkeley: University of California Press 1971.

GOVERNMENT PUBLICATIONS

Central Intelligence Agency. "World Steel Market -- Continued Trouble Ahead." May 1977. Washington, D.C.: Government Printing Office, 1977.

________. "Free World Steel Market: Supply/Demand Prospects Through 1985." Washington, D.C.: Government Printing Office, 1977.

Congressional Budget Office. "U.S. Trade Policy and the Tokyo Round of the Multilateral Trade Negotiations." xerox: March 1979.

The Eighteenth Annual Report on the Trade Agreements Program: Message from the President of the United States. Washington, D.C.: Government Printing Office, 1974.

Federal Trade Commission. "Staff Report on the United States Steel Industry and Its International Rivals: Trends and Factors Determining International Competitiveness." The Federal Trade Commission Bureau of Economics. Washington, D.C.: GPO, November 1977.

The Industrial Policy of Japan. Paris, OECD, 1972.

Japan's Industrial Structure -- A Long Range Vision. "Report of the Industrial Structure Council." An Advisory Committee of the Ministry of International Trade and Industry (Tokyo: Japan External Trade Organization, 1975).

The Murphy Commission. Appendix H "Case Studies on U.S. Foreign Economic Policy, 1965-74." Washington, D.C.: GPO 1974.

The Nineteenth Annual Report on the Trade Agreements Program: Message from the President of the United States. Washington, D.C.: GPO 1975.

U.S. Congress, Senate Committee on Finance, _The Trade Reform Act of 1973_. "Digest of Testimony Received from H.R. 10710." 93rd Congress, 2d Session. Washington, D.C.: GPO 1974.

U.S. Congress, Senate and House Committees on Finance and Ways and Means. _Trade Act of 1974_. "Summary of Provisions of H.R. 10710." 93rd Congress, 2d Session. Washington, D.C. 1974.

U.S. Congress, Senate Committee on Finance. Report of the Committee of Finance on the Trade Act of 1974. "Senate Finance Committee Report on H.R. 10710." 93rd Congress, 2d Session. Washington, D.C.: GPO 1974.

U.S. Senate, Committee on Finance. Executive Branch GATT Studies. 93rd Congress, 2d Session. Washington, D.C.: GPO 1974.

U.S. Congress, House of Representatives, Subcommittee on Trade of the House Ways and Means Committee, World Steel Trade: Current Trends and Structural Problems, 95th Congress, 1st Session. Washington, D.C. 1977.

U.S. Congress, House of Representatives, Subcommittee of the Committee on Appropriations, United States Subsidy of Foreign Steel Producers. 95th Congress, 2d Session. Washington, D.C.: GPO 1978.

U.S. Congress, Senate Committee on Finance, Report on Steel Imports. 90th Congress, 2d Session. Washington, D.C.: GPO 1967.

U.S. Congress, House of Representatives, Subcommittee on Trade of the Ways and Means Committee, oversight hearings on the Antidumping Act of 1921, 95th Congress, 1st Session. Washington, D.C.: GPO 1977.

U.S. Congress. "Report to the President: A Comprehensive Program for the Steel Industry." Anthony Solomon, chairman, Task Force, November 8, 1977. xerox.

U.S. Congress. Joint Economic Committee, U.S. International Economic Policy. 95th Congress, 2d Session Washington, D.C.: GPO 1978.

U.S. Congress. Joint Economic Committee. A Need for a New Export Policy. 95th Congress, 2d Session. Washington, D.C. GPO 1978.

U.S. Tariff Commission, Report Series, No. 128, Iron and Steel. Washington, D.C.: GPO 1938.

U.S. International Trade Commission. Stainless Steel and Allow Tool Steel. Report to the President on Investigation No. TA-201-5 Under Section 201 of the Trade Act of 1974. USITC Pub. 756, Washington, D.C. January 1976, pp. A-3 to A-7.

POPULAR MAGAZINES AND NEWSPAPERS

American Metals Market

Business Week Magazine

Congressional Quarterly

Congressional Record

The Economist

European Community (OECD)

Financial Times of London

Fortune Magazine

Iron Age Magazine

Japan Metal Bulletin

Japan Times

Journal of Commerce

National Journal

New York Times

NewsWeek Magazine

Steel Labor

Times of London

Wall Street Journal

Washington Post

Washington Star

For Product Safety Concerns and Information please contact our EU representative GPSR@taylorandfrancis.com Taylor & Francis Verlag GmbH, Kaufingerstraße 24, 80331 München, Germany

Printed and bound by CPI Group (UK) Ltd, Croydon, CR0 4YY
08/05/2025
01864373-0004